# The Judgment Seat of Christ

# The Judgment Seat of Christ

## A Biblical and Theological Study

### Revised Edition

## Samuel L. Hoyt

**Grace Gospel Press**
Duluth, Minnesota

*The Judgment Seat of Christ: A Biblical and Theological Study*
©2011 by Samuel L. Hoyt

Revised Edition, 2015

ISBN: 978-1-939110-15-2

Grace Gospel Press
201 W. St. Andrews Street
Duluth, MN 55803
U.S.A.
(218) 724-5914
www.gracegospelpress.com

Printed in the United States of America

# CONTENTS

# FOREWORD

The New Testament has much to say about the day when Christ will evaluate His Bride, the Church, when we all see Him just after the resurrection of dead believers and the rapture of living believers—which could be today! But for many centuries Christians have been confused about the timing, the participants, the seriousness, the purpose, and the final outcome of this great divine evaluation of the Church. Is it the next revealed event on God's calendar? Will all Christians be involved, or only leaders? Will any Christians suffer the loss of their salvation? Why does our Lord need to examine us in this public way? How will all of this be implemented during the millennial kingdom?

Dr. Samuel L. Hoyt wrote his doctoral dissertation on this topic in 1977. I had the privilege of serving on his advisory committee, and appreciated at that time the high quality of his work. Since then, he has interacted with many books and articles that deal with this vital topic. I highly commend his careful exegesis of relevant passages in the Bible. I know of no study that is more balanced and thorough.

What a blessing it as been for me to read this manuscript and to think of what our Lord has planned for His Bride and Body! Thank God, the issue will be the gain or loss of rewards, not of salvation! This provision of awards for faithfulness is intended by our Lord to provide tremendous motivation for His people. I need this every day I live, and so do you, dear reader!

This imminent judgment is intended by God to motivate each and every believer—not just church leaders—to serve Him in spirit and in truth. It is not designed to be a horrible threat that produces depression and fear, but, rather, an encouragement to love and serve and obey Him from the heart. In this light, may we, as born-again Christians, be more concerned than ever before about our testimony for the Savior who loves us with infinite love, and paid the ultimate price for our redemption and future glorification.

Dr. John C. Whitcomb

# PREFACE

The kaleidoscope of current theological thought is dominated by an abundance of eschatological motifs. On the stormy and changing sea of prophetic speculation one thought surfaces only to be displaced by another which is vying for prominence. Although much of today's prophetic discussions are speculative, there is available a considerable amount of fine expositional material which is derived from a careful examination of Biblical revelation. This unchanging revelation provides the necessary boundaries within which sound doctrine can be systematized and established.

For a day in which a steady stream of prophetic literature is coming from the publishing houses, there is a striking paucity of reliable material concerning the judgment seat of Christ. Indeed, it would be difficult to find another eschatological subject which is so central to practical Christian living and yet which has been subject to so much neglect and error.

This book is presented in an effort to meet the need for a systematic and comprehensive examination of the judgment seat of Christ. The task has been to glean insights from the broader fields of doctrine, specifically, Christology, soteriology, ecclesiology, and eschatology, in order to understand the nature, purpose, and significance of the eschatological topics.

I am grateful to Dr. John C. Whitcomb, Jr., former Director of Postgraduate Studies and former Professor of Theology and Old Testament at Grace Theological Seminary, under whose instruction I became interested in this subject.

Deep appreciation is expressed to the scores of teachers who have sacrificially and faithfully taught me the Word of God. Gratitude is also expressed for the literary works of others from which information and insights have been gleaned. These products of labor and research have significantly contributed to the content of this book.

Finally, this book is dedicated to my very best friend, to my gracious and loving wife, Elaine, without whose encouragement, patience, and sacrifice this book would not have been possible. She has believed in me no matter what the circumstances and has been my constant encourager.

My desire is reflected in the statement of Carl Armerding which he wrote when discussing another important issue:

> The fact that highly satisfactory answers have been given to this question need not deter us from making a fresh study of the subject. "It is the honor of kings to search out a matter." Would to God that more of us coveted this royal privilege: Not that we are in quest of something novel, but rather that we may know, not only what we believe, but why we believe it.[1]

Sam Hoyt
Founder and President of TRAIN, Inc.
www.trainministry.org

---

[1] Carl Armerding, "The Four and Twenty Elders," *Our Hope* 50 (July 1943): 29.

# CHAPTER 1

# INTRODUCTION

The judgment seat of Christ is a subject which places two great doctrinal divisions into juxtaposition. Ecclesiology and eschatology are brought side by side since this sobering event involves the future evaluation of the church. Throughout the church age, however, ecclesiology has been subjected to a wide spectrum of interpretations and applications. Likewise, eschatology has experienced numerous misinterpretations, and has also suffered from noticeable neglect until relatively recent times. As a result the doctrine of the judgment seat of Christ often has been denied or relegated to minimal consideration under the subject of a general judgment. Consequently, there has been widespread confusion concerning eschatology in general and the true nature of the judgment seat of Christ specifically.

From the plain testimony of Scripture this doctrine is of cosmic significance to each one who is a part of the true church, the body of Christ. A proper understanding of this subject has far-reaching ramifications which affect all areas of Christian life and conduct. With increased knowledge there comes increased responsibility, and increased responsibility in the present results in an increased accountability in the future.

Biblical eschatology and Christian ethics find a focal point at the judgment seat of Christ. The purpose of this awesome event is twofold: in the present to serve as a motivation for Christian living and in the future to review and reward each Christian individually. The prospect of this evaluation should incite believers to faithful and godly living against the backdrop of a future day of reckoning before the Lord Jesus Christ.

## THE NEED FOR THIS STUDY

As Christian doctrine developed throughout the centuries in a recognizable progression, systematic eschatological studies had relatively meager consideration. Historically and logically Biblical eschatology was the capstone of systematic theology. Eschatology, however, has suffered more at the hand of its interpreters than any other major field of theology. Even those who unquestionably view Scripture as the inspired Word of God interpret prophetic passages in vastly diverse ways. As a result many Bible scholars have limited their literary discussions to several major eschatological motifs, such as the resurrection of the dead, Christ's second coming, and a final judgment. This has resulted in the neglect of vast portions of prophetic Scripture.[1]

In spite of the prolonged neglect of prominent segments of doctrine, in the last two centuries increasing consideration has been given to prophetic Scriptural themes and to systematic exposition of prophetic passages. However, a careful doctrine of distinct eschatological judgments and, specifically, a separate and unique judgment for the evaluation of the works of Christians has been formulated only within the last century. The doctrine of the judgment seat of Christ, in fact, is found exclusively in relatively recent theological literature which uses as its foundation a premillennial return of Christ.

Within the church today there exists considerable confusion and debate as to the exact nature of the examination at the judgment seat of Christ. Some Bible scholars view the judgment seat as a place of intense sorrow, a place of terror, and a place where Christ will display all the believer's sins (or at least those unconfessed) before the entire resurrected and raptured church. There are those who go even further by stating that Christians must in some way experience some sort of suffering for their sins at the time of this examination.

At the other end of the spectrum is another group which holds to the same eschatological chronology and which views this event as an awards ceremony. Awards are handed out to everyone for the faithful service they have performed in the will of God through the energizing ministry of the Holy Spirit. The result of this judgment will be that each Christian will be grateful for the reward which he receives, with little or no emphasis on loss or shame.

---

[1] J. Dwight Pentecost, *Things to Come: A Study in Biblical Eschatology* (hereafter referred to as *Things to Come*), with an Introduction by John F. Walvoord (Grand Rapids: Dunham Publishing Company, 1958), p. ix.

There are also Bible scholars who espouse a mediating position between these two views. They maintain the seriousness of the examination yet emphasize the commendation aspect. Emphasis is placed on the fact that each Christian must give an account of his life before the omniscient and holy Christ. All that was done through the energy of the flesh will be regarded as worthless for reward, while all that was done in the power of the Holy Spirit will be graciously and abundantly rewarded.

With many noted pastors, Bible teachers, and theologians holding varying positions concerning the nature of this examination, it is imperative that an intensive and comprehensive investigation of Biblical revelation be made in order to discern "what saith the Scripture." Although the writer will obviously take issue with differing viewpoints, he is in no way impugning the motives or scholarship of men of God holding divergent opinions regarding this event. The purpose of this investigation is not one of rash dogmatism in relation to the contrasting points of view mentioned above. Rather, it is the writer's impelling desire that the reader achieve a greater understanding of Biblical revelation as a result of this investigation. This study seeks to expand the reader's appreciation of the Christian's salvation—fully paid, freely given, and forever enjoyed.

## THE PURPOSE OF THIS STUDY

The general purpose of this investigation is to present a Biblical, systematic statement of the judgment seat of Christ in order that it might serve as impelling motivation toward present fidelity. The specific purpose is to carefully establish the limits which define the exact nature of this examination.

The basic thesis of this book is that the judgment seat of Christ is a most solemn evaluation at which there will be no judicial condemnation, nor will there be any judicial punishment for the believer's sins, whether confessed or unconfessed, but rather commendation according to the faithfulness of the Christian's life. Though it will be an awesome experience to stand before Christ having one's life completely exposed by His searching eyes, yet this same One who judges has Himself entirely paid the penalty for all of the believer's sins. There may be some measure of shame and remorse which will result from seeing one's fleshly works rendered as unworthy of the reward which one might have received, but there will be no judicial punishment whatever for unfaithful service. There will be, however, varying degrees of reward for faithful stewardship.

This study will, therefore, seek to establish the boundaries within which this event must be Scripturally understood. Such questions as the following will be answered: In what sense is the believer judged? What is the nature and purpose of this evaluation? When will it occur? Who will be present at this examination? What will be the results? What is the nature of the rewards which will be given? Will there be qualitative differences in the eternal state? Along with answering these questions there will be a presentation and a refutation of various erroneous views, although this will not be the central thrust of the book.

## THE PROCEDURE OF THIS STUDY

In this study the term "Church" will refer to the universal aspect of the church, the body of Christ, which is composed only of saved individuals from Pentecost until the rapture. This writer will use a literal or normal hermeneutical method of interpretation for understanding prophetic[2] and non-prophetic passages. However, he will not employ crass literalism but will take into account figures of speech which teach literal truths and which are very common in predictive prophecy. The Holy Spirit has revealed truths concerning the judgment seat of Christ explicitly through plain literal statements as well as implicitly through numerous figures, illustrations, and parables. These will be examined in order to discover the literal truths which they teach regarding future accountability and future rewards.

The foundation for this book will be a thorough examination of the passages of Scripture which are related to the judgment seat of Christ. Exegetical details will be displayed only as necessary to accomplish the purpose of this study. The treatise is intended to be primarily a systematic statement of the judgment seat of Christ from a doctrinal perspective.

---

[2] An excellent work which deals with this area is the book by Paul Lee Tan, *The Interpretation of Prophecy*, with a Foreword by John C. Whitcomb, Jr. (Winona Lake, IN: BMH Books, 1974).

# CHAPTER 2

# THE GENERAL JUDGMENT THEORY

One of the prevalent themes in the Word of God is the judgment motif. Throughout the centuries this particular doctrine has been subjected to a great deal of erroneous interpretations. The most widespread of these doctrinal distortions is the general judgment theory. The proponents of this theory believe that there will be one final judgment at the consummation of the world. At this time all people of all ages, both believers and unbelievers, will be simultaneously resurrected and judged. At this event the righteous will receive reward and the unrighteous will be condemned to eternal punishment.

The issue of the general judgment theory is pertinent to the subject of this book, for if there is a general judgment then there is no value in discussing the judgment seat of Christ as a distinct and unique judgment. However, if the general judgment theory can be shown to be unsupportable from Scripture, then it is possible to demonstrate that the judgment seat of Christ will be a separate judgment only for believers of the church age.

## A PRESENTATION OF THE GENERAL JUDGMENT THEORY

The idea of a general or universal judgment has a tenacious grip on most of Christendom. This position is held by Protestants as well as Roman Catholics and by both amillennialists and postmillennialists. The necessary presupposition to this theory is that there will be one general resurrection immediately preceding the general judgment.[1] Most

---

[1] William Gilbert Bellshaw, "The General Judgment Theory" (unpublished Th.M. thesis, Dallas Theological Seminary, 1955), pp. 2-4.

premillennialists reject the general judgment and the general resurrection theories and hold to a sequence of resurrections and judgments.

The postmillennialists place the general judgment after the millennium, while the amillennialists differ among themselves with respect to the time of this judgment. Some amillennialists believe that the millennial kingdom is being fulfilled on earth during this present age, while others contend that it is descriptive of the lives of believers in heaven. Those who support these views would generally agree that the judgment takes place after the millennial kingdom which they would define individually.[2]

### *A Survey of the Historical Development of the General Judgment Theory*

In the early church the predominant eschatological view was one of a literal, premillennial return of Christ. Merrill Unger provides an excellent summary of how this position changed:

> With the advent of Origen, however, and his spiritualizing vagaries, premillennial truth became beclouded and the Church's doctrine of judgment accordingly assumed the man-made mould of one great simultaneous assize of both the righteous and the wicked. Even the great Augustine helped entrench this incipient error by the support he gave it. The Dark Ages, of course, shed no light on it, and by the time the Reformation arrived, the theological figment of a general judgment was as strongly entrenched in the Church as any of the other doctrinal distortions of the Roman Church.[3]

Unger further observes that although the Reformation "reformed" other great theological divisions, especially soteriology, it obviously failed to reform eschatology. Augustine's doctrine of a spiritualized millennial kingdom was accepted as part of Reformed theology, and thus a general judgment continued to be taught. The result was that the general judgment dogma was transposed into Reformed Protestantism. Since it had been an established doctrine for centuries and confirmed as a Biblical doctrine, prophetic research on this issue was stifled.[4]

---

[2] Ibid., pp. 6-7.

[3] Merrill F. Unger, *Great Neglected Bible Prophecies* (Chicago: Scripture Press Book Division, 1955), p. 100.

[4] Ibid.

The Reformation, however, did make a profound contribution indirectly to eschatological studies. The one great principle which resulted from this period was that of the authority of the Scriptures alone. Acting upon this principle of *sola Scriptura*, three centuries later John Darby, who wrote between the years 1835-1875, refuted the general judgment theory and gave renewed consideration to premillennialism, including the doctrine of a separate and unique judgment of the Christian's life.[5]

## *A Survey of the Confessional Development of the General Judgment Theory*

Merrill Unger again provides an excellent summary of the impact which the doctrine of the general judgment had upon Protestant confessions:

> The error of a general judgment of the pre-reformation Church as brought over into the Lutheran Reformation and into Reformed Theology and as imbedded briefly but powerfully in the great Protestant creeds, such as the Augsburg Confession, the Thirty Nine Articles, and the Westminster Confession, is too well established and attested for many otherwise great theologians to see beyond the confusion to "what saith the Scripture?"[6]

Although these confessions are necessarily brief, they unquestionably teach a general judgment. For example, the Augsburg Confession of 1530, in part one, article seventeen, states, "In the consummation of the world . . . Christ shall appear to judge, and shall raise up *all* the dead, and shall give unto the godly and elect eternal life and everlasting joys; but ungodly men and the devils shall be condemned unto endless torments."[7]

The Belgic Confession of 1561 likewise teaches a general judgment in that it says, "And then all men will personally appear before this great Judge, both men and women and children, that have been from the

---

[5] Rudolf Albert Renfer, "The Judgment-Seat of Christ" (unpublished Th.M. thesis, Dallas Theological Seminary, 1939), pp. 3-4.

[6] Unger, *Great Neglected Bible Prophecies*, p. 101.

[7] Philip Schaff, *The Evangelical Protestant Creeds, with Translations*, in vol. III of *The Creeds of Christendom, with a History and Critical Notes*, 4th ed. (Grand Rapids: Baker Book House, 1966), pp. 17-18.

beginning of the world to the end thereof."[8] A portion of Article IV of the Thirty-Nine Articles of the Church of England (1562) in speaking of Christ's ministry says, "Wherewith he ascended into Heaven, and there sitteth, until he returns to *judge all Men at the last day.*"[9] In chapter thirty-three of the Westminster Confession (1647) it speaks of a final day of judgment: "*In which day*, not only the apostate angels shall be judged, but likewise *all* persons, that have lived upon earth, shall appear before the tribunal of Christ, to give an account of their thoughts, words, and deeds."[10] These confessional statements give evidence to the fact that the general judgment theory became an integral part of Protestant dogma.

The general judgment is also an integral part of Roman Catholic eschatological dogma. A Catholic theologian, A. Suelzer, provides a summary statement of the Catholic church's support of this teaching. He writes, "The theme of a judgment upon all men on the last day is a common one in Scripture. In both the OT and the NT it is often referred to as the day of the Lord."[11] Another Catholic theologian similarly writes:

> The event of the Parousia will be followed by the Judgment and the Renewal at the end. At this time, the former corporeal condition of man will be spiritualized; that is, men will arise in some transformation (1 Cor. 15:35-57). Then will all be judged, and their eternal reward or punishment fixed (Jn. 5:28-29).[12]

### A Survey of the Theologians' Support of the General Judgment Theory

Numerous noted theologians have failed to regard the judgment seat of Christ as a distinct and unique evaluation for church-age believers. Rather, they have followed the historic Protestant confessions which advocate one simultaneous judgment for all men of all ages. As a result the church at large has adopted this doctrine as basic to their eschatological framework. For example, A. A. Hodge, a Presbyterian postmillennialist, states, "At the end of these thousand years, and before

---

[8] Ibid., p. 434.

[9] Ibid., p. 489 (Italics added).

[10] Ibid., p. 672 (Italics added).

[11] A. Suezler, "Judgment, Divine (in the Bible)," *New Catholic Encyclopedia*, 1967, VIII, 28.

[12] Robert C. Broderick, "Judgment, General," *The Catholic Encyclopedia*, 1976, 318.

the coming of Christ, there will be a comparatively short period of apostasy . . . Christ's advent, the general resurrection and judgment will be simultaneous."[13] For support of his position he turns to what he calls "authoritative statements" of this doctrine which include writings of Augustine, the Augsburg Confession, the Belgic Confession, and the Westminster Confession.[14]

Charles Hodge, who was also a Presbyterian postmillennialist, taught the general judgment theory. He writes, "The events which according to common doctrine of the Church are to attend the second coming of Christ, are first, the general resurrection of the dead; second, the final judgment."[15] W. G. T. Shedd, an amillennialist, concurs with Bates whom he quotes:

> The day of death is equivalent to the day of judgment; for immediately after it there is a final decision of men's states forever. . . . Hence at the last day all men that have lived in the several successions of ages shall appear.[16]

Louis Berkhof, a Reformed amillennialist, begins the section on the final judgment in his systematic theology by stating, "Another one of the important concomitants of the return of Christ is the last judgment, which will be general in nature."[17] Lastly, A. H. Strong, a Baptist postmillennialist, writes in his systematic theology, "Other Scriptures contain nothing with regard to a resurrection of the righteous which is widely separated in time from that of the wicked, but rather declare distinctly that the second coming of Christ is immediately connected both with the resurrection of the just and the unjust and with the general judgment."[18]

---

[13] A. A. Hodge, *Outlines of Theology* (reprinted; Grand Rapids: Zondervan Publishing House, 1972), p. 569.

[14] Ibid., p. 576.

[15] Charles Hodge, *Systematic Theology*, Vol. III (Grand Rapids: Wm. B. Eerdmans Publishing Co., 1940), p. 837.

[16] William G. T. Shedd, *Dogmatic Theology*, Vol. III (classic reprint ed.; Grand Rapids: Zondervan Publishing House, 1971), p. 500.

[17] L. Berkhof, *Systematic Theology*, 4th ed. (Grand Rapids: Wm. B. Eerdmans Publishing Co., 1941), p. 728.

[18] Augustus Hopkins Strong, *Systematic Theology* (Valley Forge, PA: Judson Press, 1907), p. 1011.

This summary makes it readily apparent that many of the major systematic theologies in print today teach the general judgment theory. With support from such noted theologians as A. A. Hodge, Charles Hodge, William Shedd, Louis Berkhof, A. H. Strong, as well as Roman Catholic theologians, one is not surprised that this theory is the accepted view of most of Christendom today.

### A Survey of the Major Propositions of the General Judgment Theory

Having surveyed the traditional supports of and spokesmen for the general judgment theory, it needs to be determined if such a doctrine is, in fact, supported by the Scriptural data. Those who espouse the general judgment theory largely assume the following:

1. That there is only one final judgment for all men of all ages, at which time both the wicked and righteous will be judged simultaneously.
2. That prophetic passages require a dual hermeneutic. Prophetic passages require a spiritualized interpretation and cannot be taken in a strictly literal sense.
3. That a general resurrection is taught in Daniel 12:2 and John 5:28-29.
4. That Matthew 25:31-46 teaches a general judgment.

In order to prove that the general judgment theory is untenable, it is only necessary to demonstrate that the Bible teaches that there will be more than one eschatological judgment.

### A Refutation of the General Judgment Theory

This section will be limited to a refutation of the general judgment theory. After it has been shown that this theory cannot stand in the light of Biblical revelation, in later chapters the writer will build an argument from Scripture for a unique and separate examination for Christians at the judgment seat of Christ.

Some premillennialists believe that there will be five major eschatological judgments. These judgments, according to Lewis Sperry

Chafer, will involve several distinct groups: church-age believers (1 Cor. 3:9-15; 2 Cor. 5:9,10); the nation of Israel (Ezek. 20:33-38; Mt. 24:37-25:30); the Gentile nations (Joel 3:2-16; Mt. 25:31-46); the fallen angels (2 Pet. 2:4; Jude 1:6); and the Great White Throne judgment (Rev. 20:11-15).[19] It is not within the purpose of this book to prove that Chafer's division of judgments is correct. However, if it can be demonstrated conclusively that there is a distinct difference between *any two* of these judgments, then the general judgment theory must be rejected.

The simple method of comparison is adequate to refute this theory. In accomplishing this, an exhaustive investigation of relevant passages will not be attempted, but a sufficient examination will be made to exhibit the irreconcilable differences between these judgments. Since there is not complete agreement among proponents of the general judgment theory in all the particulars of their view, some generalizations will of necessity be made.

### *The Spiritualizing Method of Interpretation*

Those who give support to the general judgment theory tend to use as their hermeneutical framework a spiritualizing method of interpretation rather than a literal method in the interpretation of eschatological passages. John Walvoord suggests that one's method of interpretation is the crucial issue in eschatological discussions:

> There is a growing realization in the theological world that the crux of the millennial issue is the question of *method* of interpreting Scripture. Premillenarians follow the so-called "grammatical-historical" literal interpretation while amillenarians use a spiritualizing method.[20]

Walvoord summarizes the historical roots of this spiritualizing method:

> The Alexandrian school of theology which came into prominence in the third century followed a principle of interpretation which regarded all Scripture as an allegory. . . . It remained for

---

[19] Lewis Sperry Chafer, *Systematic Theology*, Vol. IV: *Ecclesiology-Eschatology* (Dallas: Dallas Seminary Press, 1948), pp. 404-12.

[20] John F. Walvoord, *The Millennial Kingdom* (Grand Rapids: Dunham Publishing Company, 1959), p. 59.

Augustine to give a more moderate application of this principle of interpretation. In general, he held that only prophecy should be spiritualized and that in the historical and doctrinal sections of Scripture the "historical-grammatical" literal method should be used. . . . Because of the weight of Augustine in other major issues of theology where he was in the main correct, Augustine became the model of the Protestant Reformers who accepted his amillennialism along with his other teachings.[21]

Present day amillennialists generally use a combination of the spiritualizing and literal methods of interpretation. For example, Floyd E. Hamilton, an amillennialist, provides a summary of his dual method of interpreting the Scriptures. He writes:

In conclusion, then, we sum up the whole situation in regard to the fulfillment of the eschatological promises in the Old Testament by pointing out that we are to look for a literal fulfillment of these prophecies except when such literal fulfillment conflicts with truths, doctrines or principles taught in the New Testament, and unless there is plain authority in the New Testament for taking the items of the prophecy in other than a literal sense. In general we are to follow the example of the New Testament and interpret items of Prophecy symbolically when the New Testament so interprets them.[22]

The manner in which Hamilton employs this method can be seen in his interpretation of Revelation 20, in which he spiritualizes the first resurrection to be "the new birth of the believer." He concludes, "The amillennialist however believes that the first resurrection is the new birth of the believer which is crowned by his being taken to heaven to be with Christ in His reign during the interadventual period."[23]

While amillennialists accept a literal second advent of Christ and a literal final judgment of all men, they do not consistently apply a literal interpretation to the particulars of numerous passages involved. The premillennialists, however, discover several judgments which differ in time, place, subjects, and purpose because they insist on a literal

---

[21] Ibid., p. 60.

[22] Floyd E. Hamilton, *The Basis of Millennial Faith* (Grand Rapids: Wm. B. Eerdmans Publishing Co., 1942), p. 59.

[23] Ibid., p. 117.

interpretation of the details as well as the events.[24]

Numerous dangers and deficiencies are inherent in the employment of the spiritualizing method of interpretation. First, this method, if used with other passages of Scripture, would be completely ruinous to Christian doctrine. Second, this principle of interpretation is not used consistently in regard to all prophetic passages, but only where it is deemed necessary to refute premillennialism. Third, the spiritualizing method is justified because it is seen as a means of eliminating apparent problems with futuristic passages. This method originated by theological necessity rather than as a natural method of exegesis.

A fourth weakness of the spiritualizing method of interpretation is that those using this method freely employ it in non-prophetical areas when it is deemed necessary to support their theological system, specifically confusing Israel and the church. Fifth, there is no *logical* stopping point once one has embarked on such a sea of subjectivity. What is to prevent the spiritualizing method from being applied to all other areas of doctrine? If the earthly reign of Christ is spiritualized, what is there to prevent His virgin birth, His miracles, His resurrection, and His return from also being spiritualized? Sixth, it is obvious that the method of spiritualizing passages has no actual guiding principle, being checked only by the limits of the imagination of its user.[25] Dwight Pentecost has said of the spiritualizing method, "The basic authority in interpretation ceases to be the Scriptures, but the mind of the interpreter."[26] F. W. Farrar expresses this same concern: "When once we start with the rule that whole passages and books of Scripture say one thing when they mean another, the reader is delivered bound hand and foot to the caprice of the interpreter."[27] In contrast to the dangers and deficiencies of the spiritualizing method of interpreting Scripture the literal or grammatical-historical method can be defended.

## The Literal Method of Interpretation

One does not arrive at the product of an eschatological system without prior involvement in the process of applying hermeneutical

---

[24] Walvoord, *The Millennial Kingdom*, p. 110.

[25] Ibid., pp. 66-67.

[26] Pentecost, *Things to Come*, p. 5.

[27] Frederic W. Farrar, *History of Interpretation: Bampton Lectures, 1885* (reprinted; Grand Rapids: Baker Book House, 1961), pp. 238-39.

principles to the Scriptures. In his work, *Things to Come*, Pentecost puts great emphasis on hermeneutics:

> No question facing the student of Eschatology is more important than the question of the method to be employed in the interpretation of the prophetic Scripture. The adoption of different methods of interpretation has produced the variant eschatological positions and accounts for the divergent views within a system that confronts the student of prophecy. The basic differences between the premillennial and amillennial schools and between the pretribulation and posttribulation rapturists are hermeneutical, arising from the adoption of divergent and irreconcilable methods of interpretation.[28]

The literal method of interpretation invests each word with the same meaning that it would normally or customarily possess in literature, speech, or thought. The method is also called the grammatical-historical method since it emphasizes the fact that the meaning of the words and thoughts is determined by grammatical, historical, and cultural considerations.[29] Paul Tan develops a definition of literal interpretation:

> To "interpret" means to explain the original sense of a speaker or writer. To interpret "literally" means to explain the original sense of the speaker or writer according to the normal, customary, and proper usages of words and language. Literal interpretation of the Bible simply means to explain the original sense of the Bible according to the normal and customary usages of its language.[30]

The literal method of interpretation can be defended by several lines of argument. Ramm gives an excellent summary:

1. The literal method of interpretation is the usual practice in interpretation of literature. When we read a book, essay, or poem we presume the sense is literal. This is the only conceivable method of communication. . . .

---

[28] Pentecost, *Things to Come*, p. 1.
[29] Ibid., p. 9.
[30] Tan, *The Interpretation of Prophecy*, p. 29.

2. All secondary meanings of documents depend upon the previous meaning of these documents, namely, upon their literal interpretation. Parables, types, allegories, symbols, and figures of speech (metaphors, similes, hyperboles) presume that words have a more primitive reference than the sense in which they are used. The parable of the sower depends for its understanding upon the actual practice of farming. . . .

3. A large part of the Bible makes adequate and significant sense when literally interpreted. . . . All the great doctrines of the Bible rest clearly on literal exegesis. . . .

4. The literal method is the necessary check upon the imagination of men. . . . Literal interpretation is not a method followed unimaginatively or woodenly but it is really *a principle of control.*[31]

The literal method of interpretation recognizes that the Bible contains both plain literal statements and figurative language. Figurative language, however, does not demand a spiritualized interpretation. A figure of speech is simply a literary device used to communicate literal truths. In summary, Ramm lists several advantages to the literal, cultural, critical method of interpretation:

1. It seeks to ground interpretations in *facts.* It seeks to rest its case in any given passage on such objective considerations as grammar, logic, etymology, history, geography, archeology or theology.

2. It exercises a *control* over interpretation attempting to match the control which experimentation exercises over hypotheses in science.

3. This methodology has proved itself in practice. The enduring and valuable contributions to Biblical exegesis are the result of grammatical and historical exegesis.[32]

The literal method of interpretation provides the necessary principles to prevent the distortion of the Word of God. In order to understand the eschatological judgments, principles of literal interpretation must be employed in the study of both non-prophetic and prophetic passages.

---

[31] Bernard Ramm, *Protestant Biblical Interpretation: A Textbook of Hermeneutics for Conservative Protestants* (complete rev. ed.; Boston: W. A. Wilde Company, 1956), pp. 93-96.

[32] Ibid., pp. 103-4.

### Crucial Passages Frequently Misinterpreted

Those who advocate the general judgment theory understand Daniel 12:2 and John 5:28-29 to teach a general resurrection (which is an integral part of the general judgment theory). These verses need to be considered in order to determine if such an interpretation is justifiable.

### Daniel 12:2

Daniel 12:2 states, *"And many of those who sleep in the dust of the earth shall awake, some to everlasting life, some to shame and everlasting contempt."* In commenting on this passage Robert Culver gives support to a paraphrase suggested by Tregelles:

> The translation, brought to the attention of the English reading public by Tregelles . . . and advocated before him by Jewish commentators Saadia Haggon (10th century) and Aben Ezra (12th century), was favored by Seiss and Fawsett, and was fully adopted by Nathaniel West. As given by Tregelles, it is: "And many from among the sleepers of the dust of the earth shall awake; these shall be unto everlasting life; but those, the rest of the sleepers, those who do not awake at this time shall be unto shame and everlasting contempt."[33]

In Culver's argument that a general judgment is not taught here, he indicates that in the first clause (*"And many of those who sleep in the dust of the earth"*) the word "many" (*rabbîm*) appears which is less than "all" (*kōl*). If the resurrection of "all" had been intended, it would seem *kōl* (all) would have been used instead of *rabbîm* (many).[34] It is noteworthy that Edward Young, an eminent Hebrew scholar who was also an amillennialist, commented:

> We should expect the text to say *all.* In order to escape the difficulty, some expositors have taken the word *many* in the sense of *all.* However, this is forced and unnatural. The correct solution appears to be found in the fact that the Scripture at this point is not speaking of a general resurrection.[35]

---

[33] Robert D. Culver, *Daniel and the Latter Days* (Chicago: Moody Press, 1954), p. 175.
[34] Ibid., pp. 174-75.
[35] Edward J. Young, *The Prophecy of Daniel: A Commentary* (Grand Rapids: Wm. B. Eerdmans Publishing Co., 1949), p. 256.

If Daniel 12:2 were the *only* passage in Scripture that spoke of the resurrection of the dead, it is conceivable that a case might be developed for a general resurrection. However, a literal and normal interpretation of a passage which appears later in the progress of revelation clearly indicates two separate resurrections. Revelation 20:4-5 read:

> *And I saw thrones, and they sat on them, and judgment was commit-*
> *ted to them. Then I saw the souls of those who were beheaded for their*
> *witness to Jesus and for the word of God, and who had not worshipped*
> *the beast or his image, and had not received his mark on their fore-*
> *heads or on their hands. And they lived and reigned with Christ for a*
> *thousand years. But the rest of the dead did not live again until the*
> *thousand years were finished.*

Revelation 20 teaches plainly that there will be a resurrection of the righteous at the beginning of the thousand years and a resurrection of the wicked at the end of the thousand years. No other interpretation of this clear passage is possible without reverting to spiritualizing it.

Although Daniel 12:2 speaks of both the resurrection of the righteous and the resurrection of the wicked, this does not support a simultaneous resurrection. In fact, later Biblical revelation as quoted above indicates that they are separated by a thousand years. Walvoord aptly illustrates this fact:

> It is not at all unusual for the Old Testament in prophecy to in-
> clude events separated by a considerable span of time as if they
> concurred in immediate relation to each other. The passing over
> of the entire present age—the period between the first and second
> advents of Christ—in such passages as Isaiah 61:2 is familiar to all
> expositors of the Old Testament.[36]

## John 5:28-29

Another passage which is often used by those advocating a general resurrection is John 5:28-29. In these verses Christ says, *"Do not marvel at this; for the hour is coming in which all who are in the graves will hear His voice and come forth—those who have done good, to the resurrection of life, and those who have done evil, to the resurrection of condemnation."* The term "hour"

---

[36] John F. Walvoord, *Daniel: The Key to Prophetic Revelation* (Chicago: Moody Press, 1971), p. 289.

does not imply that both resurrections will occur at the same time. This term is used in the previous chapter (cf. Jn. 4:21, 23) to include the entire church age of nearly two thousand years.

Dwight Pentecost indicates what John 5:28-29 teach and what they do not teach. He states, "The Lord, in this passage, is teaching the universality of the resurrection program and the distinctions within that program, but is not teaching the time at which the various resurrections will take place."[37] Homer Kent, Jr., in a note on this passage emphasizes the same fact. He concludes, "Although this passage has been used to teach a general resurrection of all men at the same time, it actually states only the fact that all will be raised, without specifying whether there may be various stages by which resurrection will occur."[38]

Although these verses state that "all" who are in the graves shall hear Christ's voice, the term includes two separate classes, namely, the saved and the unsaved. As mentioned above, it does not indicate that both of these classes hear Christ's voice at the *same* time, nor does it say that they are raised simultaneously. The question that must be asked in such a case is: Are there other passages of Scripture that teach separate resurrections of the just and the unjust separated by a period of time? This question is readily answered in the affirmative with substantial support marshalled from Revelation 20:4, 5, 14, 15.[39] John, himself, in the progress of divine revelation clarifies that there will be an interval of one thousand years between these two resurrections.

Christ makes a sharp contrast between the two expressions "the resurrection of life" and "the resurrection of condemnation." Tan clearly explains that the resurrection of the righteous is itself part of a series of resurrections:

> Moreover, although the resurrection of the righteous is called "first" in Revelation 20:4, it is not one event but embraces a series of resurrection events. "Every man in his own order: Christ the first fruits; afterward they that are Christ's at his coming" (I Cor. 15:23). Under the single profile of the *first* resurrection, therefore, is to be comprehended the resurrection of Christ, the rapture-resurrection

---

[37] Pentecost, *Things to Come*, p. 400.

[38] Homer A. Kent, Jr., *Light in the Darkness: Studies in the Gospel of John* (Winona Lake, IN: BMH Books, 1974), p. 94.

[39] Unger, *Great Neglected Bible Prophecies*, p. 103.

of church saints, and the resurrection of tribulation saints (such as the two witnesses of Revelation 11). It also comprehends the resurrection of Old Testament saints at the end of the tribulation.[40]

From the above arguments it is concluded that there will not be a general resurrection but rather two distinct classes of resurrections separated by one thousand years.

## Matthew 25:31-46

The proponents of a general judgment mistakenly identify the judgment of the Gentiles (Mt. 25:31-46) with the judgment of the Great White Throne (Rev. 20:11-15). However, there are several striking differences between these two judgments which make it impossible to identify them as the same judgment.

|  | **Matthew 25:31-46** | **Revelation 20:11-15** |
|---|---|---|
| **Subjects** | The living Gentiles, not Christians, nor Jews (1 Cor. 10:32), nor the dead—*"All the nations will be gathered before Him"* (v. 32) | The wicked dead *"And I saw the dead"* (v. 12) |
| **Time** | *"When the Son of Man comes in His glory"* (v. 31)—before the millennium | *"But the rest of the dead did not live again until the thousand years were finished"* (v. 5)—after the millennium |
| **Basis of Judgment** | The Gentiles' treatment of Christ's brethren (v. 40) | *"According to their works, by the things which were written in the books."* (v. 12) |
| **Purpose** | To determine who inherits the kingdom (v. 34) | To determine the degree of punishment according to their works (v. 12) |

---

[40] Tan, *The Interpretation of Prophecy*, pp. 94-95.

Matthew 25:31-46 describes the judgment of the nations or Gentiles (*ethnē*). In this passage no resurrection is associated with the judgment of the *living* Gentiles. In contrast, Revelation 20:11-15 refer to the judgment of the unsaved *dead*. This passage indicates that all those who appear before the Great White Throne are resurrected individuals. John wrote, *"And I saw the dead, small and great, standing before God, and books were opened"* (Rev. 20:12). The preceding brief list of distinctions between these two judgments is sufficient to demonstrate the uniqueness of both events.

This brief comparison should sufficiently demonstrate the fallacy of the general judgment theory. It confuses the marked differences of the judgment of the living Gentiles prior to the millennium and the Great White Throne judgment following the millennium. This evidence concerning the dissimilarity of these judgments cannot be regarded lightly, for if only two judgments can be conclusively distinguished, it is sufficient evidence to disprove the theory of one general judgment for all peoples of all ages.

Because of the progressive nature of revelation there are passages, which considered in isolation, would seem to teach a general judgment. Rather than finding in these portions of Scripture the doctrine of a *general judgment*, it should be recognized that these passages are rather *general statements* of the doctrine of judgment. Taken alone they could be understood as referring to one event, but considered in the light of complete and clearer revelation they teach a series of eschatological judgments.[41] As a result of the tenacious grip which the general judgment theory has held on Christendom throughout the centuries, the judgment seat of Christ as a unique event has been mistakenly regarded as nonexistent.

---

[41] Renfer, "The Judgment-Seat of Christ," p. 17.

# CHAPTER 3

# THE ETYMOLOGICAL AND CULTURAL BACKGROUND OF THE *BEMA*

The expression "judgment seat" is a translation of a Greek word, *bēma*, which Paul borrowed from the culture of his day. One's understanding of this term in its etymological and cultural development will contribute to one's understanding of the nature of the eschatological *bēma* known as the judgment seat of Christ. Therefore, it is imperative that one has a proper understanding of the nature and function of the historical *bēma* if he is to understand the nature and purpose of the eschatological *bēma* before which each Christian will appear (2 Cor. 5:10).

## ETYMOLOGICAL CONSIDERATIONS

Etymologically, *bēma* comes from the Greek verb *bainō* which simply means to go up or ascend.[1] The primary meaning of *bēma* was a step or a raised place, and later it was used of a platform which was reached by steps. Also, it was used with reference to the Pnyx[2] which was a hill in Athens where the people assembled to make laws and decrees.

### Usage in Classical Greek

The *bēma* was of Greek origin dating back to the time of Homer. In classical Greek the word *bēma* referred to the stone pulpit or raised

---

[1] Joseph Henry Thayer, trans., *Greek-English Lexicon of the New Testament*, by C. L. Wilibald Grimm (Grand Rapids: Zondervan Publishing House, 1962), p. 101.

[2] G. Abbott-Smith, *A Manual Greek Lexicon of the New Testament* (3rd ed.; Edinburgh: T. & T. Clark, 1937), p. 80.

stand from which the orator made his delivery in a public assembly or court of law.[3]

## Usage in the Septuagint

In the Septuagint version of the Old Testament the term *bēma* is found twice. It is translated to mean a pulpit or wood platform and again to mean a foot breadth or the space which the foot covers. For example, in Nehemiah 8:4 it says, *"So Ezra the scribe stood on a pulpit[4] of wood, which they had made for the purpose."* In Deuteronomy 2:5 God speaks saying, *"For I will not give you any of their land, no, not so much as one footstep."*[5]

## Usage in the New Testament

The word *bēma* appears twelve times in the New Testament. Two of the occurrences have reference to the same eschatological event, namely, the judgment seat of Christ. The other ten occurrences describe various historical events.[6] In 2 Corinthians 5:10 the expression *tou bēmatos tou christou* (literally "the *bēma* of the Christ") appears. In the other prophetic passage, Romans 14:10, the phrase *tō bēmati tou theou* occurs. In this latter reference there is good manuscript evidence that the reading *theou*, and not *christou*, is correct.[7] The editors of the United Bible Societies' Greek New Testament as expressed by Bruce Metzger state: "At an early date (Marcion, Polycarp, Tertullian, Origen) the reading *theou*, which is supported by the best witnesses . . . was supplanted by *christou* probably because of influence from 2 Cor. 5:10."[8]

---

[3] Arthur Penrhyn Stanley, *The Epistle of St. Paul to the Corinthians with Critical Notes and Dissertations*, 4th ed. (London: John Murray, 1876), p. 418.

[4] *Bēma* is used to translate the Hebrew word *migdāl* which means an elevated stage or pulpit of wood according to Francis Brown, S. R. Driver, and Charles A. Briggs, eds., *A Hebrew and English Lexicon of the Old Testament with an Appendix Containing the Biblical Aramaic* (Oxford: Clarendon Press, 1907), pp. 153-54. Also see 1 Esdras 9:42 and 2 Maccabees 13:26.

[5] In the Septuagint *bēma* is used to translate the Hebrew expression *kap rāgel.*

[6] The eschatological references are Romans 14:10 and 2 Corinthians 5:10. The historical references are Matthew 27:10; John 19:13; Acts 7:5; 12:21; 18:12, 16, 17; 25:6, 10, 17.

[7] This reading is supported by such noted manuscripts as Sinaiticus, Alexandrinus, Vaticanus, and Ephraemi Rescriptus. Kurt Aland *et al.*, eds., *The Greek New Testament*, 2nd ed. (Stuttgart: United Bible Societies, 1968), p. 568.

[8] Bruce M. Metzger, *A Textual Commentary on the Greek New Testament* (London: United Bible Societies, 1971), p. 531 (ellipsis added).

The difference of terms that are used in 2 Corinthians 5:10 and Romans 14:10 presents no real problem. W. Robert Cook suggests an explanation for the difference in these references: "In 2 Corinthians 5:10 this judgment is called the "judgment-seat of Christ" and thus the person of the one before whom we will stand is emphasized, but in Romans 14:10, where the same judgment is in view, it is called the 'judgment-seat of God" (A.S.V.) for there the emphasis is upon the deity of the one before whom we will stand."[9]

In Acts 7:5 the basic meaning of *bēma* is a step, and in Acts 12:21 it refers to a rostrum or a speaker's platform. The remaining eight occurrences in the New Testament refer to an official raised seat or platform of a judge. An examination of the eight occurrences of *bēma* illustrates how this term was used with regard to judicial proceedings. The first occurrence of this word is in Matthew 27:19 with Jesus before Pilate: *"When he [Pilate] was sitting on the judgment seat [bēma], his wife sent to him, saying, Have nothing to do with that just Man: for I have suffered many things today in a dream because of Him."* Then in verse twenty-six it says, *"Then he released Barabbas to them; and when he had scourged Jesus, he delivered Him to be crucified."*[10]

The term *bēma* is also used with regard to Paul's appearances before Gallio, Festus, and Caesar. In Acts 18:12 it states, *"When Gallio was proconsul of Achaia, the Jews with one accord rose up against Paul and brought him to the judgment seat"* (cf. also vv. 16-17). On another occasion Paul appeared before Festus and there requested to appear before Caesar's *bēma* in Acts 25:6, 10:

> And when he [Festus] had remained among them more than ten days, he went down to Caesarea. And the next day, sitting on the judgment seat [*bēma*], he commanded Paul to be brought. . . .
> So Paul said, "I stand at Caesar's judgment seat [*bēma*], where I ought to be judged."

Lexicographers and expositors consider this judicial usage in their explanation of the term. Thayer says it was, "a raised place mounted

---

[9] William Robert Cook, "The Judgment-Seat of Christ as Related to the Believer's Walk" (paper presented to the professor of Systematic Theology, Dallas Theological Seminary, May, 1953), pp. 2-3.
[10] For a parallel passage see John 19:13-16.

by steps; a platform, tribune: used of the official seat of a judge, Mt. xxvii.19."[11] Arndt and Gingrich describe this term as referring to a tribunal and say it was used especially of a bench.[12] Expositor Alfred Plummer gives a rather lengthy description of the usage of the term *bēma*:

> The *bēma* is the *tribunal*, whether in a basilica for the *praetor* in a court of justice, or in a camp for the commander to administer discipline and address the troops. In either case the *tribunal* was a platform on which the seat (*sella*) of the presiding officer was placed. In LXX, *bēma* commonly means a platform or scaffold rather than a seat (Neh. viii.4; 1 Esdr. ix.42; 2 Macc. xiii.26). In N.T. it seems generally to mean the seat (Mt. xxvii.19; Jn. xix.13; Acts xviii.12; xxv.6, etc. Seven times in Acts in this sense). But in some of these passages it may mean the platform on which the seat was placed.[13]

The conclusion can be drawn, therefore, that in the New Testament the term *bēma* has several specific meanings depending upon the context, but each stems from the basic meaning of a step or a raised seat and denotes a place of prominence, dignity, and authority. However, there was another usage of this word in New Testament times which is significant in this study. It will be discussed in the following section.

## CULTURAL CONSIDERATIONS

The *bēma* in the Grecian world was not known primarily as the seat from which a judge passed sentence in a legal case as it was in Roman usage. An examination of the Grecian games, from which Paul gathered numerous illustrations of the Christian life, will be made. This will be followed by a consideration of the use of the word *bēma* in the Roman Court.

---

[11] Thayer, *Greek-English Lexicon of the New Testament*, p. 101.

[12] William F. Arndt and F. Wilbur Gingrich, trans., *A Greek-English Lexicon of the New Testament and Other Early Christian Literature*, by Walter Bauer, 4th ed. (Chicago: University of Chicago Press, 1957; Cambridge: Syndics of the Cambridge University Press, n.d.), p. 139.

[13] Alfred Plummer, *A Critical and Exegetical Commentary on the Second Epistle of St. Paul to the Corinthians*, in the *International Critical Commentary* (Edinburgh: T & T Clark, 1915), p. 156.

## THE GRECIAN GAMES

The *bēma* was the seat upon which the appointed judges sat as they observed the athletic contests and awarded prizes to the winning contestants. Since Paul's allusion to the *bēma* was drawn in part from the athletic usage of the term (cf. 1 Cor. 9:24-27; 2 Tim. 2:5; 2 Tim. 4:7-8), it will be helpful to examine its usage more carefully as it relates to the Grecian games.

### *Historical Background of the Games*

In Paul's first epistle to the believers in Corinth he referred to an event with which every Corinthian was thoroughly acquainted. In 1 Corinthians 9:24-27 Paul made reference to the Isthmian games. The apostle frequently sought to convey spiritual truths in such a way that unfamiliar spiritual concepts were illustrated by familiar secular concepts.

During the life and ministry of the apostle Paul Greece was under Roman domination. However, much of distinct Grecian culture continued to thrive, for conquest of another kingdom did not necessarily insure the conquest of that culture. In particular, the Greeks and the Romans had distinct tastes in relationship to public games. Victor Pfitzner summarizes these differences:

> This desire for supremacy in achievement, as a characteristic of the Greek mind, can also be observed by comparing the Greek and Roman public games. The Greek Agones provided the citizens with the opportunity to pit their strength and skill against each other. The Roman "Ludi" [games] . . . on the other hand contained no vestige of this ideal. Here the citizens were passive spectators, observing the bloody contests of the gladiators merely for the sake of entertainment.[14]

There were four great Panhellenic games which were in essence national as well as religious attractions:

> The Olympic and Pythian games were held at four-yearly intervals; the Isthmian and Nemean were biennial, the Isthmian

---

[14] Victor C. Pfitzner, *Paul and the Agon Motif: Traditional Athletic Imagery in the Pauline Literature* (Leiden: E.J. Brill 1967) p. 17.

held in Olympic and Pythian years, the Nemean in the years between. In the period before Christ the Olympic years are those divisible by four. Thus, for example, 396 B.C. is an Olympic and Isthmian year, 395 Nemean, 394 Pythian and Isthmian, 393 Nemean and so on.[15]

Since the biennial Isthmian games were held at Corinth, the Corinthian Christians were doubtless well acquainted with these games. These games were held in honor of Poseidon,[16] the god of the *sea,* who had a spruce grove dedicated to him from which the victor's wreath was taken. Oscar Broneer describes some of the mythological significance of these games:

> The chief deity of the Isthmian sanctuary was Poseidon, who had right to possession of the Isthmus as the god of the sea and as the wielder of subterranean forces that cause the earth to tremble. The Isthmus of Corinth, less than four miles wide and frequently shaken by earthquakes, lies between two bodies of water, the Saronic Gulf on the east and the Corinthian Gulf on the west. The Corinthians accounted for Poseidon's possession of the Isthmus by the myth of a strife between Poseidon, god of the sea, and Helios, the sun god. As a result of arbitration, Poseidon received the Isthmus and Helios came into possession of Akrokorinthos. This story of a struggle between two elemental forces, sun and sea, typifies the competitive nature of the games in which men vied with each other for the prize of victory.[17]

There is some question whether Paul actually attended the Isthmian games during his eighteen month residency in Corinth (cf. Acts 18:11). The games were held in the spring, sometime in April or early May. The date of Paul's stay in Corinth can be ascertained with a measure of certainty according to the date of the proconsulship of Gallio which is mentioned in Acts 18:12. Some Bible scholars believe that Gallio

---

[15] H. A. Harris, *Greek Athletes and Athletics,* with an Introduction by the Marquess of Exeter (n.p.: Indiana University Press, 1964), p. 36.

[16] The Olympian games were held in honor of Zeus (Jupiter) at Olympia, the Pythian games were held in honor of the sun god Apollo near Delphi, and the Nemean games were held in honor of Zeus in the valley of Nemea.

[17] Oscar Broneer, "Paul and the Pagan Cults at Isthmia," *Harvard Theological Review* 64 (April-July 1971): 171.

entered office in July of the year A.D. 51,[18] and others believe it was in July of A.D. 52.[19] In either case since the Isthmian games were held every two years, there is a good possibility that Paul's eighteen month stay in Corinth and the biennial Isthmian games overlapped. Although one cannot be dogmatic at this point, it seems highly probable that Paul was in Corinth at the time of the games. Conybeare and Howson go so far as to assert that it is "highly probable" that Paul personally attended these games.[20] Likewise, A. T. Robertson says, "Probably Paul often saw these athletic games."[21]

Eric Sauer rejects the theory that Paul gained knowledge of these pagan athletic contests by attending such games. Rather, Sauer suggests:

> The early Christians did not obtain their knowledge of heathen sporting customs by visiting these institutions, or by personal participation in the games, *after* their conversion to Christ. For Paul even *before* his conversion a visit to these festivals was completely excluded. For every orthodox Jew, to which company Paul as an earnest Pharisee belonged, such participation was forbidden in advance.[22]

Pfitzner explains the reason that a strict Jew would not attend the games. He states, "The competitive spirit of the games was as far removed from Jewish thinking as it could have been, quite apart from the offence in the sight of God caused by the nakedness of the athlete, whether training or competing."[23] Whether Paul actually attended the games is not expressly revealed in Scripture. Therefore, one cannot dogmatically assert whether he received his information directly or

---

[18] F. F. Bruce, *Commentary on the Book of the Acts: The English Text with Introduction, Exposition, and Notes,* In the *New International Commentary on the New Testament,* ed. by F. F. Bruce (Grand Rapids: Wm. B. Eerdmans Publishing Co., 1954), p. 374.

[19] Merrill C. Tenney, *New Testament Survey* (rev. ed.; Grand Rapids: Wm. B. Eerdmans Publishing Co. 1961), p. 288.

[20] W. J. Conybeare and J. S. Howson, *The Life and Epistles of St. Paul,* new ed. (Grand Rapids: Wm. B. Eerdmans Publishing Company, 1966) p. 540.

[21] A. T. Robertson, *Word Pictures in the New Testament,* Vol. IV: The Epistles of Paul (Nashville: Broadman Press, 1931), p. 148.

[22] Eric Sauer, *In the Arena of Faith: A Call to a Consecrated Life* (Grand Rapids: Wm. B. Eerdmans Publishing Company, 1955), p. 50.

[23] Pfitzner, *Paul and the Agnon Motif: Traditional Athletic Imagery in the Pauline Literature,* p. 16.

indirectly, but it is obvious that Paul was keenly aware of the specific details of the games.

### Qualifications for the Games

In 1 Corinthians 9:24-25 Paul writes:

> Do you not know that those who run in a race all run, but one receives the prize? Run in such a way that you may obtain it. And everyone who competes for the prize is temperate in all things. Now they do it to obtain a perishable crown, but we for an imperishable crown.

There is little doubt but that Paul is making reference to the local Isthmian games which were so well-known to the Corinthians. The Isthmian games included such events as foot races, horse races, chariot contests, jumping, wrestling, boxing, and throwing the discus and the javelin.[24]

In order to participate in these events certain conditions were required. The applicant was required to be a citizen. He had to demonstrate that he was of pure Greek parentage, for no foreigners were allowed to enter the contests. Neither were slaves allowed to participate; instead only free men became contestants. No immoral men nor criminals could enter the games, but only those who were above reproach. Thus citizenship, freedom, and purity of life were requirements, and bodily strength and expertise were essential.[25]

Before the games each contestant was required to be involved in ten months of rigorous training under the direction of the judges who had themselves received instruction for a similar period concerning the details of the games. M. R. Vincent quotes Epictetus who describes the dietary aspect of this training. Epictetus states, "Thou must be orderly, living on spare food; abstain from confections; make a point of exercising at the appointed time, in heat and in cold; nor drink cold water nor wine at hazard."[26]

Before the contestants actually entered the games, they were required to make a vow before the image of their god that they had complied with

---

[24] Arthur M. Ross, "Games," *Pictorial Bible Dictionary*, ed. by Merrill C. Tenney (Grand Rapids: Zondervan Publishing House, 1964), p. 298.

[25] Sauer, *In the Arena of Faith: A Call to a Consecrated Life*, p. 55.

[26] M. R. Vincent, *Word Studies in the New Testament*, Vol. II (Mac Dill AFB, FL: MacDonald Publishing Company, n.d.), p. 781.

all the rules in their preliminary training,[27] and that they would follow all the rules of the games.[28] Gardiner describes the important relationship between athletics and religion:

> Sports were definitely placed under the patronage of the gods, and the victorious athlete felt that he was well pleasing to the gods and owed his success to them. Further, the athlete felt that any violation of the rules of the games, especially any unfairness or corruption, was an act of sacrilege and displeasing to the gods. This feeling undoubtedly tended to preserve the purity of sport at Olympia even when corruption was rife elsewhere.[29]

Paul makes reference to the adherence to the rules of the games in 2 Timothy 2:5: *"And also if anyone competes in athletics, he is not crowned unless he competes according to the rules."*

### The Herald for the Games

Another feature of the Panhellenic games that is alluded to by Paul is the herald (*kēryx*). In 1 Corinthians 9:27 Paul writes, *"But I discipline my body and bring it into subjection, lest, when I have preached [kēryxas] to others, I myself should become disqualified."*

In the Grecian games the herald acted as the master of ceremonies. He announced each competitor by calling out his name and the city he represented. Thomas Horne describes some of the other duties of a herald:

> A herald called over their names, recited to them the laws of the games, encouraged them to exert all their powers, and expatiated upon the blessings and advantages of victory. He then introduced the competitors into the stadium, led them around it, and, with a loud voice, demanded if any one in that assembly could charge any of the candidates with being infamous in his life and morals, or could prove him a slave, a robber, or illegitimate. They were then conducted to the altar, and a solemn

---

[27] Oscar Broneer, "The Apostle Paul and the Isthmian Games," *The Biblical Archaeologist* 25 (1962): 29.

[28] Pfitzner, *Paul and the Agnon Motif: Traditional Athletic Imagery in the Pauline Literature*, p. 19.

[29] E. Norman Gardiner, *Athletics of the Ancient World* (Oxford: Clarendon Press, 1930) p. 33.

oath exacted from them, that they would observe the strictest honour in the contention.[30]

After an athletic event was finished, the herald announced the victor, his father's name, and the city from which he came.[31] Paul indicated in 1 Corinthians 9:27 that he kept his body under subjection lest after he had acted as a herald and announced the rules to others, that he, himself, should be disqualified for the prize.

### The Judges of the Games

The judges of the athletic events were men of unquestionable integrity. The judges varied in number from one to twelve, but after 348 B.C. the number was always ten. They observed the contestants as they competed to guard against any transgression of the rules.[32] Any breakage of the rules meant automatic disqualification of the athlete for the prize.

The judges were easily distinguished by the purple robes which they wore. After an event was completed and the herald had announced the winner, the contestant had to appear before the raised seat or the *bēma* of the umpire in order to receive the victor's wreath. In this act the judge represented the god in whose honor the games were held.[33]

### The Prizes for the Games

The victors of the various contests were each awarded a prize. William Smith in summarizing says, "Successful athletes were rewarded at the great games by a wreath consisting in the apostolic age of wild olive (Olympian), parsley (Nemean), laurel (Pythian), or pine (Isthmian)."[34]

---

[30] Thomas Hartwell Horne, *An Introduction to the Critical Study and Knowledge of the Holy Scriptures*, Vol. II, new ed. (Philadelphia: Desilver, Thomas & Co., 1836), p. 192.

[31] Fred H. Wright, *Manners and Customs of Bible Lands* (Chicago: Moody Press, 1953), p. 295.

[32] "Games," *The People's Bible Encyclopedia*, 1921, p. 395.

[33] Sauer, *In the Arena of Faith: A Call to a Consecrated Life*, p. 60.

[34] William Taylor Smith, "Games," *The International Standard Bible Encyclopedia*, 1955, pp. 1172-73. Broneer indicates that a pine wreath was not always used at the Isthmian games. He summarizes the general periods in which different wreaths were used. Pine was used from the foundation of the Isthmian games until the early fifth century B.C. Celery was used from the early fifth century until the second century B.C. Pine and/or celery was used from the second century B.C. to the end of the

Paul made an analogy to such a prize in 1 Corinthians 9:24 and also in Philippians 3:14 which states, *"I press toward the goal for the prize [brabeion] of the upward calling of God in Christ Jesus."* The word *brabeion* simply means a prize which is awarded in a contest.[35] It is used in this latter reference figuratively of the award of victory which Paul expected to receive.

At the Isthmian games a spray was cut from a fir tree in the sacred grove which was in the vicinity of the contests. The wreath which was made for the victor had no intrinsic worth. The wreath did not, therefore, arouse any mercenary motives in the competitors. The spectators saw not the worth of the wreath, but rather the worth of the men who were found worthy to wear these wreaths. The wreath was simply a perishable symbol of the dignity, worth, and accomplishment of its wearer. Paul compares the believer's prospect of an award with this fading wreath in 1 Corinthians 9:25: *"And everyone who competes for the prize is temperate in all things. Now they do it to obtain a perishable crown [wreath], but we for an imperishable crown."*

During the victory celebration which followed the athletic contests, the contestant returned to his home town in a triumphal procession. There in his home town he would place his wreath upon the altar of his deity. Any honor which was bestowed upon the victor was subsequently conveyed to the god he represented in the contest.[36] In Revelation 4 the apostle John saw in his heavenly vision the twenty-four elders around the throne of God wearing golden wreaths. John wrote in verses four, ten, and eleven:

> Around the throne were twenty-four thrones, and on the thrones I saw twenty-four elders sitting, clothed in white robes; and they had crowns [*stephanous*] of gold on their heads. . . . The twenty-four elders fall down before Him who sits on the throne and worship Him who lives forever and ever, and cast their crowns before the throne, saying, "You are worthy, O Lord, to receive glory and honor and power."

second century A.D. and perhaps later. Oscar Broneer, "The Isthmian Victory Crown," *American Journal of Archaeology* 64 (1962): 263.

[35] Arndt and Gingrich, *A Greek-English Lexicon of the New Testament and Other Christian Literature*, p. 146.

[36] Pfitzner, *Paul and the Agnon Motif: Traditional Athletic Imagery in the Pauline Literature*, p. 20.

Perhaps the Grecian games came to the readers' minds as they read this account for this was what was done by a winner in the games. The honor which he received was given to his god. This was a public acknowledgment that it was only because of his god that he was able to stand as the victor.

Paul's knowledge and his readers' knowledge of this athletic motif permitted him to use secular concepts to convey spiritual concepts. Paul used these athletic references with eschatological significance as he portrayed the Christian life in relation to the prize which is the hope for every believer. Throughout this book reference will be made to aspects of the games which relate to the *bēma* and the victors' awards.

## THE ROMAN COURT

Previously in this chapter it was mentioned that the term *bēma* was used of Roman judicial affairs. In contrast to the Grecian court of law in which two stands were used, one for the accuser and one for the defendant, in the Roman law court the term *bēma* was applied to the official seat or tribunal of a Roman magistrate.[37] This tribunal of the Roman magistrate was the most august representation of justice which was in existence at that time.[38]

Two Greek words are translated in the authorized English version by the expression "judgment seat": *bēma* in Romans 14:10 and 2 Corinthians 5:10 and *kritērion* in James 2:6. This latter verse reads, *"But you have dishonored the poor man. Do not the rich oppress you and drag you into the courts?"* The word in this verse exclusively refers to a law court or court of justice, a lawsuit or some kind of legal action.[39] Merrill Unger makes an important observation concerning Paul's use of *bēma* rather than *kritērion* in relation to the believer's future evaluation. He states:

> The use of the term "Bema" for this august and solemn scene is very appropriate and apt. Paul does not use the apparently less fitting word *kritērion* (Jas. 2:6), which is frequently employed in

---

[37] W. E. Vine, *An Expository Dictionary of New Testament Words with their Precise Meanings for English Readers* (Westwood, NJ: Fleming H. Revell, 1940), p. 282.

[38] Stanley, *The Epistles of St. Paul to the Corinthians with Critical Notes and Dissertations*, p. 418.

[39] Arndt and Gingrich, *A Greek-English Lexicon of the New Testament and Other Early Christian Literature*, p. 455.

the Papyri to mean "a court of justice," and is connected with the root *krisis* (judgment, condemnation). This thought has no place in any assize for the believer, and Paul evidently studiously avoids it.[40]

He further states concerning the *bēma*:

> The dignity of the term is illustrated by the fact that it is used of the tribunal of the Roman magistrates in general, and of Caesar's august judgment seat in particular (Acts 25:10), to which Paul appealed as a Roman citizen. It is very appropriate that he uses this significant word in writing to the Romans (Rom. 14:10) where he describes the appearance of all Christians before the greater than Caesar, the Lord Jesus Himself.[41]

Paul's reference to the *bēma* must have made an indelible impression upon the minds of the Roman Christians who were intimately familiar with the structure and functioning of Roman government.

If, indeed, there is a demonstrable difference in these two words as Unger suggests, *kritērion* must be the stronger word in reference to justice, judgment, and condemnation. The word *bēma*, as mentioned earlier, comes from *bainō* and basically means a step or a raised place or platform. It refers to the physical character of a place and conveys the concepts of prominence, dignity, and authority.[42] The word *kritērion* comes from *krinō* and basically refers to a place of judicial proceedings, that is, a law court. *Bēma* generally denotes a place of prominence, while *kritērion* specifically refers to a place of prosecution. The former can be and frequently is used of judicial situations at which evaluations are made in regard to the life and conduct of an individual.

In this chapter the term *bēma* has been shown to have as its root-meaning a step, and then it was used of a raised platform and a speaker's platform. In the Grecian games *bēma* referred to the platform from which the judges viewed the contestants as they competed and from which the victorious competitors were awarded wreaths. In the Roman law court it referred to the official seat or raised platform on which the magistrate or ruler sat, thus conveying the ideas of prominence,

---

[40] Unger, *Great Neglected Bible Prophecies*, pp. 120-21.

[41] Ibid., pp. 121-22.

[42] Pentecost, *Things to Come*, p. 220.

dignity, and authority. Having considered the essential background regarding the usage of the term, an examination will be made of the eschatological setting of the Christian's *bēma* experience.

# CHAPTER 4

# THE SETTING OF THE CHRISTIAN'S JUDGMENT

The fact of a future examination of Christians in order to review their lives and to reward their faithfulness is acknowledged by virtually all scholars who accept the Bible as the Word of God. Those who hold to a general judgment place the *bēma* with the judgment of all men at the end of the age. This theory has been demonstrated to be untenable in light of an examination of Scriptural passages dealing with the judgment motif. Since there will not be a general judgment the question remains: When will the Christians then be judged? After this question is answered, the place of and participants in this judgment will be considered.

## THE PERIOD OF THE JUDGMENT

The period of time within which the judgment seat of Christ will occur can be ascertained from Scriptural evidence. The purpose of this portion of the investigation will be twofold: to establish the time boundaries of the judgment seat, and to suggest possibilities for its duration.

### *The Boundaries of the Judgment*

The time boundaries for the Christian's future examination can be established with a great measure of certainty through concrete Scriptural evidence. First, in Luke 14:14 Christ indicates that the time of reward occurs at the resurrection of the righteous: *"for you shall be repaid at the resurrection of the just."* Specifically, for the church-age believer the resurrection will occur at the rapture of the church according to 1 Thessalonians 4:14-17:

> For if we believe that Jesus died and arose again, even so God will bring with Him those who sleep in Jesus. For this we say to you by the word of the Lord, that we who are alive and remain until the coming of the Lord will by no means precede those who are alseep. For the Lord Himself will descend from heaven with a shout, with the voice of an archangel, and with the trumpet of God. And the dead in Christ will rise first. Then we who are alive and remain shall be caught up together with them in the clouds to meet the Lord in the air. And thus we shall always be with the Lord.

Second, other portions of Scripture also implicitly or explicitly indicate that the judgment seat of Christ will occur after the Lord comes for the saints. For example, in 1 Corinthians 3:13 Paul states, *"Each one's work will become clear; for the Day will declare it, because it will be revealed by fire; and the fire will test each one's work, of what sort it is."* "The day" is most likely the subject of the verb *apokalyptetai.* This day is one which shall be revealed with fire. It is not the fire of eternal punishment, but rather it is a metaphor picturing a refiner's fire for testing the quality of a material. Paul makes this clear in his statement, *"And the fire will test each one's work, of what sort it is."* This verse, therefore, speaks of a day of evaluation for each Christian's works; but when does this day occur?

The context which follows this verse develops much the same thought and answers the question which has been raised. Paul says in 1 Corinthians 4:5, *"Therefore judge nothing before the time, until the Lord comes, who will both bring to light the hidden things of darkness and reveal the counsels of the hearts. Then each one's praise will come from God."* Clearly, then, the *bēma* does not occur until Christ returns for the church.

To buttress this conclusion several more verses will be considered. Revelation 22:12 indicates that Christ will bestow rewards upon His people at His coming: *"And, behold, I am coming quickly, and My reward is with Me, to give to every one according to his work."* In 1 Peter 5:4 the apostle Peter writes concerning the time of reward for faithful pastors: *"And when the chief Shepherd appears, you will receive the crown of glory that does not fade away."* Paul speaks of his anticipation of his reward which will occur at a specific future time as revealed in Philippians 2:16: *"Holding fast the word of life, so that I may rejoice in the day of Christ that I have not run in vain or labored in vain."* Scofield writes of this day, "The 'day of Christ' relates wholly to the reward and blessing of saints at His coming, as 'day of the Lord' is connected with judgment."[1] Merrill Unger further describes this event:

> The coming of the Lord for his own, moreover, marks the commencement of "the day of Christ" (Phil. 1:6, 10; I Cor. 1:8; II Tim. 4:8). This is the day of Christ's presence with His saints in the heavenlies, where their service is tested, their crowns awarded (II Cor. 5:10; Rom. 14:10; I Cor. 3:11-15), and the marriage of the Lamb celebrated. In heaven it is the day of Christ, but on earth it is the day of Antichrist (II Thess. 2:1-12). The day of Christ embraces also the resurrection of tribulation saints (Rev. 6:9-11; Rev. 20:4-6), the gleaning of the harvest, and ends with the revelation of Christ in glory, when He returns in power to the earth to inaugurate the day of the Lord.[2]

Another verse which indicates the time of this evaluation is 2 Timothy 4:8. Paul says, *"Finally, there is laid up for me the crown of righteousness, which the Lord, the righteous Judge, will give to me on that Day, and not to me only but also to all who have loved His appearing."*

The above verse indicates that Paul did not expect to receive his reward immediately after his death. Nor are any Christians rewarded individually immediately following death. Paul expected to receive his reward "at that day," a particular day when all the other Christians would also be given their rewards. L. Sale-Harrison comments concerning the *bēma*:

> It cannot be a piecemeal examination when the Lord is conducting it. It must be when their earthly work is completed, and when the united family is there. Again we must repeat: the Judgment Seat of Christ is a family matter; not for a portion of the family, but the whole.[3]

---

[1] C. I. Scofield, ed., *The Scofield Reference Bible*, p. 1212.

[2] Unger, *Great Neglected Bible Prophecies*, pp. 118-19.

[3] L. Sale-Harrison, *The Judgment Seat of Christ: An Incentive and a Warning* (London: Pickering & Inglis, 1938; Harrisburg, PA: Evangelical Press, 1938), p. 36.

The Scriptural evidence presented above indicates that the judgment seat of Christ will take place following the rapture of the church. In light of the fact that Christ's return for the saints is imminent, I. M. Haldeman says, "According to the Word of God, the testimony of the Son of God, and the corroborative and unbroken testimony of the Apostles, *there is not the thickness of tissue paper between us who are Christians and the Judgment Seat of Christ.*"[4] Robert Gromacki also concludes, "The judgment seat of Christ, therefore, could take place at any moment, even today."[5] For this reason James exhorts his readers, *"You also be patient. Establish your hearts, for the coming of the Lord is at hand. Do not grumble against one another, brethren, lest you be condemned. Behold, the Judge is standing at the door!"* (Jas. 5:8-9).

Having established the *terminus a quo* for the *bēma*, namely the church glorified in the heavenlies, it remains to establish the *terminus ad quem* of this event. A careful examination of Revelation 19 provides evidence for the time by which the judgment seat must be completed. This examination must be terminated prior to the marriage supper of the Lamb for when Christ returns to the earth for the marriage supper of the Church, His bride is already arrayed in *"the righteousness [righteousnesses] of the saints."* Revelation 19:7-8 states:

> Let us be glad and rejoice and give Him glory, for the marriage of the Lamb has come, and His wife [bride] has made herself ready. And to her it was granted to be arrayed in fine linen, clean and bright, for the fine linen is the righteous acts of the saints.

Pentecost comments on verse eight:

> When the Lord returns to the earth with His bride to reign, the bride is seen to be already rewarded. This is observed in Revelation 19:8, where it must be observed that the "righteousness of the saints" is plural and cannot refer to the imparted righteousness of Christ, which is the believer's portion, but the righteousnesses which have survived examination [the judgment seat] and have become the basis of reward. . . . Thus it must be observed that the

---

[4] I. M. Haldeman, *Ten Sermons on the Second Coming of Our Lord Jesus Christ* (reprinted; Grand Rapids: Baker Book House, 1963), p. 166.

[5] Robert Glenn Gromacki, *Are These the Last Days?* (Old Tappan, NJ: Fleming H. Revell Company, 1970), p. 157.

rewarding of the church must take place between the rapture and the revelation of Christ to the earth.[6]

The believer's judgment, therefore, will occur essentially within the time span of the tribulation period which will take place on earth. The termini for the judgment seat are the coming of the Lord for His saints, that being the rapture, and the coming of the Lord with His saints, that being His revelation in glory on the earth where the marriage supper will be celebrated.

### The Duration of the Judgment

Although the limits within which the judgment seat must occur can be established with a great deal of certainty, the duration of this judgment is a matter subject to considerable speculation. There are several differing views concerning the length of time that this awesome event will take. Lehman Strauss, for example, suggests that this event could be instantaneous. He states:

> However one thing is certain, as Henry W. Frost has said: "A divine judgment need not take long." It is absurd even to conceive of a problem of space when we think of the vast expanse in the heavens. "It is possible that this judgment of the saints will be instantaneous, and that each Christian will rise into the air to enter at once into his proper place and appointed rewarding."[7]

Although not being as explicit as Strauss, Leon Wood suggests that the judgment of Christians could occur within a short period of time. He cautiously comments:

> The time of this judgment of Christians is best placed shortly after the rapture and certainly sometime within the seven-year period of the tribulation. This is supported, first, by logical deduction. If Christians are to be judged for works done prior to the rapture, it is reasonable to believe that such a judgment would follow the rapture as soon as possible. It seems logical to let those judged know

---

[6] Pentecost, *Things to Come*, pp. 220-21.

[7] Lehman Strauss, *We Live Forever: A Study of Life After Death* (New York: Loizeaux Brothers, 1947), p. 73.

the results of their judgment sooner rather than later. Second, in Luke 14:14, Jesus states that the recompense for works done will be meted out "at the resurrection of the just," and this occasion occurs, as has been seen, at the time of the rapture. Third, both First Corinthians 4:5 and Revelation 22:12 indicate that Christ will bestow rewards at the time of His coming for His own, with the implication that this will happen at *a moment very near that time*.[8]

Haldeman takes another position regarding the duration of the judgment seat of Christ. He concludes, "It [the judgment seat of Christ] will continue for three years and a half and then Satan, the Devil, will be cast out of heaven."[9] Haldeman further explains his position by stating that during the first three and one-half years Satan is pictured as being in heaven as the accuser of the brethren (cf. Rev. 12:10) before the judgment seat of Christ. This event is concluded just prior to Satan's expulsion from heaven.[10]

There are other reputable Bible scholars who suggest that the judgment seat will take the entire seven year period. Herman Hoyt says, "It will probably begin immediately after the rapture and will continue until shortly before the revelation, at which time the bride of Christ, now having made herself ready, is joined in wedlock to the heavenly Bridegroom (Rev. 19:7-8)."[11] M. R. DeHaan, likewise, concludes:

> When will this judgment seat of Christ for believers occur? . . . It will begin when the Church is caught away in the rapture, will continue for seven years during the tribulation period while God judges the nation of Israel, and the nations here upon the earth. The judgment seat of Christ will occur in the air, in the heavens, and will run simultaneously with the judgment of the nations and Israel here upon the earth. The judgment seat of Christ will end just before Jesus returns with His Church at the close of the tribulation.[12]

---

[8] Leon J. Wood, *The Bible and Future Events: Introductory Survey of Last-Day Events* (Grand Rapids: Zondervan Publishing House, 1973), pp. 49-50 (italics added).

[9] Haldeman, *Ten Sermons on the Second Coming of Our Lord Jesus Christ*, p. 361.

[10] Ibid., pp. 363-64.

[11] Herman A. Hoyt, *The End Times* (Chicago: Moody Press, 1969), p. 218.

[12] M. R. DeHaan, *The Judgment Seat of Christ: A Scriptural Examination of the Three Judgments of the Believer—Past, Present, Future* (Grand Rapids: Radio Bible Class, n.d.), p. 5.

George Ladd argues that seven years is not long enough to carry out the individual examination of millions of Christians. Ladd writes:

> If a period of time must intervene for this judgment to take place, will seven years be enough? It is estimated that there are two hundred million living Christians. In seven years, there are just over two hundred million *seconds*. How much of a fraction of a second is necessary for the judgment of each believer? If an interval of time is needed, then far more than seven years will be required.[13]

Ladd uses this objection to refute the pretribulational rapture position, and he suggests, "Perhaps the first period of the millennial reign will be devoted to the apportioning of kingly authority on the basis of the faithfulness manifested in earthly existence."[14] Walvoord answers Ladd's objection very pointedly:

> This argument [i.e. Ladd's] would seem to border on the ridiculous— God is not subject to the same limitations as men. Ladd's own solution is that "perhaps the first period of the millennial reign will be devoted" to this judgment. The natural question is, if seven years is too short, would one hundred years be long enough— approximately fourteen seconds to judge each of Ladd's estimated two hundred million? The problem is further complicated because Ladd's computation involves only living Christians and does not include those raised from the dead. If seven years is too short for the church, then the millennium is also too short. The obvious refutation of Ladd's argument is that God is not limited.[15]

The enormity of the task of evaluating each Christian staggers the imagination. If, indeed, there will be millions upon millions of Christians present with each one possessing unique gifts, opportunities, advantages, and disadvantages, the evaluation and rewarding of each one with unerring exactness is only possible by an omniscient Judge. God has not chosen to reveal the logistics of this great event, or how it will be

---

[13] George Eldon Ladd, *The Blessed Hope* (Grand Rapids: Wm. B. Eerdmans Publishing Company, 1956), p. 103.

[14] Ibid.

[15] John F. Walvoord, *The Rapture Question* (Grand Rapids: Dunham Publication of the Zondervan Publishing House, 1957), p. 92.

accomplished within an available time period of seven years. Although the contemplation of the magnitude of the event is overwhelming, one finds confidence in the fact that with God all things are possible.

To corroborate that a judgment of a vast multitude of individuals in a relatively short period of time is possible, the judgment of Israel and the judgment of the nations need only be briefly considered. Both of these judgments will occur after the second advent of Christ and prior to the establishment of the millennial kingdom. Both will involve judgment of individuals. Ezekiel 20:37 says of the judgment of Israel, *"I will make you pass under the rod, and I will bring you into the bond of the covenant."* In Matthew 25:31-46 Christ describes the judgment of the nations. The criterion for this judgment will be how the Gentiles treated "my brethren," the Jews. This treatment of the Jews is an evidence of the individual Gentile's faith in God and his reception of the preaching of the gospel of the kingdom. At this judgment God will separate saved Gentiles who will enter the millennial kingdom from unsaved Gentiles who will be slain to await final judgment at the Great White Throne. This judgment is on an individual basis rather than a national basis. A nation is made up of individuals who each must choose to believe and follow after God, or who each choose to reject God. No nation is made up of any entirely regenerate population.[16] Therefore, if Christ can individually judge Israel and the nations in the apparent seventy-five day period[17] between the second advent and the establishment of the millennial kingdom, it is certainly possible to individually examine all Christians at the judgment seat within the seven year period or in considerably less time. God is not shackled by such time restrictions.

## THE PLACE OF THE JUDGMENT

Having determined the time of the judgment seat of Christ, the question concerning the place of this event is easily established. Since the *bēma* is subsequent to the rapture, the examination cannot occur on earth. In 1 Thessalonians 4:17 Paul states that at the rapture Chris-

---

[16] For a more complete argument that the judgment of the nations will be on an individual basis see Pentecost, *Things to Come*, pp. 417-22.

[17] Antichrist is cut off by Christ at the end of 1260 days (cf. Rev. 12:6f; 13:5; Dan. 9:27; 7:25) after which time there is a 75-day interval apparently for these judgments (cf. Dan. 12:11-12).

tians will "meet the Lord in the air." Since the judgment seat of Christ is completed prior to Christ's return to earth with the saints, it can be generally stated that it will occur in the sphere of the heavenlies. The specific location, however, is subject to some debate.

Because of Paul's statement in 1 Thessalonians 4:17 some believe that the *bēma* evaluation will be "in the air." For example, James M. Gray writes:

> It was stated that this judgment is scheduled for the time when we shall meet the Lord in the air, but this is not to say that He and we shall remain there in the air. That is our meeting-place with the Lord, but not necessarily our abiding place. It serves as the location of the judgment and for the adjudication of our rewards of our places in the coming Kingdom.[18]

Others contend that this examination will occur in heaven itself. E. Schuyler English states, "Some say that it [the judgment seat of Christ] is in the air, that is, in the heavens. It is my thought that it will be in heaven itself."[19] These two suggestions are apparently the only two options for the place of the *bēma*. Although the Bible does not make explicit statements concerning the precise location of the *bēma*, nevertheless, Scripture is suggestive in reference to the location of this event.

In 2 Corinthians 5:10 Paul writes, *"For we must all appear before the judgment seat of Christ."* The term *emprosthen* ("before") means "in that local region which is in front of a person or a thing."[20] Perhaps such a statement implies that Christians will appear before the throne of God which is associated with heaven itself (cf. Ps. 11:4; Rev. 4:2, 10). In Revelation 4:10 the twenty-four elders which are pictured as around the throne cast their crowns before the throne. It would seem logical to conclude that it is from this throne these crowns were bestowed, and that before this throne these crowns were received. Although one cannot be dogmatic at this point, it seems reasonable to concur with such men as Lewis Sperry

---

[18] James M. Gray, "Christ the Executor of All Future Judgments," in *Christ and Glory: Addresses Delivered at the New York Prophetic Conference, Carnegie Hall, November 25-28, 1918*, ed. by Arno C. Gaebelein (New York: Publication Office "Our Hope," n.d.), pp. 201-2.

[19] E. Schuyler English, "The Church at the Tribunal," in *Prophetic Truth Unfolding Today*, ed. by Charles Lee Feinberg (Old Tappan, NJ: Fleming H. Revell Company, 1968), p. 25.

[20] Thayer, *Greek-English Lexicon of the New Testament*, p. 208.

Chafer[21] and Herman Hoyt[22] who understand Scripture as indicating that the *bēma* examination will take place in heaven itself.

## THE PARTICIPANTS IN THE JUDGMENT

In any judgment there are two parties present, namely, the one who judges and the one who is being judged. Likewise, at the judgment seat of Christ the Judge, Jesus Christ, and those who are to be judged, the Christians, will be present.

### *The Judge—Christ*

Many Scriptural passages may be cited which indicate explicitly and implicitly that the Judge at the *bēma* is Jesus Christ. John 5:22 clearly states, *"For the Father judges no one, but has committed all judgement to the Son."* Thus Christ acts as the mediating Judge on behalf of God the Father in the exercise of judgment. This position was given to Him not solely on the basis of His deity, though this is essential, but rather because of His humanity. John 5:27 reveals this: *"And [the Father] has given Him authority to execute judgement also, because He is the Son of Man."* In the Greek the absence of the article before "Son of man" indicates not His title, but His essence. He was appointed as Judge because He Himself is wholly man, while at the same time being wholly God.

Verse twenty-two states that *all* judgment is committed to Christ. Likewise, Acts 17:31 states that Christ, the righteous man, will judge more than just believers: *"Because He [God] has appointed a day on which He will judge the world in righteousness by the Man whom He has ordained. He has given assurance of this to all by raising Him from the dead."* As the resurrected Man, He has been appointed the Judge of all mankind. Thus, common to all eschatological judgments will be Jesus Christ, the perfect Son of man, Who will be the Judge.[23]

---

[21] Chafer, *Ecclesiology-Eschatology*, p. 406.

[22] Hoyt, *The End Times*, p. 218.

[23] Also Christ's universal judgment is taught in Acts 10:42 which says, *"It is He [Christ] who was ordained of God to be Judge of the living and the dead."* 1 Peter 4:5 also states, *"They will give an account to Him [Christ] who is ready to judge the living and the dead."*

In the Christian's future evaluation the very expression, "the judgment seat of Christ," indicates Who the Judge will be. In Romans 14:10 where the expression, "the judgment seat of God," is mentioned, it must be understood that the Father is functioning in judgment through His Son Who is Himself God. Here the deity of the One Who exercises judgment is emphasized.

In 2 Timothy 4:8 Paul describes the supreme qualification of Christ, the Judge. He writes, *"Finally, there is laid up for me the crown of righteousness, which the Lord, the righteous Judge, will give to me on that Day."* There will be no inequity in the evaluation for rewards. Neither will there be any partiality shown for *"and there is no partiality with Him"* (Eph. 6:9). The task of accurately and righteously examining the complicated lives of millions of believers is incomprehensible. However, He is omniscient, so every detail will be infallibly considered.

Not only will He take into account the outward acts of service and apparent faithfulness, but He will expose the motives which prompted the actions. In 1 Corinthians 4:5 Paul writes, *"Therefore judge nothing before the time, until the Lord comes, who will both bring to light the hidden things of darkness, and reveal the counsels of the hearts."* In the previous verse Paul also identifies specifically Who his Judge will be: *"He who judges me is the Lord"* (1 Cor. 4:4).

Christ, the Adjudicator, was seen by the prophet Isaiah in His preincarnate state. Isaiah beheld Him upon His throne in all His indescribable holiness.[24] Approximately three score years after Christ's death, resurrection, and ascension the apostle John received a vision of the glorified Christ as recorded in the Apocalypse. In the first chapter He is majestically described as Judge:

> *His head and hair were white like wool, as white as snow, and His eyes like a flame of fire; His feet were like fine brass, as if refined in a furnace and His voice as the sound of many waters; He had in His right hand seven stars, out of His mouth went a sharp two-edged sword, and His countenance was like the sun shining in its strength* (Rev. 1:14-16).

---

[24] The fact that Isaiah saw Christ in this vision is confirmed by a careful reading of John 12:37-41.

Christ Who is wholly man and wholly God *"was in all points tempted as we are, yet without sin"* (Heb. 4:15). It is He Who stands as the only One Who is infallibly qualified to be the Judge at the *bēma*.

### The Judged—Christians

The judgment seat of Christ is limited in regard to its time, to its place, and to its participants. These considerations as well as the fact that it is also limited in its purpose make the *bēma* a unique eschatological judgment with regard to those who will be judged at this time.

#### Only the Church-Age Believers

The time at which the *bēma* occurs suggests that this judgment is limited in regard to its participants. The fact that it occurs prior to the resurrection of the wicked suggests that this event will not include unbelievers who will instead stand before God at the Great White Throne judgment (Rev. 20:5, 11-15).

Since this examination will commence immediately after the rapture of the church-age saints, those that espouse faith in Jesus Christ during the tribulation and during the millennium cannot be included in this unique event. The only other possible group of believers that could be present would be the resurrected Old Testament saints. However Daniel 12:1-3 indicate that the resurrection of the Old Testament saints will not be prior to the tribulation period but immediately after it. Therefore, this resurrection is subsequent to the judgment seat evaluation, and thus the Old Testament saints will be excluded from this adjudication.[25] As a result, there is left to consider only those Church-age saints who are living or have lived between Pentecost and the rapture; and it is deduced from Scripture that these will be the only ones who will stand before the *bēma* of Christ.

The above conclusion that only the church-age saints will be present at the judgment is further supported by Romans 14:10 and 2 Corinthians 5:10. In Romans 14, Paul identifies himself with those who will come before the *bēma*. He says, *"For we shall all stand before the judgment seat of Christ."* The preceding context establishes that Paul

---

[25] Arthur B. Walton, "The Judgment Seat of Christ: A Study of the Doctrinal Importance of the Judgment" (unpublished theology paper, Dallas Theological Seminary, January, 1968), p. 14.

is making reference to believers, for in verse eight he says, *"Therefore, whether we live or die, we are the Lord's."*

Both Corinthian epistles were clearly written to believers. In 1 Corinthians 1:2 Paul writes, *"To the church of God which is at Corinth, to those who are sanctified in Christ Jesus, called to be saints, with all who in every place call on the name of Jesus Christ our Lord."* Again in 2 Corinthians 1:1 he says, *"To the church of God which is at Corinth, with all the saints who are in all Achaia."*

In 2 Corinthians 5 Paul identifies himself with these believers by using the first person plural, "we," twenty-six times. An examination of these references reveals that every occurrence of "we" refers to believers. In verse ten Paul states, *"For we must all appear before the judgment seat of Christ."* Pentecost presents a convincing summary:

> There can be little doubt that the bema of Christ is concerned only with believers. The first personal pronoun occurs with too great frequency in 2 Corinthians 5:1-19 to miss this point. Only the believer could have "an house not made with hands, eternal in the heavens." Only the believer could experience "mortality . . . swallowed up of life." Only the believer could experience the working of God, "who also hath given us the earnest of the Spirit." Only the believer could have the confidence that "whilst we are at home in the body, we are absent from the Lord." Only the believer could "walk by faith, not by sight."[26]

Therefore, it must be concluded that this examination is all-inclusive, including all of the church-age saints, as well as all-exclusive, excluding unbelievers and saints of other ages. At the judgment seat of Christ only church-age believers will appear, with no unsaved person present. Neither will Old Testament saints, tribulational saints, nor millennial saints be present at this examination. This unique assize is limited to those dead saints who will be resurrected at Christ's return and those living believers who will be caught up together to meet the Lord in the air at the end of this present age.

**All the Church-Age Believers**

The fact that this adjudication will be a universal experience for all believers of this dispensation needs only little consideration. Romans

---

[26] Pentecost, *Things to Come*, p. 221.

14:10 states, *"For we shall all [pantes] stand before the judgment seat of Christ."* Similarly, 2 Corinthians 5:10 says, "For we must all [*pantes*] appear before the judgment seat of Christ." The plural adjective used substantivally in both of these verses suggests the totality or universality of Christians who will be at the *bēma* examination. W. E. Vine writes, "In the plural it [*pas*] signifies the totality of the persons or things referred to."[27]

The conclusion must be drawn that no church-age believer will be exempt from appearing before Christ's *bēma*. Whether he be the most noted apostle or the most obscure believer; whether he be carnal or spiritual, unfaithful or faithful; each and every Christian will be summoned to appear before the judgment seat of Christ. Thus the *bēma* will be for only church-age believers and for all church-age believers without exception.

---

[27] Vine, *An Expository Dictionary of New Testament Words with Their Precise Meanings for English Readers*, 46.

# CHAPTER 5

# THE NATURE OF THE CHRISTIAN'S JUDGMENT

All believers of this present dispensation, as it has been shown, will be the only ones who stand before the judgment seat of Christ. Although it appears that they will be present *en masse* before the *bēma*, the question remains: Will Christians be judged individually or corporately? After considering this question there will be an investigation concerning the exact nature and purpose of this examination.

## THE INDIVIDUALITY OF THE JUDGMENT

The plain statements of the New Testament provide the answer to the question of whether Christians will be judged individually or corporately. Second Corinthians 5:10 indicates that the *bēma* evaluation will be individual in nature: *"For we must all appear before the judgment seat of Christ; that each one may receive the things done in the body, according to what he has done, whether good or bad."* The Greek word, *hekastos*, which simply means "each" or "every," specifically indicates that this evaluation will be conducted on an individual basis. Vine writes that this word "is used of any number separately."[1]

Another verse which, likewise, teaches the individualized nature of the *bēma* is Romans 14:12. Just prior to this verse the judgment seat of God (Christ) is mentioned. Verse twelve reads, *"So then each*

---

[1] Vine, *An Expository Dictionary of New Testament Words with Their Precise Meanings for English Readers*, II, 9.

*[hekastos] of us shall give account of himself to God."* First Corinthians
3:8 supports the conclusion that each Christian will be evaluated in
some sense individually. Verse eight reads, *"Now he who plants and he
who waters are one, and each one [hekastos] will receive his own reward
according to his own labor."* Paul continues by writing in verses thirteen
through fifteen:

> *Each one's [hekastou] work will become clear; for the Day will
> declare it, because it will be revealed by fire; and the fire will
> test each one's [hekastou] work of what sort it is. If anyone's
> [tinos] work which he has built on it endures, he will receive a
> reward. If anyone's [tinos] work is burned, he will suffer loss;
> but he himself [autos] will be saved, yet so as through fire.*

Throughout this passage and the previously mentioned verses the
individual nature of this judgment is accentuated. Robert Gromacki
discusses the individual aspect of the Christian's evaluation as mentioned
in 2 Corinthians 5:10:

> Although Christians will stand as one corporate group before
> Christ, they will not be judged as a group but as individuals.
> Notice the change from "we" and "all" to "every one." I will not
> give an account for you, and you will not give an account for
> me. I will be judged for my life, and you will be judged for your
> experience.[2]

Similarly, Alfred Plummer concludes, "We shall not be judged
*en masse*, or in classes, but one by one, in accordance with individual
merit."[3]

The individual aspect of the judgment seat of Christ might be compared to graduation from a large university. Although thousands may
be graduated in a relatively brief period of time, they each receive individual attention. Each is awarded his appropriate degree based upon his
individual grades and academic performance. Although the graduation
ceremony is completed relatively quickly, each graduate is evaluated
and honored on an individual basis. Even though Scripture does not

---

[2] Gromacki, *Are These the Last Days?* pp. 159-60.
[3] Plummer, *A Critical and Exegetical Commentary on the Second Epistle of Paul to the
Corinthians*, p. 157.

indicate the logistics of the judgment seat, such an individualized evaluation is not only possible, it is certain in light of Biblical revelation.

## THE JUDGMENT IN THEOLOGICAL PERSPECTIVE

Having considered the individualized nature of the judgment seat of Christ the issue which needs to be discussed is the reason for this evaluation. Perhaps this issue is the most difficult and most highly debated question in regard to the *bēma*. Some writers believe that Christians will face their unconfessed sins, while others believe that the believer's sins, whether confessed or unconfessed, will have no place at the *bēma*. Some view the judgment seat as a place of great fear; others see it as a place of great anticipation. These issues will be considered after an examination is made of the nature and implications of the three other judgments which have a direct bearing upon Christians: the judgment of the cross, the self-judgment of the believer, and the disciplinary or chastening judgment of the believer. Without an accurate understanding of these judgments the nature of the judgment seat of Christ is subject to hopeless confusion.

### *The Judgment of the Cross*

The question of the nature of the judgment seat of Christ is vitally related to the doctrine of soteriology. The problem which the Bible student confronts is: To what extent did the work of Christ on the cross relate to sins in the Christian's life? In light of Christ's past dealing at the cross with sin, how does God deal with them in the present and in the future? What does Scripture teach concerning justification and God's grace?

In order to comprehend the significance of the death of Christ on the sinner's behalf, it is essential that relevant portions of Scripture be carefully considered. Although the writer does not desire this section to be unduly wearisome, it is considered necessary to quote numerous verses which relate to the purpose of Christ's death and to the imputation of His righteousness by which the believer is judicially and positionally declared righteous.

Many verses indicate that the Christian will never face condemnation; that is, he will never face eternal punishment for sin. For example, John

3:18 states, *"He who believes in Him [Christ] is not condemned; but he who does not believe is condemned already."* John 5:24 reads, *"Most assuredly, I say to you, he who hears My word and believes in Him who sent Me has everlasting life, and shall not come into judgment, but has passed from death into life."* Romans 8:1 says, *"There is therefore now no condemnation to those who are in Christ Jesus."*

Other portions of Scripture teach that Christ died in the believer's place to pay for his sins. Paul writes in 2 Corinthians 5:21, *"For He [God] made Him [Christ] who knew no sin to be sin for us, that we might become the righteousness of God in Him."* First Peter 2:24 states, *"Who Himself bore our sins in His own body on the tree, that we, having died to sins, might live for righteousness—by whose stripes you were healed."*

Many passages teach that by faith a person is justified or declared righteous in God's sight. To be justified is to be declared righteous by God. It is to have a new standing before God in which the believer is regarded as righteous in His sight. Thus no legal charge can be brought against the believer whereby he must pay for his sins. Romans 5:1, 9 read, *"Therefore, having been justified by faith, we have peace with God through our Lord Jesus Christ. . . . Much more then, having now been justified by His blood, we shall be saved from wrath through him."* Similarly, Romans 3:22-24 state, *"Even the righteousness of God, through faith in Jesus Christ, to all and on all who believe. For there is no difference; for all have sinned and come short of the glory of God, being justified freely by His grace through the redemption that is in Christ Jesus."* Romans 8:33 reads, *"Who shall bring a charge against God's elect. It is God who justifies."*

As a result of the believer's justification God sees the Christian clothed in the righteousness of Christ. This righteousness is an imputed righteousness and not an attribute of God's righteousness which is possessed by the believer. To be justified is to be legally *declared* righteous, not to be *made* experientially righteous by God. Paul writes in 1 Corinthians 1:30, *"But of Him you are in Christ Jesus, who became for us wisdom from God—and righteousness and sactification and redemption."* Philippians 3:8-9 state, *"Yet indeed I also count all things loss for the excellence of the knowledge of Christ Jesus my Lord, for whom I have suffered the loss of all things, and count them as rubbish, that I may gain Christ and be found in Him, not having my own righteousness, which is from the law, but that which is through faith in Christ, the righteousness which is from God by faith."*

Finally, the believer's sins are fully and eternally paid for according to Hebrews 9:26-28: *"He then would have had to suffer often since the foundation of the world; but now, once at the end of the ages, He has appeaared to put away sin by the sacrifice of Himself. And as it is appointed for men to die once, but after this the judgment, so Christ was offered once to bear the sins of many."* Likewise, Hebrews 10:10, 14, 17 read:

> *By that will we have been sanctified through the offering of the body of Jesus Christ for all. . . . For by one offering He has perfected for ever those who are being sanctified. But the Holy Spirit also witnesses to us; for after He had said before. . . . Their sins and their lawless deeds I will remember no more.*

Through an abundance of clear Scriptural teaching it must be concluded that every believer has been declared righteous through faith in Christ. There is, therefore, no future forensic judgment or forensic punishment for sin. Forensic judgment or punishment denotes a legal or judicial exercise of punishment resulting from a judicial system which demands just payment for an offense to satisfy the demands of the law. For the believer Christ made the full payment for all of his sin in order that the demands of God's justice might be completely satisfied. John Walvoord comments on the implications of Christ's death as it relates to sin:

> The moment we really trusted Christ our judgment for the guilt of sin became effective once and for all. It was accomplished for us at the cross of Christ. For a Christian there is no future judgment for sin. There is no future condemnation for sin, "for there is no condemnation to them which are in Christ Jesus."[4]

Lewis Sperry Chafer summarizes the Scriptural teaching of justification for the Christian:

> Justification causes no one to be righteous. It is not the bestowment as such of righteousness. It rather proclaims one to be justified whom God sees as perfected in His Son. Therefore, this may be stated as the correct formula of justification: The

---

[4] John F. Walvoord, *The Return of the Lord* (Grand Rapids: Zondervan Publishing House, 1955), p. 116.

sinner becomes righteous in God's sight when he is in Christ; he is justified by God freely, or without a cause, because thereby he is righteous in His sight.[5]

Because of the Christian's justification God does not impute sin. Not just part of the believer's sins, but all of his sins prior to and subsequent to his conversion, were fully paid for by Christ Himself. The question of sin and the forensic payment for sin in regard to God's justice has been forever satisfied in the mind of God by the all-sufficient death of His Son. Chafer writes, "Sin has been judged by Christ as Substitute for all on behalf of whom He died. The believer has been in court, condemned, sentenced, and executed in the Person of his substitute."[6]

Therefore, the believer in this life and in the life to come will never be called upon to render any judicial payment or experience any judicial suffering for any of his sins, since the complete payment for his sins has been fully and forever paid. God the Father sees the believer clothed in the righteousness of Christ. He can find no more to forensically accuse in the Christian than He can find to accuse in Jesus Christ.

Some might object that Colossians 3:24-25 does teach that there will be some sort of future punitive action taken against the sinning Christian by the Lord. These verses state:

> Knowing that from the Lord you will receive the reward of the inheritance; for you serve the Lord Christ. But he who does wrong [ho adikōn] will be repaid [komisetai] for what he has done, [ho ēdikēsen] and there is no partiality.

The problem which is raised by this passage is the meaning and implications of the expression *"he who does wrong will be repaid for what he has done."*

The verb *komisetai* is a future middle indicative of *komizō* which means to receive back, to get for oneself, or to receive pay or wages.[7] This is also the same word which appears in 2 Corinthians 5:10 where the *bēma* is specifically mentioned. This verse states, *"For we must*

---

[5] Lewis Sperry Chafer, *Systematic Theology*, Vol. VII: *Doctrinal Summarization* (Dallas: Dallas Seminary Press, 1948), p. 222.

[6] Ibid., p. 214.

[7] Arndt and Gingrich, *A Greek-English Lexicon of the New Testament and Other Early Christian Literature*, p. 443.

*all appear before the judgment seat of Christ, that each one may receive [komisētai, first aorist middle subjunctive] the things done in the body, according to what he has done, whether good or bad."*

Both of these passages teach that there will be a "paying back" or a "receiving back" both for the good things which are done in the Christian's life as well as for the wrong or bad things which are done. In the light of the analogy of faith and clear teachings from the Word of God previously mentioned, it must be concluded that this "receiving back" for the wrongs which have been done cannot refer to any judicial payment for those wrongs. It should be carefully noted that what the disobedient believer will receive back for his wrongdoing is *not* mentioned in either of these two passages. To read into these passages judicial punishment or some form of chastisement in the future life is to go beyond the bounds of sound exegesis and to do injustice to the analogy of faith.

In order to determine what the disobedient Christian shall receive for his wrongdoing one could go to such passages as 1 Corinthians 3:15 and 1 John 2:28. These verses indicate that wrongdoing does have eternal consequences, namely, the loss of eternal rewards which one could have received and the experiencing of shame before the Lord of glory. To the degree that a Christian is unfaithful he will experience loss of reward at the judgment seat of Christ. This loss will be a real and eternal loss which can never be regained.

### The Self-Judgment of the Christian

The past aspect of judgment was accomplished by Christ at the cross *"in that, while we were yet sinners, Christ died for us"* (Rom. 5:8). In the present God deals with believers as sons. First John 3:1 states, *"Behold what manner of love the Father has bestowed on us, that we should be called children of God."*[8] As a son a twofold judgment is operative, namely, the self-judgment by the believer himself which is a preventive judgment; and disciplinary judgment by God which is basically a corrective or remedial judgment.

The self-judgment of the believer is mentioned by Paul in 1 Corinthians 11:31. He writes, *"For if we would judge [diakrinō] our-*

---

[8] See also such verses as Romans 8:14; Hebrews 12:5-11; and 1 John 3:2.

*selves, we should not be judged [krinō]."* The word *diakrinō* means to self-evaluate or to self-examine. Here this self-examination is to determine if there is any unconfessed sin that would hinder fellowship with God. The resultant purpose for this judgment is to avoid the Lord's chastisement as stated in the following verse: *"But when we are judged [krinō], we are chastened [paideuō] of the Lord, that we may not be condemned [katakrinō] with the world"* (v. 32). James Boyer in elaborating on this self-judgment, writes:

> This judgment which we might avoid by self-judgment is the chastening of the Lord. Here, then, is a present judgment of the believer's sins. If we judge ourselves, and deal with our sins in the appointed manner, God's purpose for our lives will be realized.[9]

God's appointed manner for the believer in dealing with his sins is succinctly expressed in 1 John 1:9: *"If we confess our sins, He is faithful and just to forgive us our sins and to cleanse us from all unrighteousness."* Confession brings forgiveness and cleansing which results in restored fellowship with God. This principle of the believer judging and confessing his own sins is also found in Proverbs 28:13 which states, *"He who covers his sins will not prosper, but whoever confesses and forsakes them will have mercy."*

### The Disciplinary Judgment of the Christian

According to 1 Corinthians 11:30-32 chastisement or discipline follows if the believer does not exercise self-judgment through confessing and forsaking his sin. These verses state, *"For this reason many are weak and sick among you, and many sleep. For if we would judge ourselves, we should not be judged. But when we are judged, we are chastened [paideuometha] of the Lord, that we may not be condemned with the world."* To call this disciplinary judgment some sort of punishment is to misunderstand the work of God *for* the believer and the work of God *in* the believer. Even the extreme form of discipline by which God brings an end to the life of an unrepentant believer is not punishment in the sense of an expression of

---

[9] James L. Boyer, *Prophecy: Things to Come: A Study* (Winona Lake, IN: BMA Books, 1973), p. 100.

God's wrath. It is rather the removal of opportunity for any further reward because of continued disobedience. Those believers who will not accept God's instruction because of a rebellious heart render themselves irretrievable for this life. Therefore, the opportunity for faithfulness in this life and further reward in the life to come is brought to an abrupt halt by God. This is not punishment in a judicial sense, but rather Paul calls it chastening.

Hebrews 12:5-11 teaches that God in some sense chastens *all* of His sons in order that they might bring forth the peaceable fruit of righteousness. Verse eleven states, "Now no chastening [*paideia*] for the present seemeth to be joyous, but grievous: nevertheless afterward it yieldeth the peaceable fruit of righteousness unto them which are exercised thereby." God cannot and will not condone sins in the lives of believers. He cannot overlook them. Discipline turns the eyes of the wayward believer Godward so that he will confess and forsake his sin.

The Greek term *paideuō*, which appears in 1 Corinthians 11 and in Hebrews 12, is translated by the word "chastise" which corroborates that forensic punishment for the sake of satisfying God's justice is not in view. Vine indicates that the Greek verb *paideuō* (and the Greek noun *paideia*) "primarily denotes to train children, suggesting the broad idea of education."[10] The verb refers to the act of training or instructing a child, being derived from the Greek verb *pais* which means "a child."[11] The word appears in 2 Timothy 3:16 in its basic meaning as it relates to the Word of God: *"All Scripture is given by inspiration of God, and is profitable for doctrine, for reproof, for correction, for instruction [paideian] in righteousness."*

In light of the fact that Christ satisfied all of God's righteous demands for any judicial punishment for sin, this chastisement cannot stem from any forensic payment for sin which the believer must render to God in order to satisfy His justice.[12] Punishment is a judicial act whereby a person must render payment for his sin by suffering. Correction is not in view. Rather it is an act of judicial retribution. Chastisement is a family act between a father and a son whereby the son is dealt with

[10] Vine, *An Expository Dictionary of New Testament Words with Their Precise Meanings for English Readers*, I, 183.

[11] Ibid.

[12] Erwin Lutzer, "Are We Making Sin Too Easy?" *Moody Monthly*, July-August, 1976, pp. 45-47. This is a helpful article both theologically and practically for understanding and applying these truths to the lives of believers.

in order to correct his waywardness. Discipline is an act of restoration rather than an act of retribution. Punishment and chastisement view an act from different perspectives. Chastisement does not primarily look back at the sin, but rather forward to restoration and growth. Punishment looks back at the offense and cries that the demands of justice be satisfied by future payment. Chastisement is a loving act between a father and a son. Punishment is a legal act between a judge and a criminal. Although both may involve suffering to accomplish their unique purposes, chastisement involves remedial suffering while punishment involves retributive suffering.

God's chastening or discipline in some cases may seem like punishment for the sins committed by the recipient in the sense that a measure of suffering may be involved. Rather than satisfying His justice, however, God is in loving affection instructing the believer in holy living. Hebrews 12:10 states, "For they [earthly fathers] verily for a few days chastened us after their own pleasure; but he for our profit that we might be partakers of his holiness."

The writer of Hebrews clearly states, *"For whom the Lord loves He chastens, and scourges[13] every son whom he receives. If you endure chastening, God deals with you as with sons; for what son is there whom a father does not chasten?"* (Heb. 12:6-7). Chafer explains that love is the divine motive in chastisement rather than justice:

> Because of the comfort which it secures and because of the fact respecting the character of God which is revealed therein, the truth that love is the divine motive in every instance where chastisement is employed should not be overlooked. No attempt to expound this important doctrine should be made which fails to indicate that divine chastisement arises in the infinite compassion of God and is administered under the influence of infinite, divine affection.[14]

---

[13] Homer A. Kent, Jr. discusses the use of the term "scourge" (*mastigoō*) as it is used in Hebrews 12:6. He writes: "It is used here figuratively of God's chastising of His children. This clause, although an instance of Hebrew poetic parallelism in the quotation, seems to add the idea of corrective discipline to the more general reference to child training. The point is that proper training must include correction of faulty behavior. This should bring no discouragement, however, but realization that God is concerned about the healthy spiritual development of His children." *The Epistle to the Hebrews: A Commentary* (Grand Rapids: Baker Book House, 1972), pp. 261-62.

[14] Lewis Sperry Chafer, *Systematic Theology*, Vol. VI: *Pneumatology* (Dallas: Dallas

D. Martin Lloyd-Jones gives a superb illustration of the believer's position under love rather than law and its effect in providing a greater motivating force for righteous living. In his comments an Romans 8:1 he writes:

> You who are Christians, even when you sin, do not go back "under condemnation." The reason is, as he tells us in the next verse, that you have finished with the Law. He has already told us that in the words "Ye are not under law, but under grace." You must never again feel "under condemnation."
>
> We can put it in the form of an illustration. The difference between an unbeliever sinning and a Christian sinning is the difference between a man transgressing one of the laws of England or any other State, and a member of a family doing something that is displeasing to another member of the family. In the one case a man commits an offence against the State; in the other a husband, say, has done something that he should not do in his relationship with his wife. He is not breaking a law, he is wounding the heart of his wife. That is the difference. It is no longer a legal matter, it is a matter of personal relationship now, and that a relationship of love. The man does not cease to be the husband of the woman, nor the woman to be the wife of the husband. Law does not come into the matter at all; it lies outside that realm. In a sense it is now something much worse than a legal condemnation. I would rather offend against a law of the land objectively outside me, than hurt someone whom I love.[15]

Some might object that such teaching (though it is thoroughly Biblical) makes for a "cheap grace" which reduces the leverage for holy living. Rather, God intended grace to apply leverage to holy living, for in Titus 2:11-13, Paul writes:

> *For the grace of God that brings salvation has appeared to all men, teaching us that, denying ungodliness and worldly lusts, we should live soberly, righteously, and godly in the present age, looking for that blessed hope and glorious appearing of our great God and Savior Jesus Christ.*

---

Seminary Press, 1948), pp. 242-43.

[15] D. M. Lloyd-Jones, *Romans: An Exposition of Chapters 7.1-8.4: The Law: Its Function and Limits* (Grand Rapids: Zondervan Publishing House, 1973), p. 278.

Lutzer comments on this issue:

> When someone says that God's unlimited forgiveness gives license to sin, it shows that he's beginning to understand the incredible generosity of God's grace!
>
> When Paul argued that through Christ we can be freely forgiven, he knew that if he made his point clear, his readers would object by saying, "Let us continue in sin that grace might increase!" (Rom. 6:1). Once we have grasped the unlimited favor God gives to us, the human reaction is to assume that such teaching will encourage people to sin. Paul's answer is direct: "God forbid. How shall we, that are dead to sin, live any longer therein?" (Rom. 6:2).[16]

Lutzer further explains:

> Undoubtedly, some have deliberately sinned, flippantly presuming on God's grace. (I think if we were honest, we'd all admit that we've been guilty of that sometimes.) But when this happens, God assumes the responsibility of disciplining His children. God does not punish us, because Christ has already borne our punishment. But God does discipline us. He brings consequences into our lives that will teach us to live in constant fellowship with Him.[17]

Although the believer is not forensically punished for his sin, nevertheless, there will be temporal consequences as well as eternal consequences. Present unconfessed sin results in a loss of desire for service as one is out of experiential fellowship with God. Unconfessed sin also results in loss of power in the believer's life since the sin grieves the Holy Spirit. Furthermore, unconfessed sin results in loss of opportunity since the sinning believer is not living according to the will of God. Although these are three present consequences of unconfessed sin in the believer's life, likewise, there are future consequences. When a believer is not walking in experiential fellowship with God, he is passing up opportunities for reward which he will never have again. As a result he will lose the reward that God would have so lavishly bestowed upon him had he been faithful. This will be a real and eternal loss indeed.

---

[16] Lutzer, "Are We Making Sin Too Easy?" p. 46.
[17] Ibid.

In regard to confessed or even unconfessed sin it must be concluded that God's justice was completely satisfied in the substitutionary death of Christ. Because the Christian is a member of the family of God, any unconfessed sin in his life invites God's discipline, which has as its purpose restoration to fellowship rather than retribution through judicial punishment. Thus God's disciplinary judgment in the believer's present experience is not a matter of justice but rather a matter of loving correction. Doubtless, discipline takes varying forms and degrees of severity. Some children, like wayward Christians, are very strong-willed, and they might require severe discipline to achieve any real change. Other children can be rebuked and corrected by just a word. The question is not how much punishment should be meted out in light of the offense, but what is necessary to bring the child back to proper behavior. The omniscient heavenly Father is an all-wise disciplinarian, apportioning corrective chastening to the unique need of the individual Christian.

### The Evaluative Judgment of the Christian

The expression "the judgment seat of Christ" in the English Bible has tended to cause some to draw the wrong conclusion about the nature of the evaluation at the *bēma*. A common conclusion which is drawn from this English translation, "judgment seat," is that God will mete out a just retribution for sins in the believer's life, and some measure of retributive punishment for sins will result. However, as shown earlier, Christ has borne the guilt of the believer's sins. The Christian will stand glorified before Christ without his old sin nature. He will, likewise, be without guilt because he has been declared righteous. There will be no need of forensic punishment for Christ has forever borne it. However, sin will have its eternal effect of loss of reward which was within the grasp of the believer. There will be no need for discipline for he will be entirely perfected and cannot morally improve in his experiential holiness.[18] Paul writes, *"So that you come short in no gift, eagerly waiting*

---

[18] Hebrews 11:40 speaks of Old Testament saints as not yet being made perfect. It should be noted that "perfect" has several meanings: perfect in standing at the moment of regeneration; perfect in sinlessness after death; and perfect in completion after the resurrection. Hebrews 12:23 indicates that Old Testament saints' spirits are made perfect. Apparently this has reference to the fact that Christ's sacrifice for

*for the revelation of our Lord Jesus Christ, who will also confirm you to the end, that you may be blameless in the day of our Lord Jesus Christ"* (1 Cor. 1:7-8). Again the apostle writes in 1 Thessalonians 3:12-13, *"And the Lord make you increase and abound in love to one another and to all, just as we do to you, so the He may establish your hearts blameless in holiness before our God and Father at the coming of our Lord Jesus Christ with all His saints."*[19]

Discipline in the present life is designed to lead the believer back to fellowship, but without the sin nature the Christian will be morally perfect as Christ is morally perfect. Paul describes the glorified church in Ephesians 5:27: *"That He might present her to Himself a glorious church, not having spot or wrinkle or any such thing, but that she should be holy and without blemish."* That which is true of Christians' moral condition corporately is true individually. Christians will be beyond the point where discipline will have any meaning in relationship to purification or separation in the eternal state.

The only question which will remain concerns the faithfulness of a believer's life as a member of the body of Christ. What will be examined is his entire life as a servant of God and as a steward of the abilities, opportunities, and privileges which have been entrusted to him by the Master. The result of this examination will be rewards for faithfulness or loss of rewards for unfaithfulness.

## SUGGESTED PURPOSES OF THE JUDGMENT

In order to facilitate greater understanding of the judgment seat of Christ, consideration will be given to various erroneous views. As it will be seen, there are reputable and respected Bible teachers and theologians who hold greatly varying positions in regard to the purpose and nature of this judgment. Though exception will be taken with their

---

sins has actually brought about removal of their sins. Hebrews 11:40 states that these Old Testament saints should not be made perfect without "us," that is, New Testament believers. This has reference to the fact that their spirits have not yet been reunited with their bodies, which will occur at the resurrection of Old Testament saints subsequent to the resurrection of New Testament saints. This means that their spirits are morally perfect in the intermediate state in the sense that they are unable to sin. They are in a fixed state awaiting the evaluation of their earthly lives.

[19] Also see Colossians 1:21-22.

conclusions, their sincerity and scholarship is in no way impugned by this writer.

### *The Judgment Seat and Salvation*

Many reputable scholars, primarily of the general judgment persuasion, believe that at the judgment seat of Christ there will be a determination of who will enter heaven and who will not. For example, Louis Berkhof writes, "The last judgment determines, and therefore naturally leads on to, the final state of those who appear before the judgment seat. Their final state is either one of everlasting misery or one of eternal blessedness."[20] Similarly Charles Hodge reveals the extent to which this view is advocated and describes the purpose of this final judgment. He writes:

> By the Church doctrine is meant that doctrine which is held by the Church universal; by Romanists and Protestants in the West, and by the Greeks in the East. That doctrine includes [the fact that] . . . the final judgment is a definite future event . . . when the eternal destiny of men and of angels shall be finally determined and publicly manifested.[21]

Although the above are noted scholars, their conclusion that the judgment seat will deal with the issue of salvation is derived from the faulty assumption that there will be a general judgment. It has been shown that only church-age believers will be present at the *bēma*. Since the issue of one's eternal destiny was irreversibly determined the instant he believed on the Lord Jesus Christ, it will never come up at the judgment seat.

As seen earlier the *bēma* does not involve the question of salvation because no unsaved will be present. Neither does it involve the question of a believer having "earned" salvation. In Arminian doctrine, salvation is made a sort of reward which is capable of being retained by perseverance. John Gates, in his summary of the Arminian doctrine, writes, "While the Remonstrants [advocates of Arminius' teachings] are cautious on the matter, they imply that if a saved person does not continue to cooperate with Christ he will become 'devoid of (saving) grace.'" Arminianism teaches

---

[20] Berkhof, *Systematic Theology*, p. 735.
[21] Hodge, *Systematic Theology*, III, 845 (brackets added).

that it is possible for those who are Christians to fall from a state of saving grace. To the Arminian and the Roman Catholic, being in a state of "grace" at the time of death is essential for salvation. Lloyd-Jones comments on this false notion in his exposition of Romans 8:1:

> There are many who misunderstand this [truth of no condemnation for the believer]. They seem to think of the Christian as a man who, if he confesses his sin and asks for forgiveness, is forgiven. At that moment he is not under condemnation. But then if he should sin again he is back once more under condemnation. Then he repents and confesses his sin again, and asks for pardon, and he is cleansed once more. So to them the Christian is a man who is constantly passing from one state to the other; back and forth; condemned, not condemned. Now that, according to the Apostle, is a wholly mistaken notion, and a complete failure to understand the position. The Christian is a man who can never be condemned; he can never come into a state of condemnation again.[22]

Such confusion concerning the issues of salvation and condemnation at the judgment seat is widespread. Salvation is never conditioned upon human merit (cf. Eph. 2:8-9 and Ti. 3:5) but solely upon faith apart from good works. P. E. Hewitt has succinctly summarized the distinction between salvation and reward:

1) Salvation is a free gift; reward is earned.
2) Salvation is by faith; reward is by faithfulness.
3) Salvation is without merit; reward is meritorious.
4) Salvation is the result of a work by God for man; reward is the result of the work by God in man.
5) Salvation is the start of the race; reward is the finish of the race.[23]

For the Christian, salvation is eternally secure because full and adequate payment for his sins has already been efficaciously made by Christ. Therefore, salvation will not be an issue at the judgment seat of Christ.

---

[22] Lloyd-Jones, *Romans: An Exposition of Chapters 7.1-8.4: The Law: Its Function and Limits*, p. 271.

[23] P. E. Hewitt, *Coming Events: A Handbook of Bible Prophecy* (Grand Rapids: Zondervan Publishing House, 1942), p. 37.

## The Judgment Seat and Punishment

Another erroneous view of the judgment seat which is common in various theological circles teaches that God will punish believers for all their unconfessed sins and for carnal living. George Dollar, for example in the glossary of his book, *A History of Fundamentalism in America*, defines *bēma*. He writes:

> It is the judgment of the believer that will take place after the rapture of the Church but before the Lord's return to earth. Its purpose is to make manifest and *deal with the sins of the believer that he has not dealt with in self-judgment*. Its purpose is not condemnation but examination and the meting out of rewards.[24]

Dollar believes and teaches much more concerning the judgment seat of Christ than that which is revealed in this book. In a sermon he commented on the parable of the talents in Matthew 25:14-30. Verse thirty reads, "And cast ye the unprofitable servant into outer darkness: there shall be weeping and gnashing of teeth." Dollar states that this unprofitable servant "was a self-centered, carnal, selfish, wicked, lustful, bad Christian."[25] His fleshly works are burned up at the judgment seat of Christ. Dollar describes what Christ said to the profitable servants:

> I'm going to make you ruler . . . and during the millennial reign he will rule. He will have a throne. He will rule and reign with Christ for a thousand years. . . . Do you think wicked Christians are going to rule in the millennial reign? One thousand times never.[26]

Dollar then continues by describing the lot of the unprofitable Christian. Dollar believes and teaches that the carnal Christian is to be cast into outer darkness for a thousand years. He states:

---

[24] George W. Dollar, *A History of Fundamentalism in America* (Greenville, SC: Bob Jones University Press, 1973), p. 378 (italics added).
[25] George W. Dollar, "Rewards," a tape-recorded sermon preached at Faith Baptist Church, La Crosse, WI, n.d.
[26] Ibid.

For a thousand years when the Lord rules and reigns over the earth, you'll not rule. . . . But throughout that one thousand years, up there in the outer darkness there shall be weeping and gnashing of teeth. You don't care now, you will care. . . . You'll have a thousand years, my friend, and I am a friend to your soul to warn you. . . . Lazy, unprofitable, wicked servants, you will have one thousand years of remorse. . . . He's going to take the good and faithful servants with Him; they will rule with Him over the earth. But He's going to send all of the wicked, lazy, unprofitable Christians . . . to outer darkness for one thousand years and they shall weep and there shall be gnashing of teeth.[27]

Such a view misinterprets and misapplies this parable, for the unprofitable servant is not a saved individual, but an unsaved man facing eternal damnation.[28] To apply this to a Christian, even to a carnal Christian, is contrary to the whole tenor of Biblical revelation. Kenneth Dodson also writes of punishment at the judgment seat of Christ:

Justice toward His children demands that God reward them for both "good works" and "bad works" at the "Judgment Seat of Christ." There will be crowns and rewards for "good works." There will be chastisement and *"stripes"* for *"bad works."*[29]

Likewise, William Narum pointedly concludes, "There will be punishment, then, as through fire, in the judgment for our evil works."[30] However, Scripture teaches that for the believer God's *justice* has already been fully and forever satisfied at the cross in relation to the believer's sins. If God were to judicially punish the believer for his sins, He would be requiring two payments for sin and would, therefore, be unjust. Such a concept erroneously disparages the all-sufficiency of Christ's death on the cross. Hebrews 10 removes any question in regard to the finality of

---

[27] Ibid.

[28] For further support for this conclusion see George Zeller, "Weeping and Gnashing of Teeth: Will This Be the Fate of True Christians?" http://www.middletownbible church.org/doctrine/hodgesgn.htm (accessed March 17, 2011).

[29] Kenneth F. Dodson, *The Prize of the Up-Calling or Paul's Secret of Victory* (Grand Rapids: Baker Book House, 1969), p. 82 (italics added).

[30] William H. K. Narum, "A Study of the Eschatological Motifs of the Christian Life" (unpublished Th.D. dissertation, Princeton Theological Seminary, 1951), p. 299.

payment for sin. Verse twelve reads, *"But this Man, after He had offered one sacrifice for sins forever, sat down at the right hand of God."* The writer then applies this truth to Christians: *"For by one offering He has perfected forever those who are being sanctified"* (Heb. 10:14). His conclusion is stated in Hebrews 10:17-18: *"Their sins and their lawless deeds I will remember no more. Now where there is remission of these, there is no longer an offering for sin."* Therefore, the idea that the judgment seat of Christ is a place where forensic punishment will be meted out for the believer's sins must be rejected. The believer does sin. All unfaithfulness in relationship to his stewardship responsibility is sin. James 4:17 reads, *"Therefore, to Him who knows to do good and does not do it, to him it is sin."* But Christ paid the penalty for all of the believer's post-conversion sins. He will forfeit rewards which he could have received, but he will not be punished in a judicial sense of "paying" for his sins.

### The Judgment Seat and Chastisement

Related to the preceding idea of punishment at the *bēma* is the erroneous view that God will chasten unfaithful Christians at the judgment seat. For example, Robert T. Ketcham concludes:

> The question as to the continuance of such a process of disciplinary judgment at and after the Judgment Seat of Christ immediately involves the *character* of the age to come. *This* is purely an *age of grace.* The age to come seems to be purely one of *justice or judgment.*[31]

He further explains: "Now, if in this day of *grace* we admit (and we all *do*) that disciplinary measures are used of God in dealing with His own, why not admit the reasonableness of their continuance in the coming age which is purely *disciplinary and judicial?*"[32] Dodson, likewise, believes there will be chastisement at the *bēma*. As quoted earlier, he states, "There will be chastisement and 'stripes' for 'bad works.'"[33]

Several arguments can be considered in refutation of such a position. First, as one examines such passages as Hebrews 12 and 1 Corinthians 11

---

[31] Robert T. Ketcham, *Why Was Christ a Carpenter? and Other Sermons* (Des Plaines, IL: Regular Baptist Press, 1966), p. 134.

[32] Ibid., p. 135.

[33] Dodson, *The Prize of the Up-Calling or Paul's Secret of Victory*, p. 82.

it is obvious that the Bible only mentions chastisement in relation to the present life of the believer. It is never mentioned in relationship to the judgment seat of Christ or with reference to the believer's life in heaven. L. Sale-Harrison writes:

> We must not confuse condemnation with chastisement. The Lord chastens us, but He Himself bore all judgment due to us. *Chastisement has to do with this life, and not with the Judgment Seat of Christ.* Chastisement is for the purpose of discipline and not for condemnation; *also all need for disciplinary measures is over when we leave this earthly pilgrimage.*[34]

Second, the reason for chastisement in this life, as it has been shown earlier, is to foster holy living, not for the purpose of retributive punishment. Hebrews 12:10 and 11 read:

> *For they indeed for a few days chastened us as seemed best to them, but He for our profit, that we may be partakers of His holiness. Now no chastening seems to be joyful for the present, but painful; nevertheless, afterward it yields the peaceable fruit of righteousness to those who have been trained by it.*

At the judgment seat the believer will already be in his glorified body, without the old sin nature, and morally perfect as Christ is morally perfect. No further moral improvement in his character or conduct will be possible. Any development in experiential sanctification is limited to the Christian's life on earth. Chafer and Walvoord concur, "It is not a matter of sanctification such as is experienced in present chastisement for failure to confess sin . . . because the believer is already perfect in the presence of God."[35] Therefore, chastisement will have no purpose in the life to come.

Third, those who teach that chastisement will have a place at the *bēma* erroneously consider it as a form of punishment or retribution rather than a method of instruction and restoration for the purpose of

---

[34] Sale-Harrison, *The Judgment Seat of Christ: Incentive and a Warning*, pp. 36-37 (italics added).

[35] Lewis Sperry Chafer, *Major Bible Themes: 52 Vital Doctrines of the Scripture Simplified and Explained*, rev. by John F. Walvoord (rev. ed.; Grand Rapids: Zondervan Publishing House, 1974), pp. 285-86.

sanctification in this life. As demonstrated earlier, the judgment seat does not involve judicial punishment for sin.

### The Judgment Seat and Unconfessed Sins

The question to be considered now is: Will the believer ever face his unconfessed sins? At one end of the spectrum are the Roman Catholics and their doctrine of purgatory, and at the other end are those who teach that unconfessed sins will not be an issue.

## Purgatorial View of Unconfessed Sins

The Roman Catholic doctrine of purgatory is categorically rejected by Protestants. Even Protestants who hold a severe view in regard to the judgment seat do not consider the suffering which results as any kind of purgatorial suffering. Dodson, who holds a rather harsh position, writes:

> In all of Paul's teaching, as well as that of the Lord Jesus, there is no room for the Roman Catholic Church's doctrine of purgatory. Though some of its writers have attempted to use some of these Scriptures to teach a sort of "intermediate hell," into which all Catholics must go to be "purged" from their "venial sins," before they can go into heaven, neither the Lord Jesus nor Paul taught any such thing.[36]

Catholics, however, do teach that if anyone dies having committed some venial sin which has not been duly confessed, that person will enter purgatory in order to make expiation or full atonement for his sin. This involves an undetermined length of suffering in fire which eventually purifies the person so that he may enter into eternal bliss. They teach that the duration and intensity of the suffering are in proportion to the guilt and impurity of the sufferer. J. F. X. Cevetello provides a concise statement of the Catholic doctrine of purgatory. He writes: "According to the teaching of the Church, [purgatory is] the state, place, or condition in the next world, which will continue until the last judgment, where the souls of those who die in the state of grace, but not yet free from all imperfection, make expiation from unforgiven venial sins or for the

---

[36] Dodson, *The Prize of the Up-Calling or Paul's Secret of Victory*, p. 89.

temporal punishment due to venial and mortal sins that have already been forgiven and, by so doing, are purified before they enter heaven."[37]

In refutation of the doctrine of purgatory several objections can be raised. First, for the Christian, God's wrath is not involved. His wrath for the believer's sins was fully satisfied at the cross. Second, it is impossible for fallen man to atone for his own sins through suffering. Third, the doctrine of purgatory has no Scriptural support. Although Catholics have supposed 1 Corinthians 3:15 to support their doctrine of purgatory, this passage provides no corroboration for such a position.

Patrick Henry has compiled a list of arguments which demonstrate that Paul did not intend to teach any doctrine of purgatorial fire in 1 Corinthians 3:15:

1. Absolutely nothing is said in this passage about purification from sins. . . .
2. The sins of people are not in question in this passage. Nothing is said of sins. This passage is addressed to justified believers.
3. Nowhere is it said that this fire inflicts pain. The fire in this passage destroys works but does not inflict pain. It is not the individual who is burned but his works.
4. The Catholic Church teaches that purgatory is a present condition, that is, people are burning there now. The reference in this passage is to the second coming of Jesus Christ and has nothing to say about the intermediate state between death and judgment.[38]

Another unscriptural assumption concerning the Roman doctrine of purgatory is that the Pope and his subordinates have power to retain or to remit the sins of departed souls, and to deliver them from the purgatorial fires or to allow them to suffer in its torments.[39] However, God alone has the power to forgive sins (cf. Mark 2:7; 1 Tim. 2:5).

Although Protestants openly reject the doctrine of purgatory, some approximate this Roman Catholic doctrine in their writing on the judgment seat of Christ. For example, Theodore Epp writes concerning

---

[37] J. F. X. Cevetello, "Purgatory," New Catholic Encyclopedia, 1967, XI, 1034.

[38] Patrick David Henry, "What Are the Works that Shall Be Burned as Mentioned in I Corinthians 3:15?" (unpublished B.D. monograph, Grace Theological Seminary, 1946), pp. 39-40.

[39] C. Hodge, Systematic Theology, III, 758.

the *bēma*, "Here we shall be judged for every idle word and every deed done in the flesh. This is not a judgment for condemnation, but a judgment for purification."[40] Similarly, H. H. Savage states, "So there must not only be a purging of sin in the heavenly places themselves as we have already seen, but there must also be a purging of sin in the believer so that the remaining imperfections can be eliminated."[41]

Some fiery evangelists and Bible teachers go so far as to portray the judgment seat as a place of weeping and wailing and gnashing of teeth. Again, Dollar states, "But He is going to send all the wicked, lazy, unprofitable Christians to outer darkness for one thousand years and they shall weep and there shall be gnashing of teeth."[42]

In his discussion on Luke 16:14-31 concerning the rich man and Lazarus, G. H. Lang states that the rich man who was suffering and who was "tormented in this flame" may have been a carnal believer. He writes:

> It is on Christians that this certainty is pressed, in order that we may not be weary in communicating of our substance, in doing well, by working that which is good toward all men. . . . A Dives [the supposed Latin name for the rich man in Luke 16:19] may be a degenerate believer. Scripture and fact assert it. Who dare deny it?[43]

Lang further comments on this passage:

> That death introduces a complete break in moral state and experience is refuted. On the contrary, moral condition persists and governs experience. The law of sowing and reaping operates rigidly and fully. *Eternal* consequences have indeed been cancelled for the repentant by the sufferings of Christ on the cross; but temporal consequences prevail in the period between death and resurrection.[44]

---

[40] Theodore H. Epp, *The Sinning Christian and His Judgment* (Lincoln, NE: Back to the Bible Publishers, n.d.), p. 45.

[41] Henry H. Savage, *The Heavenlies: Purified Places, Perfected Peoples, Perpetual Plans* (Grand Rapids: Diadem Music and Publishing Company, 1964), p. 125.

[42] Dollar, "Rewards."

[43] G. H. Lang, *Pictures and Parables: Studies in the Parabolic Teaching of Holy Scripture* (London: The Paternoster Press, 1955), p. 266 (brackets added).

[44] Ibid., p. 262.

In his concluding remarks Lang writes:

> Believers have been buoyed up with the fictitious notion that they go from their death-bed to the glory of heaven, and the salutary warning has been lost that their unrepented misdeeds must be faced directly after death.[45]

Such conjectures and interpretations go beyond the bounds of sound Biblical exposition. Walvoord supplies a concluding argument:

> Although some have attempted to make this a Protestant purgatory, i.e., a time of punishment for unconfessed sin, it seems clear from the general doctrine of justification by faith that no condemnation is possible for one who is in Christ. Discipline such as is administered in this life will be of no value to those already made perfect in heaven.[46]

## Public Exposure View of Unconfessed Sins

Many expositors with varying degrees of severity describe the judgment seat of Christ as the place where the Christian will be faced with his unconfessed sins. Some writers picture the *bēma* scene as one of public humiliation. Dodson writes:

> The whole Bible teaches that God is a God of absolute justice and holiness, Who will bring every word and deed of human beings into judgment. *He has a video-tape of every human life*, with all the lines of human influence that have gone from that life into other human lives, *and He will play back all of these video-tapes of all humanity*. This will be "God's Drama of History."[47]

Similarly, Clarence Mason writes of public humiliation in heaven:

> Many expositors believe that this scene will not be individual and private, but overt and public. How much better to go to a brother and make things right now, so that we shall not hang

---

[45] Ibid., p. 268.

[46] John F. Walvoord, "The Church in Heaven," *Bibliotheca Sacra* 123 (April-June 1966): 99.

[47] Dodson, *The Prize of the Up-Calling or Paul's Secret of Victory*, p. 77 (italics added).

our heads in shame at Christ's Judgment-seat. *Secret sin on earth is open scandal in Heaven.*[48]

Most writers who believe that unconfessed sins will be an issue at the *bēma* are not as extreme in their positions as the above. Many simply state that unconfessed sins will be judged or confessed at that time. M. R. DeHaan is rather vague concerning the effects of unconfessed sin. He states, "While the sin question is settled at Calvary, our walk is judged by God's chastening in this life, and all unconfessed sin will be taken care of at the Judgment Seat of Christ."[49] Sale-Harrison says the unconfessed sins must be exposed. He writes, "Therefore if we do not confess our sins, that unrighteousness—which has not been cleansed—must be manifested (exposed) at the Judgment Seat of Christ."[50] Savage elaborates on the need for confession of wrongs committed while in this life at the judgment seat of Christ. He explains:

> Those at the judgment seat of Christ are going to have to confess before Him the things that still need to be confessed. Those who are critics, those who are faultfinders, those who are character assassins, those who are doing everything they can to bring about schisms and difficulties in the church will have to report to Him. They have to confess to Him what sort of influence they have had on earth.[51]

As seen by the above quotations the view that the believer will be confronted publicly with unconfessed sins is widely held. Some writers further develop this thought by stating that wrongs will not only be exposed, but they will be made right by the offending Christian at the judgment seat of Christ. Haldeman presents his conception of what will transpire at this awesome event. He writes:

> If any one owes you a debt, it will have to be acknowledged and paid. If a Christian has wronged you in any fashion, hurt

---

[48] Clarence E. Mason, Jr., "A Study of Pauline Motives as Revealed in 2 Corinthians 4:16-6:4a," *Bibliotheca Sacra* 111 (July 1954): 221 (italics added).

[49] M. R. DeHaan, *The Believer's Judgments* (Grand Rapids: Radio Bible Class, 1963), pp. 16-17.

[50] Sale-Harrison, *The Judgment-Seat of Christ: An Incentive and a Warning*, p. 53.

[51] H. H. Savage, "What Will the Faithful Do in Heaven?" in *Moody Founder's Week Conference Messages: February 5-11, 1962* (Chicago: Moody Bible Institute, n.d.), p. 49.

you by an idle word or the spreading of a false and irresponsible report, such an one will have to apologize to you before high heaven and the assembled host.[52]

The above mentioned writers, although they may differ in specific details of this future examination, would all agree that if a believer confesses his sins he is forgiven on the basis of his confession. However, if he refuses or somehow fails or forgets to confess any of his sins, God will confront him with those unconfessed sins at the judgment seat of Christ.

## Present Experience View of Unconfessed Sins

In contrast to the view that Christians will be confronted with all of their unconfessed sins at the *bēma*, other equally respected and reputable Bible teachers and Bible scholars reject this position as erroneous. They emphasize that Scripture teaches that all sins, both confessed and unconfessed, have been borne by Christ on the cross, and the Christian will never be faced with either at the judgment seat of Christ. Gromacki states that the believer will never face punishment for unconfessed sins:

> Will God punish believers for all those sins which were committed *after* receiving Christ? No, because God has removed all of our transgressions (past, present, future) from us as far as the east is from the west (Psalm 103:12). The believer will never be punished for sins because Christ bore that punishment in His body on the cross. . . . Some have suggested that the Christian will be punished for all *unconfessed* sin, but Christ paid the penalty for *all* sin, both confessed and unconfessed. Unconfessed sin brings immediate loss of divine blessing to the child of God; this is his loss.[53]

Scriptural support can be presented to demonstrate that when God removes sin from the believer, He does it completely. For example, God says, *"I have blotted out, like a thick cloud, your transgressions, and like a cloud, your sins"* (Isa. 44:22). The Psalmist writes, *"As far as the*

---

[52] Haldeman, *Ten Sermons on the Second Coming of Our Lord Jesus Christ*, p. 341.
[53] Gromacki, *Are These the Last Days?* p. 160.

*east is from the west, so far has He removed our transgressions from us"* (Ps. 103:12). Micah declares, *"You will cast all our sins into the depths of the sea"* (Mic. 7:19). Isaiah again writes, *"For You have cast all my sins behind Your back"* (Isa. 38:17). Both the Old and New Testaments record God's declaration, *"For I will be merciful to their unrighteousness, and their sins and lawless deeds I will remember no more"* (Jer. 31:34; Heb. 8:12). Using these verses and others as background Pentecost writes:

> There are others who hold the view that is kin to this last [that all post-conversion sins of Christians will be punished] and is likewise erroneous. They claim that if a believer *confesses* his sins, he is forgiven those sins on the basis of his confession. But if he refuses, or fails, or forgets to confess a sin, God is going to judge him at the Judgment Seat of Christ and make him confess and then be punished for all the sins he failed to confess. . . . This presupposes the fact that my sins have not been completely and perfectly dealt with by the blood of Christ. It presupposes that God is keeping a record of all my iniquities so that He can present them before me when I stand in His presence. Such is contrary to the holiness of God and to the finished work of the Lord Jesus Christ.[54]

In another one of his works Pentecost pointedly states:

> To bring the believer into judgment concerning the sin question, whether his sins before his new birth, his sins since his new birth, or even his unconfessed sins since the new birth, is to deny the efficacy of the death of Christ and nullify the promise of God that "their sins and iniquities will I remember no more" (Heb. 10:17).[55]

Lehman Strauss, likewise, concludes that punishment for sin will not be an issue at the *bēma*. Strauss writes:

> So perfectly and completely did our Saviour's blood cleanse us that God can find nothing in us for which to condemn us. The Christian's judgment for sins is past, so that the Judgment Seat

---

[54] J. Dwight Pentecost, *Prophecy for Today: An Exposition of Major Themes on Prophecy* (Grand Rapids: Zondervan Publishing House, 1961), p. 153 (ellipsis added).
[55] Pentecost, *Things to Come*, p. 222.

of Christ is not a judgment for sins committed either before or after one has been saved.[56]

Chafer and Walvoord concur with the preceding writer's conclusion. They state:

> With reference to sin, Scripture teaches that the child of God under grace shall not come into judgment (John 3:18; 5:24; 6:37; Rom. 5:1; 8:1; 1 Cor. 11:32); in his standing before God, and on the ground that the penalty for all sin—past, present, and future (Col. 2:13)—has been borne by Christ as the perfect Substitute, the believer is not only placed beyond condemnation, but being in Christ is accepted in the perfection of Christ (1 Cor. 1:30; Eph. 1:6; Col. 2:10; Heb. 10:14) and loved of God as Christ is loved (John 17:23).[57]

Again Chafer writes concerning the *bēma*, "It cannot be too strongly emphasized that the judgment is unrelated to the problem of sin, that it is more for the bestowing of rewards than the rejection of failure."[58]

The men who have been quoted above all emphasize in their writings the perfect position of every believer before God. They emphasize the fact that Christ's death has fully paid for all of the Christian's sins—past, present, and future. All are in agreement that the believer's sins, even his unconfessed sins, will not in any way be charged against him at the judgment seat of Christ.

Other arguments which these writers use as support for their position lend additional light in regard to the reason for their beliefs. Pentecost, for example, argues that Paul's usage of the term *bēma* in the second Corinthian epistle was one that was familiar to the readers. The historical event that would come to their minds was the Isthmian games, which have been considered in detail earlier in this work. The contestants would compete for the prize under the careful scrutiny of the judges to make sure that every rule of the contest was obeyed. The victor of a given event who participated according to the rules was led by the judges to the

---

[56] Lehman Strauss, *God's Plan for the Future* (Grand Rapids: Zondervan Publishing House, 1965), p. 108.

[57] Chafer, *Major Bible Themes: 52 Vital Doctrines of the Scripture Simplified and Explained*, p. 282.

[58] Chafer, *Ecclesiology-Eschatology*, p. 406.

platform called the *bēma*. There a laurel wreath was placed upon his head as a symbol of victory.

Pentecost concludes that Paul is picturing the believer as a contestant in a spiritual contest. As the victorious Grecian athlete appeared before the *bēma* to receive his perishable award, so the Christian will appear before Christ's *bēma* to receive his imperishable award. The judge at the *bēma* bestowed rewards to the victors. He did not whip the losers. Pentecost summarizes, "Thus the apostle is speaking not in the area of sin, but in the area of reward for the child of God."[59]

Another argument which supports the position that the Christian's sins will not be an issue at the *bēma* relates to the present effect of unconfessed sins. Some would argue that unconfessed sins relate to fellowship in this life. Any unconfessed sin stands as a barrier to fellowship and growth in one's present relationship to God. Confession brings immediate forgiveness and restoration of fellowship between the Christian and God. This is present tense forgiveness and deals with "family" forgiveness. For example, 1 John is a "family" epistle addressed to the "born ones" or to *teknion mou* ("my little children"). In the first chapter, "family" or experiential forgiveness is referred to: *"If we confess our sins, He is faithful and just to forgive us our sins and to cleanse us from all unrighteousness"* (1 Jn. 1:9). Gromacki writes of this family relationship:

> The sense of fellowship, however, can be broken by sinful acts and attitudes. . . . The Father-son relationship is not broken by sin; only the sweet fellowship is lost by the believer. This is what the prodigal son had to learn. After wasting his riches and life, he decided to return home. When he arrived, he said, "Father, I have sinned against heaven, and in thy sight, and am no more worthy to be called thy son" (Lk. 15:21). He underestimated the love and understanding of his father. Did the father grant his request? No. Rather, he said, "Bring forth the best robe, and put it on him; and put a ring on his hand, and shoes on his feet: And bring hither the fatted calf, and kill it; and let us eat, and be merry: For this my son was dead, and is alive again; he was lost, and is found. And they began to be merry" (Lk. 15:22-24). The son felt that the father-son relationship should

---

[59] Pentecost, *Prophecy for Today: An Exposition of Major Themes on Prophecy*, pp. 153-54.

be dissolved because of his actions, but fathers do not think that way. There was no criticism by the father. He did not give his son a lecture nor beat him. Rather, he opened his arms, his heart, and his home to the blessings of renewed fellowship. So it is with God.[60]

The daily forgiveness of those who are within the family of God is distinguished from judicial and positional forgiveness which was applied forensically to all of a person's sins the moment he believed in the Lord Jesus Christ. Paul writes of this forensic forgiveness in Colossians 2:13: *"And you, being dead in your trespasses and the uncircumcision of your flesh, He has made alive together with Him, having forgiven you all trespasses."* The point Paul makes is that the believer is completely forgiven legally before the sin is even committed. The question that arises concerning a believer's sins is between the Father and a son, and not between a judge and a criminal. The legal side has already been settled. The question is now of a contemporaneous relationship between the Father and a son. If there is a barrier which arises through the son offending his Father, there must be family forgiveness. It is not forensic forgiveness for that has been eternally granted and efficaciously applied the moment he became a son. Gromacki further explains the differences and implications between these two aspects of forgiveness. He writes:

> There is a difference between judicial and daily forgiveness. It is comparable to the once-for-all bath of regeneration and the daily cleansings of the believer's walk. The forgiveness of sins, at the moment of believing faith, gives the new child of God a proper relationship to, or an acceptable standing before, God. Daily forgiveness is necessary to maintain fellowship with the Father and to enjoy the daily blessings of the Father-son relationship. When a child of God sins, he needs restoration, not a new regeneration. Daily forgiveness is obtained through daily confession. . . . Daily sin will make the Christian feel bad or ashamed, but he will not sense the concept of guilt or liability to eternal punishment. He has been forgiven all of his sins judicially by God.[61]

---

[60] Robert Glenn Gromacki, *Salvation Is Forever* (Chicago: Moody Press, 1973), p. 99.
[61] Ibid., 60 (ellipsis added).

Perhaps an underlying concern of those who differ with this position is raised and answered by Lloyd-Jones in his outstanding exposition of Romans 8:1 regarding the fact that Paul says there is "no condemnation" for believers. Lloyd-Jones boldly writes:

> But why does the Apostle say this, and on what grounds does he say it? Is it not a dangerous thing to say? Will it not incite people to sin? If we tell Christians that their past sins, their present, and their future sins have already been put away by God, are we not more or less telling them that they are free to go out and sin? If you react in that way to my statements I am most happy, for I am obviously a good and true interpreter of the Apostle Paul. It was because he preached such things that people said, "What shall we say then? Shall we continue in sin that grace may abound?" (chapter 6:1). That is the very charge they were bringing against him. . . . The Apostle has already given the answer in chapters 6 and 7, proving that there is no risk at all, but rather the opposite.[62]

Lloyd-Jones supplies the answer which he alluded to above:[63]

> That is why there is no risk in the Apostle's statement. Being in this state and relationship as a Christian gives me a much higher standard, and makes sin much more offensive to me, much more hateful, something to be shunned. There is no risk here at all. The man who is in Christ Jesus, and who knows it, is a man who will fight sin and hate it and avoid it much more than the man who is "under the law."[64]

In conclusion, one thing is certain; in neither passage in which the judgment seat of Christ is explicitly found is the issue of sin in general, or unconfessed sins in particular, referred to by Paul. The penalty for the believer's sins has been fully paid. The issue at the judgment seat will therefore not be the Christian's sin but the Christian's service.

---

[62] Lloyd-Jones, *Romans: An Exposition of Chapters 7.1-8.4: The Law: Its Function and Limits*, pp. 272-73.

[63] It would be helpful for the reader to read Lloyd-Jones' argument in entirety.

[64] Lloyd-Jones, *Romans: An Exposition of Chapters 7.1-8.4: The Law: Its Function and Limits*, p. 278.

# CHAPTER 6

# THE PURPOSE OF THE CHRISTIAN'S JUDGMENT

The purpose of the judgment seat of Christ is not to consider the issue of salvation. Neither is the purpose to render judicial punishment for the believer's sins, whether they be pre-conversion or post-conversion sins, or whether they be confessed or unconfessed. To make the believer's sins and their resultant punishment the issue at the judgment seat is to deny the sufficiency and efficacy of Christ's death in paying the full penalty for all sin and completely satisfying God's justice. God cannot justly exact payment twice for sin.

The issue at the *bēma* is, therefore, not a question of sin to be punished, but rather a question of service. The believer's life will be examined and evaluated in regard to his faithfulness as a steward of the abilities and opportunities which God had entrusted to him. Faithfulness will be graciously rewarded while unfaithfulness which is sin according to James 4:17, will go unrewarded. Thus the primary purpose of the judgment seat of Christ is to reveal and review the Christian's life and service and then to reward him for what God deems worthy of reward. Not only is the purpose of this event future manifestation, but it also should serve as present motivation for contemporary godly living. These primary purposes will be considered in the light of the major passages that describe the judgment seat.

## PRESENT MOTIVATION

The New Testament writers frequently exhorted Christians to godly living in light of the necessity of eventually having their lives examined by the Lord. Paul, himself, expressed this as a motive of his life and service in 2 Corinthians 5:9-11:

*Therefore we make it our aim, whether present or absent, to be well pleasing to Him. For we must all appear before the judgment seat of Christ, that each one may receive the things done in the body, according to what he has done, whether good or bad. Knowing, therefore, the terror of the Lord, we persuade men; but we are well known to God, and I also trust are well known in your consciences.*

In verse nine Paul writes, *"we make it our aim [philotimoumetha], whether present or absent, to be well-pleasing [or acceptable] to Him."* The reason that Paul gives for desiring to be well-pleasing to the Lord is given in verse ten: *"For [gar, which expresses the ground or reason] we must all appear before the judgment seat of Christ."* Paul regarded this as a worthy motive for Christian service in order *"to be well pleasing to Him."* This was a great compelling force in Paul's life that kept him faithful in the midst of overwhelming obstacles and opposition. In Philippians 3:8, 14 Paul writes:

*Yet indeed I also count all things loss for the excellence of the knowledge of Christ Jesus my Lord, for whom I have suffered the loss of all things, and count them as rubbish, that I may gain Christ. . . . I press toward the goal for the prize of the upward call of God in Christ Jesus.*

Then he exhorts in verse fifteen that as many as are spiritually mature to be thus minded. Paul lived his life in light of eternity. His great consuming ambition was to be well-pleasing to the Lord in every area of his life.

In 2 Corinthians 5:11 Paul mentions that he is impelled by the *"terror [phobos] of the Lord"* to persuade men. This verse begins with the causal participle *eidotes* which could be translated in context "since we know therefore the terror of the Lord." The *phobos* of the Lord motivated Paul in his ministry. The question is what did Paul mean by the expression "the *phobos* of the Lord"?

The Greek word *phobos* is generally translated "fear." Arndt and Gingrich indicate that when this word is used in relationship to God it conveys the idea of reverence and respect.[1] Vine expands this basic idea of reverence when he writes, "[It is] reverential fear . . . of God, as a controlling motive

---

[1] Arndt and Gingrich, *A Greek-English Lexicon of the New Testament and Other Early Christian Literature*, p. 871.

of the life, in matters spiritual and moral, not a mere fear of His power and righteous retribution, *but a wholesome dread of displeasing Him.*"[2] Perhaps G. Campbell Morgan conveys the thought and intent of the apostle Paul's statement when he writes:

> What is the fear of the Lord? The old way of defining the fear of the Lord is that I used to be afraid that God would hurt me. Now the fear is, or should be, that I should hurt Him, that I should grieve Him, that I should cause sorrow to the Holy Spirit.[3]

Although the apostle made no attempt to explain his statement, it does suggest the seriousness of the occasion. The interpreter is left with the task of deciding if the phrase *phobon tou kyriou* is best understood as an objective genitive or a subjective genitive. If it were a subjective genitive, the noun in the genitive, "Lord," *produces* the action. In such a case the Lord would produce the terror or fear because of what He might do to the unfaithful believer. If it were an objective genitive, the noun "Lord" *receives* the action. In such a case it would be the respect or reverence given to the Lord because of the believer's recognition of His person, power, and position. The latter appears to be supported by the preceding context since Paul stated that it was his impelling desire to be well-pleasing to the Lord. He desired to please the Lord in all that he did. This is, likewise, the tenor of the New Testament. The believer is not afraid of what his heavenly Father will do to him, but rather he seeks to please Him in all that he does because of love and respect for his heavenly Father.

The desire of Paul's heart was to be with the Lord, as stated in 2 Corinthians 5:8, *"We are confident, yes, well pleased rather to be absent from the body and to be present with the Lord."* Then he states that he desires to be well-pleasing to the Lord. Walvoord, commenting on Paul's motive for service, writes, "This fear is of the possibility that his life will be revealed as one wasted and spent in selfishness rather than in devotion and complete obedience to Christ."[4] W. Robert Cook further explains that this was not due to any thought of condemnation, but rather of displeasing his Lord. Cook states:

---

[2] Vine, *An Expository Dictionary of New Testament Words with Their Precise Meanings for English Readers*, II, 84 (brackets and italics added).

[3] G. Campbell Morgan, *The Corinthian Letters of Paul: An Exposition of I and II Corinthians* (New York: Fleming H. Revell Company, 1946), p. 242.

[4] Walvoord, "The Church in Heaven," p. 100.

Not to be overlooked as a motive for service is the element Paul describes in 2 Corinthians 5:11 as "the fear of the Lord." This fear is the result of the realization that each will receive the things done in the body whether they be good or bad. It is by no means fear of condemnation, for there is "now no condemnation to them that are in Christ Jesus" (Rom. 8:1), but rather it is the same fear to which the apostle alludes in 1 Corinthians 9:27.[5]

Other passages in the New Testament, likewise, suggest that this future evaluation serves as a motivation for faithful service and godly living. For example, 1 Corinthians 15:58 states, *"Therefore, my beloved brethren, be steadfast, immovable, always abounding in the work of the Lord, knowing that your labor is not in vain in the Lord."* The apostle John writes of the need for holy living:

> *Beloved, now we are children of God; and it has not yet been revealed what we shall be, but we know that when He is revealed, we shall be like Him, for we shall see Him as He is. And everyone who has this hope in Him purifies himself, just as He is pure.* (1 Jn. 3:2-3).

From such explicit and implicit exhortations as referred to in this section, it is clear that the present purpose of the judgment seat of Christ is to incite the believer to faithful service and holy living in order to be well-pleasing to the Lord.

Believers wrestle with the difficulty of running the Christian race in a world that is full of obstacles and opposition. God knows the dilemma that each one faces. He has provided this motivating truth concerning future reward to foster present faithfulness. This truth should cause the believer to focus on the consequences of his behavior. His behavior will be considered either worthy of reward or not worthy of reward as it is evaluated at the judgment seat of Christ. As a believer is captured by this truth he recognizes the importance of living a holy and faithful life now since present fidelity determines future reward.

## FUTURE MANIFESTATION

Not only is the judgment seat of Christ motivational, it is also revelational; that is, its purpose is to reveal the true character of the believer's

---

[5] Cook, "The Judgment-Seat of Christ as Related to the Believer's Walk," p. 4.

life and service. At this event the omniscient Christ, whose *"eyes are as a flame of fire,"* reveals the true nature of the believer's thoughts, words, and deeds. Second Corinthians 5:10 begins with the causal conjunction "for" (*gar*) which gives the explanation or reason for Paul's desire to please the Lord. This verse begins, *"For we must all appear before the judgment seat of Christ."* The word "appear" by itself does not convey the meaning of the Greek word *phaneroō*. "Appear" simply implies that one is present at the judgment seat in a geographical sense, whereas *phaneroō* connotes the idea of the Christian being made manifest or being revealed for what he really is. In this verse *phanerōthēnai* is an aorist passive infinitive suggesting that the act of revealing is caused by another agent. Arndt and Gingrich indicate that *phaneroō* in the passive voice means to be revealed or to be made known.[6] This verse thus begins, *"For it is necessary for all of us to be made manifest before the judgment seat of Christ."* Merrill Unger further explains:

> The word is forceful—*phanerootheenai* [sic], meaning to *be made manifest, be revealed in true character, be made plain or evident.* The very character of each Christian will thus be laid bare. His inmost motives and purposes will be ascertained. Only the unerring and omniscient vision of Christ, whose "eyes are as a flame of fire" (Rev. 1:14), could ever do this. The purpose of this penetrating and all-piercing investigation is *hina*, "in order that" each one "may receive (as reward or loss of reward) the things done (works) in the body, according to what he hath done (works again!), whether it be good or bad (worthless).[7]

Vine likewise defines *phaneroō*: "The true meaning is to uncover, lay bare, reveal."[8] From this it must be concluded that there is a revelational aspect with the *bēma*.

The believer's works will be brought under examination. The verse reads, *"That every one may receive the things done in the body, according to what he has done."* The preposition *dia* is used instrumentally here. The

---

[6] Arndt and Gingrich, *A Greek-English Lexicon of the New Testament and Other Early Christian Literature*, p. 860.

[7] Merrill F. Unger, "The Doctrine of the Believer's Judgment," *Our Hope* 58 (January 1952): 433.

[8] Vine, *An Expository Dictionary of New Testament Words with Their Precise Meanings for English Readers*, III, 36.

body is the instrument or channel by or through which deeds are done. Thus the verse should read, "The things done by means of the body" or "through the body." The body is the instrument or vehicle of action. Herman Hoyt explains:

> The *place* where these deeds are centered is the body. Hence the expression, "in the body," more accurately, "through the body," refers to the instrument by which these deeds were performed. No doubt the background of Greek philosophy, depreciating the importance of the body and exalting the meaning of the spirit, led him to say this. This sort of philosophy had promoted the lowest forms of physical excess under the guise that it was the spirit alone that mattered.[9]

This judgment is not merely an external judgment which considers only the observable; but rather it examines the essential character and underlying motives of each believer. Not only *what* the believer has done, but also *why* the believer has done it will be exposed. In 1 Corinthians 4:5 Paul uses this same word *phaneroō* with reference to the Christian's motives. He writes, *"Therefore judge nothing before the time, until the Lord comes, who will both bring to light the hidden things of darkness and reveal [phanerōsei] the counsels of the hearts."* Hoyt again explains:

> A work has three aspects: motive, means, result. Most people are occupied with the last. Fewer consider also the means. Almost none are concerned with the motive. But God looks at all three, starting with the motive. Therein lies the inner essence of a deed. In order for a work to receive God's approval, the motive must be for His glory (1 Cor. 10:31).[10]

The believer's motive can be either selfish or selfless; to bring glory to God or to bring glory to self. The Pharisees did that which would exalt themselves in the eyes of men. To them Jesus said, "Assuredly, I say to you, they have their reward." (cf. Mt. 6:2, 5, 16).

The means are, likewise, important in considering the true character of a work. That which a believer does in the energy of the flesh, though

---

[9] Herman A. Hoyt, "The Examination and Rewarding of the Chuch" (unpublished sermon text, Winona Lake, IN. n.d.), p. 4.
[10] Ibid., p. 6.

it accomplishes apparent results, is unworthy of reward in God's sight. Reward is determined on the basis of that which a believer does in the energy of the Spirit for the glory of God. Paul asked the Galatian believers, *"Are you so foolish? Having begun in the Spirit, are you now being made perfect by the flesh?"* (Gal. 3:3).

In 2 Corinthians 5:10 Paul indicates that when the believer's works are made manifest, they will fall into one of two classes: *agathos* or *phaulos*; that is, good or bad. The Greek term that Paul used for "bad" was not the usual word for that which is morally evil or corrupt (*kakos* or *ponēros*). Rather, he used *phaulos* which Trench explains:

> [It is] evil under another aspect, *not so much that either of active or passive malignity, but that rather of its good-for-nothingness,* the impossibility of any true gain ever coming forth from it. . . . This notion of worthlessness is the central notion of *phaulos*.[11]

Arndt and Gingrich indicate that *phaulos*[12] can be used in a moral sense as well. Their definitions are: "worthless, bad, evil, base."[13] Gromacki comments on the meaning of *phaulos* as it is used in the context of 2 Corinthians 5:10:

> Paul said that our work will fall into two categories: "good or bad." The word for "bad" here does not mean that which is wicked or sinful. It means something which is worthless or not up to par.[14]

Pentecost provides an illustration for the non-ethical use of this word. He explains:

> The words were used in two senses in the original text. "Good or bad" could be used in reference to sins and righteousnesses,

---

[11] Richard Chenevix Trench, *Synonyms of the New Testament* (Marshallton, DE: National Foundation for Christian Education, n.d.), pp. 296-97 (brackets and italics added).

[12] It must be acknowledged that *phaulos* can and does carry a moral or an ethical connotation depending on the context. The word can be used of sin and unrighteousness, or as Trench said, it can be used of something that is worthless or good for nothing.

[13] Arndt and Gingrich, *A Greek-English Lexicon of the New Testament and Other Early Christian Literature*, p. 862.

[14] Gromacki, *Are These the Last Days?* p. 161.

or in reference to something that was usable or unusable, acceptable or unacceptable, apart from an ethical or moral significance. What the apostle is saying here is that every one is going to be examined to see whether that which he has done is acceptable or unacceptable, whether it is suited to a designated use or is unsuited to a designated use. Sometimes as a do-it-yourself carpenter you will try to use a tool to do a job for which it was not designed at all. A pair of pliers is perfectly good when it is used for its intended purpose, but if you try to convert the pliers into a hammer, you will have nothing but a bent nail as the result of your effort. The pliers are perfectly good but unacceptable as a substitute for a hammer. The apostle is not speaking of that which is morally good as opposed to morally bad, but of that which is usable or useful as opposed to that which is useless.[15]

In agreement with Pentecost's understanding of the term *phaulos* Frederick Tatford writes:

The examination at the judgment seat will determine what is acceptable and what is worthless. (The word *phaulos*, translated "bad" in II Corinthians 5:10, does not imply what is ethically or morally evil, but rather what is worthless).[16]

It must be agreed by all that Paul does not use the common term, *kakos*, which is normally used to denote moral evil or wickedness. As concluded earlier, this judgment is not for the purpose of punishing sin as such. Unfaithful stewardship is sin, but payment for that sin has been made. The issue which remains is what works of the believer are worthy of reward and what works are unworthy of reward. The purpose is not to chasten the believer for sin but to reward for faithful service done in the power of the Holy Spirit for the glory of God. Gromacki illustrates:

Think of Mary and Martha (Luke 10:38-42). Mary was commended by Christ for choosing the *good* part. What did she do? She sat at the feet of Jesus enjoying His fellowship and eating

---

[15] Pentecost, *Prophecy for Today: An Exposition of Major Themes on Prophecy*, pp. 154-55.

[16] Frederick A. Tatford, *God's Program of the Ages* (Grand Rapids: Kregel Publications, 1967), p. 75.

of the spiritual bread which came out of His mouth. Martha was busy out in the kitchen fixing supper. What Martha did was not sinful or wrong in itself. Most good hostesses would have done the same thing, and this was Martha's protest about her sister. However, there are some things more important, more vital, more life-satisfying than busy work for the Master. To be with Him is better than to serve Him when He wants you at His feet. Mary's action was good; Martha's was bad.[17]

At the judgment seat the Lord will expose or make manifest each believer's works, revealing their essential character.

## FUTURE EVALUATION

Closely related to the manifestation of the believer's life at the judgment seat of Christ is the unerring evaluation which the Lord will make as described in 1 Corinthians 3. In order to understand the teaching of 1 Corinthians 3 two questions must first be answered: Is Paul referring to Christian ministers or Christians in general? Does the material refer to persons or doctrines?

### Difficulties Examined

In order to answer the first question it should be noted in verse nine that Paul says, *"For we are God's fellow workers; you are God's field, you are God's building."* "We" refers definitely to the "ministers through whom you believed" (v. 5). "You" refers to the Christians that composed the Corinthian church. The builders of this local church are primarily the leaders included in the term "we." However, there are implications in this passage that suggest Paul intended to broaden the application to refer to Christians in general. James Boyer comments on this issue:

> In this context, which is dealing with a proper understanding of the work and function of the human leaders in the church, Paul must have in mind primarily Apollos and Cephas and other human leaders (v. 5). . . . Thus, the main thrust of this illustration must be the function of the human leaders of the church, not a general function of all Christians.[18]

---

[17] Gromacki, *Are These the Last Days?* pp. 161-62.
[18] James L. Boyer, *For A World Like Ours: Studies in 1 Corinthians* (Winona Lake, IN: BMH Books, 1971), pp. 48-49.

However, there are several indications that Paul here intends to expand the application. Notice the indefinite and general terms he employs (v. 10, "another," "each one"; vv. 11, 12, 14, 15, 17, "anyone"). While the responsibility for church building is especially upon those whom God puts in the places of leadership it is also true that every member of the body has a part to contribute to the edification or building of the church (Eph. 4:16).

Such a conclusion concerning this extended application is, likewise, supported by the fact that the examination described in 1 Corinthians 3 and 2 Corinthians 5:10 is the same judgment. The latter passage clearly indicates that it is for all Christians: *"For we must all appear before the judgment seat of Christ, that each one may receive the things done in the body."*

The second question to consider is: Do the materials mentioned in this passage refer to persons or doctrines? Verse ten indicates that Paul laid the foundation of the Corinthian church, and verse eleven indicates that this foundation was Jesus Christ. Most commentators would agree that Paul is referring to the doctrine of Jesus Christ that he laid, for a church is begun and built by acceptance of and adherence to the gospel message concerning Jesus Christ. Christ had already lived, died, risen from the dead, and ascended to the Father. Thus, Paul was simply preaching the gospel concerning Christ, and it was with this gospel message that Paul did the foundational work at Corinth.

In verse ten Paul writes, *"I have laid the foundation, and another builds on it."* It would seem that if Paul's foundational work was the doctrine of the gospel of Jesus Christ, those who built upon this elementary gospel message would also build with doctrine. In fact, at the beginning of this chapter Paul states, *"I fed you with milk and not with solid food; for until now you were not able to receive it, and even now you are still not able"* (1 Cor. 3:2). The milk and meat metaphorically refer to the Word of God.

Paul had given them milk, but they were as yet unable to assimilate the deeper truths of God. Therefore, if indeed the foundation were doctrine, that which was built upon it would likewise seem to be doctrine. Verse six also supports this conclusion: *"I have planted, Apollos watered, but God gave the increase."* Paul sowed the seed of the Word of God, and Apollos came along and nurtured it. Verse five indicates that these men were *"ministers through whom you believed."* The doctrine of the gospel of Jesus Christ is that which is appropriated by faith.

Although 1 Corinthians 3 is not primarily referring to an examination of deeds but doctrines, 2 Corinthians 5:10 does present the fact that each believer will be examined for the deeds done in his body. By way of application in 1 Corinthians 3 the materials could be extended to refer indirectly to the work of teaching these doctrines since believers will be evaluated not only for the content of what they say but also for the motivation and means of their teaching. Is one's life and ministry for the glory of God and the edification of the body of Christ, or is it for the glory of self and the elevation of the teacher? Is it done through the energizing of the Spirit or is its source in the old fleshly nature? Although the interpretation of this passage is that the materials refer to doctrines, there seems to be justification for application to Christian service in general. Not only does Paul refer to Christian leaders in particular, he also alludes to Christians in general, who have a part in building the church through the ministry of their individual spiritual gifts.

### Doctrine Established

First Corinthians 3:13 states, *"Each one's work will become clear; for the Day will declare it, because it will be revealed by fire; and the fire will test each one's work, of what sort it is."* The word *phaneros* (manifest) which occurs in this verse is the noun form of the same word which is translated "appear" in the phrase *"we must all appear before the judgment seat of Christ"* in 2 Corinthians 5:10. This is a time not only of manifestation but also a time of evaluation. The term *hēmera* (day) appears with the definite article and thus refers to the specific time of the *bēma* evaluation. At this time "the fire" shall try or test every man's work in order to determine of what sort it is. This reference to "what sort it is" is parallel to Paul's statement in 2 Corinthians 5:10 which indicates that every believer's deeds will be evaluated in order to determine if they are worthy of reward or unworthy.

The fire referred to is metaphorically used to represent Christ's judgment which will test or evaluate the believer's works. The metaphor of fire is found frequently in Scripture to denote judgment (cf. Isa. 4:4; Mal. 3:2; Mt. 3:10-12; 2 Th. 1:8; Heb. 12:29; Rev. 1:14). In 1 Corinthians 3:15 the fire does not burn the worker but the work. In other words Christ will evaluate the work in order to determine of what sort or of what quality it is. Thus Paul figuratively states that the real worth of each believer's work will be examined. The fire which destroys worthless works is the same fire that approves worthy works.

Although God is interested in both the quality of the believer's service as well as the quantity, the fire will try every man's work *"of what sort it is"* not *"how much it is."* In terms of that which is worthy of reward, actual faithfulness is more important than apparent fruitfulness. Outward results can be deceiving, but the Lord's omniscient scrutiny will examine not only the outward results but the inward character. Many believers have labored unknown with little visible results to show for their efforts, but they have been faithful.

Paul teaches in verse six that it is God who determines the quantity of the results: *"I have planted, Apollos watered, but God gave the increase."* Noah, for example, (though understandably not of the present dispensation) was a man who was faithful, yet who had no converts except for his own family to show for one hundred and twenty years of service. God will reward on the basis of faithfulness not fruitfulness. God in one sense primarily determines the quantity, while the believer determines the quality of the service.

The figure Paul uses indicates that God gives no preferential treatment for quantity. In verse twelve he figuratively describes the believer's work: *"Now if anyone builds on this foundation with gold, silver, precious stones, wood, hay, stubble."* Fire does not give heed to quantity. A mountain of stubble is quickly consumed by fire while gold is only purified. Quality is the underlying criterion for reward. God is concerned with the character of the work rather than just the amount. That work which is worthy of reward is done for the glory of God through the enablement of the Spirit of God according to the will of God. All other service is simply a passing edifice to self-interest and self-effort.

The list of six materials which the apostle uses to characterize the believer's work can be divided into two classes: imperishable ("gold, silver, precious stones") and perishable ("wood, hay, stubble"). Paul does not ascribe meaning to the individual materials listed here. Many commentators have sought to explain the significance of each of the various materials. Paul, however, seems to be content to leave these materials unexplained other than that one group perishes when subjected to fire and the other group of materials endures the flame. This is sufficient to illustrate the point which he seeks to make, namely, that the true character of the believer's service will be examined in order to determine that which is worthy of reward and that which is unworthy. Pentecost gives a simple illustration of this truth. He writes:

May I illustrate it by referring to two Sunday school teachers. One teaches out of a heart prompted by the Spirit of God, is faithful before the Lord in preparation, and teaches not for her own pleasure, not to satisfy someone who has asked her to teach, not to gain reputation for being a good teacher, but teaches faithfully for the glory of the Lord. On the other hand, the second is a teacher who desires a position of prominence, likes to be influential, wants to be respected for having an interest in spiritual things. They both have done the *same thing*, but at the bema of Christ, God is going to say to the one, "That is acceptable to Me because it brought glory to Me." And to the other He will say, "That is unacceptable to Me because it brought glory to you and I got no glory out of it whatsoever." One could stand in a pulpit and preach because he loves to preach, or because of the influence that it brings to him, or the admiration and respect. God would say, "I disown all of it. It is of no use to Me," and it would be swept away as wood, hay, and stubble. It is not the fact that one has preached that will gain a reward, but it is the question of one's motive. What was my reason? What was my desire in discharging that ministry?[19]

The true quality of a work is not only revealed in *what* is done, but *why* it is done. All self-seeking and fleshly motivation will go unrewarded. Haldeman picturesquely writes:

Like wood, hay and stubble, it is big, bulks greatly, gives the idea of being busy, occupied, doing things; but like wood, hay and stubble, the bigger the bulk the bigger the bonfire it will make; for all such religious rubbish will be burned away on the day of the Lord.[20]

God desires that the believer have pure motives and methods in his Spirit-empowered and Word-directed service, with the sole desire that the believer may be well-pleasing to the Lord (2 Cor. 5:9). The purpose of the judgment seat of Christ is to motivate to godly living and faithful service, to reveal the essential character of the believer's life, and to evaluate that which is worthy of reward.

### FINAL COMMENDATION

A primary purpose of the judgment, as considered above, is to review the believer; but the resultant purpose is to reward him for

---

[19] Pentecost, *Prophecy for Today: An Exposition of Major Themes on Prophecy*, p. 158.
[20] Haldeman, *Ten Sermons on the Second Coming of Our Lord Jesus Christ*, p. 358.

faithful service. In 1 Corinthians 3:14-15, Paul writes, *"If anyone's work which he has built on it endures, he will receive a reward. If anyone's work is burned, he will suffer loss; but he himself shall be saved, yet so as though fire."* The specific kinds of rewards will be considered later. The fact that God will bestow rewards is clearly seen in this passage as well as others.

### Reception of Rewards

In the Grecian games the participant sought to win the prize. This too was Paul's desire in the spiritual race: *"I press toward the goal for the prize of the upward call of God in Christ Jesus"* (Phil. 3:14). In 1 Corinthians 9:24-25 Paul encourages believers to run the race of life in such a manner that they may receive a prize:

> Do you not know that those who run in a race all run, but one receives the prize? Run in such a way that you may obtain it. And everyone who competes for the prize is temperate in all things. Now they do it to obtain a perishable crown, but we for an imperishable crown.

In order to receive a prize each participant must compete according to the rules: *"And also if anyone competes in athletics, he is not crowned unless he competes according to the rules"* (2 Tim. 2:5).

Although rewards are sourced in the grace of God, yet it is true that in a sense they are earned. Paul states in 1 Corinthians 3:8, *"Now he who plants and he who waters are one, and each one will receive his own reward according to his own labor."* The preposition *kata* with the accusative in this context establishes the standard or "the norm according to which a judgment is rendered, or rewards or punishments are given."[21] Herman Hoyt elaborates:

> The *present* will have its issue in the future as marked by the phrase "according to." Since the phrase means literally "as measured by," this means that the future judgment will be measured by the deeds done in the present. This speaks of a rule of measure, and with God there is a yardstick, a scale, a test tube. This phrase means that there will be a confronting of every deed. Every

---

[21] Arndt and Gingrich, *A Greek-English Lexicon of the New Testament and Other Early Christian Literature*, p. 408.

deed of the believer in this life will pass into the next and have its issue at the Bema of Christ. With God there are precise mathematics.[22]

The standard or norm for the believer's rewards is given as *ton idion kopon* (his own labor). Boyer explains:

> Workers are distinct in responsibility and reward (v. 8b). The emphatic words here are "his own," occurring twice. Each worker has his own reward. The word used means "pay for work done." This is not a "reward" in the sense of a gracious gift, but "wages" for work that has been accomplished. This reward shall be "according to his own labor."[23]

Paul indicates that rewards will be commensurate to one's labor. In this sense the believer earns his reward through his labors in this life.

Similarly, in 2 Corinthians 5:10 Paul writes again, *"For we must all appear before the judgment seat of Christ; that each one may receive the things done in the body, according to [pros] what he has done, whether good or bad."* Instead of using the preposition *kata* as he did in 1 Corinthians 3:8, Paul uses the preposition *pros* here to denote the commensurate relationship between deeds done in this life and rewards received in the next. There is a direct relationship between the two. Arndt and Gingrich suggest that in this verse *pros* means "in accordance with" or "in comparison with."[24] The more quality works that a believer does for the Lord in this life, the more he will receive from the Lord in the next life.

The obvious conclusion is that not all believers will receive an equal reward. The fact that there will be varying degrees of rewards is taught in numerous passages (cf. Mt. 16:27; 1 Cor. 3:14-15; 2 Cor. 5:10; Rev. 2:23; 22:12; etc.). Such verses as those quoted and listed above reveal a direct relationship between the reward bestowed and the work worthy of reward.

Some might object that rewards are a selfish and mercenary motive for service. They might say that believers are to serve the Lord out of love rather than with the anticipation of what they might receive in return for their service. In response to such an objection one could ask, "Could the apostle

---

[22] Hoyt, "The Examination and Rewarding of the Church," p. 3.

[23] Boyer, *For a World Like Ours: Studies in 1 Corinthians*, p. 48.

[24] Arndt and Gingrich, *A Greek-English Lexicon of the New Testament and Other Early Christian Literature*, p. 717.

Paul be accused of selfishness when he penned Philippians 3:14?" He wrote, *"I press toward the goal for the prize of the upward call of God in Christ Jesus."* Again, could the apostle Paul have erred when he exhorted believers to strive for the prize? He emphatically wrote in 1 Corinthians 9:24: *"Do you not know that those who run in a race all run, but one receives the prize? Run in such a way that you may obtain it."* The conclusion that must be drawn from such clear teaching is that such motivation is indeed Scriptural. In the New Testament, Moses is given as an Old Testament example of one who lived this life in the light of anticipated rewards. Hebrews 11:26 states that Moses esteemed *"the reproach of Christ greater riches than the treasures in Egypt; for he looked to the reward."*

Although the doctrine of rewards is found in Scripture as legitimate motivation for service, it is nonetheless only partial motivation. The predominant thrust of Scripture emphasizes not the reward but the Rewarder. Rewards are like an afterthought compared to the preeminence given to the Rewarder by the Biblical writers. In the Old Testament, God was not only viewed as the Giver of rewards but as the ultimate reward Himself. God declared to Abraham, *"I am your shield, your exceedingly great reward"* (Gen. 15:1). In the New Testament the apostle John also indicates the supremacy of the Rewarder. He states:

> *The twenty-four elders fall down before Him who sits on the throne and worship Him who lives forever and ever, and cast their crowns before the throne, saying: "You are worthy, O Lord, to receive glory and honor and power; for You created all things, and by Your will they exist and were created"* (Rev. 4:10,11).

God desires to acknowledge the faithfulness of His children through the bestowal of rewards. Though Christians may forget the service they rendered to God and the sacrificial service of others, God cannot forget. Hebrews 6:10 states, *"For God is not unjust to forget your work and labor of love which you have shown toward His name, in that you ministered to the saints, and do minister."* He alone has the ability to faithfully and generously keep His promise.

The greater an individual reward the greater will be his ability to give glory to Christ eternally. The greater the believer's faithfulness, the greater will be the glory given to God in this life and greater will be his capacity to glorify God in the life to come.

### Recipients of Rewards

With the promise of rewards for faithful service the question remains: Will all Christians receive some reward or will some go unrewarded in heaven? Will those believers whose works will be classified as wood, hay, and stubble and who suffer loss, receive any measure of reward at the judgment seat of Christ? There is some measure of disagreement concerning this issue. Ironside concludes, "If you are in Christ, the Holy Spirit of God is dwelling in you, and in that coming day it will be made manifest that every Christian has accomplished something for God for which he can be rewarded."[25]

Other writers suggest the opposite, namely, that all believers will not receive a reward at the judgment seat of Christ. Robertson's and Plummer's comments on 1 Corinthians 4:5 reflect this position. They write:

> "And *then*, and not till then, *the* measure of praise that is due will come to each from God." "He will have *his* praise" (R.V.), what rightly belongs to him, which may be little or *none*, and will be very different from the praise of partizans here.[26]

According to their translation of this verse they indicate that it does not primarily refer to the universality of rewards among believers, but *the appropriate or fitting praise that is due each one*. Robertson reaffirms this interpretation in his voluminous grammar. He writes, "In 1 Cor. 4:5 *ho epainos* means the praise due to each one."[27] Again in his *Word Pictures* he writes, "The praise (note article) due him from God (Rom. 2:29) will come to each then (*tote*) and not till then. Meanwhile Paul will carry on and wait for the praise from God."[28]

Such an interpretation would fit the context since chapter three closes with the thought that the Corinthians had been glorying in their human

---

[25] H. A. Ironside, *Addresses on the First Epistle to the Corinthians* (New York: Loizeaux Brothers, Publishers, 1938; Oakland, CA: Western Book and Tract Co., 1938), p. 147.

[26] Archibald Robertson and Alfred Plummer, *A Critical and Exegetical Commentary on the First Epistle of St. Paul to the Corinthians*, in the *International Critical Commentary*, ed. by C. A. Briggs, et al., 2nd ed. (Edinburgh: T & T Clark, 1914), p. 78.

[27] A. T. Robertson, *Grammar of the Greek New Testament in the Light of Historical Research* (Nashville: Broadman Press, 1934), p. 757.

[28] A. T. Robertson, *Word Pictures in the New Testament*, Vol. IV: *The Epistles of Paul* (Nashville: Broadman Press, 1931), p. 104.

leaders rather than in Christ. Paul warns them of such a practice in chapter four and verse six. They had been giving exaggerated praise to selected teachers. But Paul suggests that they wait till the day when the *fitting* praise or the praise that is *rightly due* each will be granted them from (*apo*) God. His is the only praise that ultimately matters. The Corinthians were superficial and premature in their judgments of their favored leaders.

The primary point that Paul is making is not the universality of praise but rather the fitting praise that was due the various leaders as stewards of God in light of the fact that their real motives will be exposed at the *bēma*. Although this passage does not explicitly teach that every believer will receive some reward, it is nonetheless indirectly suggestive of that fact in its use of *hekastos*. Since its primary interpretation must refer to the church leaders whom Paul had previously mentioned, one must not conclude dogmatically from *this* passage that every believer will receive a reward. John Marchbanks gives a suitable answer to this question, although perhaps not inherently satisfying. He cautiously writes:

> What about those who have been saved on their death beds, for example, and those who died in infancy? Will they have a reward? About this the Word is silent. Certainly, however, they will have no fleshly works to be burned. About such we can know and say: "Shall not the Judge of all the earth do right?" (Gen. 18:25).[29]

The issue for any given believer should not be, "Will I live my life as a Christian and go unrewarded?" but "How can I live my life so that I will be rewarded?" As Deuteronomy 29:29 aptly states, *"The secret things belong to the Lord our God, but those things which are revealed belong to us and to our children forever, that we may do all the words of this law."* God Who is the Judge of all the earth will do right. Will every believer receive a reward? Perhaps only God knows with certainty. However, each believer can be assured of reward for his faithful service.

---

[29] John B. Marchbanks, "Question Box," *Our Hope* 62 (January 1956): 415.

# CHAPTER 7

# THE STANDARDS OF THE CHRISTIAN'S JUDGMENT

In the previous chapter the purpose of the judgment seat of Christ was considered. The examination of the purpose of this event has of necessity alluded to the standards for this judgment. In this chapter the standards of the *bēma* evaluation will be separately examined in greater depth in order to ascertain the criteria that God has for the believer's life and service. Although not every believer has been called to full-time Christian service, all believers have been called to full-time Christian living. God has at least three significant standards which relate to the believer's future evaluation. One relates to the Christian himself, another relates to the stewardship responsibility committed to him, and the final one relates to the work which is done. Each of these standards will be considered in light of the Scripture which reveals these truths.

## THE SERVANT: WAS HE DISCIPLINED?

The first standard of service to be considered is pictured in the figure of an athlete who disciplines himself in order that he may win the prize. Paul writes, *"And everyone who competes for the prize is temperate in all things. Now they do it to obtain a perishable crown, but we for an imperishable crown."* (1 Cor. 9:25). The word translated "temperate" (*egkrateuomai*) means to control oneself, or in this context, to exercise self-control in all respects as an athlete.[1] This word is derived from *en* and *kratos* (power or strength) thus literally meaning to have power over oneself.[2] In doing the will of God the believer receives his direction from the Word of God and his dynamic or power from the Spirit of God. The Holy Spirit energizes a life that is in submission to God in order to give moment by moment victory over the desires of the flesh.

The apostle Paul compares the rigid discipline an athlete exercises "in all things" to the discipline needed for the Christian life. This self-discipline involves the physical realm of one's body as well as the moral realm of one's behavior. If a contestant were to win, he must be physically fit which only comes through rigid personal discipline in such areas as eating, sleeping, and exercise. He was required to participate in a ten-month training program prior to the contest during which time the athlete disciplined himself in order to gain physical superiority over all his opponents.

Self-discipline in the physical realm was in itself insufficient in order for the athlete to be a prize-winner in the games. An athlete had to exercise discipline in the moral realm. Paul writes, *"And also if anyone competes in athletics, he is not crowned unless he competes according to the rules"* (2 Tim. 2:5). Although a contestant might be physically superior to all his opponents, yet if he did not follow the rules of the games he would be disqualified (1 Cor. 9:27). Arthur Ross writes:

> The competitor had to "strive lawfully" or else he was not crowned (II Tim. 2:5), i.e. he had to observe the conditions of the contest, keeping to the bounds of the course, having previously trained himself for ten months with chastity, abstemious diet, enduring cold, heat, and severe exercise.[3]

Through his physical training and discipline the athlete prepared himself so as to run, *"not with uncertainty,"* and to fight *"not as one who beats the air."* Through his moral training and discipline he prepared himself to compete lawfully.

---

[1] Arndt and Gingrich, *A Greek-English Lexicon of the New Testament and Other Early Christian Literature*, p. 215.

[2] Vine, *An Expository Dictionary of New Testament Words with Their Precise Meanings for English Readers*, I, 235.

[3] Ross, "Games," p. 299.

This figure of the athlete competing in the Isthmian games has an obvious application to the life of the Christian. In 1 Corinthians 9:18 Paul asks, "What is my reward then?" In verses eighteen through twenty-three he describes his own ministry of sacrifice and renunciation of personal liberty in order to further the Gospel. For Paul the anticipation of future reward drove him on in faithful, sacrificial service. He realized that his pay would not necessarily be in this life. He was storing up treasure in heaven. He could not take earthly compensation with him, but he could send it on ahead.

Then in verses twenty-four through twenty-seven he illustrates the principle that reward depends upon the nature and quality of the service which has been done for God. Paul guarded his body and kept it under subjection in order that he might *"make no provision for the flesh, to fulfil its lusts"* (Rom. 13:14), lest through some carnal or casual service he would be disqualified for the prize. The spiritual athlete must not only avoid sin but must likewise avoid anything that would hinder him from being completely effective.

Self-control extended to the moral realm of Paul's life for he made it his ambition to be well-pleasing to the Lord (cf. 2 Cor. 5:10). In order to live a life of self-control Paul depended upon Spirit-control. In Galatians 5:16 he writes, *"Walk in the Spirit, and you shall not fulfill the lust of the flesh."* Then a few verses later he lists self-control as one of the fruits of the Spirit in the believer's life (v. 23). Self-control and Spirit-control, therefore, are not contradictory but complementary. The believer who lives and serves under the control of the Holy Spirit will have the power which is necessary to discipline his life to be well-pleasing to the Lord in all that he does. Self-discipline harnesses the natural desires of the flesh through the power of the Holy Spirit to bring them into subjection to the will of God.

In order for a Christian to receive his full reward at the judgment seat of Christ, he must be self-controlled moment by moment in all areas of life. Otherwise, he will be disqualified for the prize. If self-renunciation is essential for the athlete who strives for a perishable wreath, how much more is it necessary for the believer who is running for an imperishable reward? For the faithful, spiritual athlete there must be a renunciation of all halfhearted service and a demonstration of a wholehearted endeavor, with the willingness to set aside personal liberties and comforts in order to attain the heavenly prize. As an athlete for Christ, one strives not for his own cause and honor, but for the purpose and glory of Him Who has called him to run.

## THE STEWARDSHIP: WAS IT DISCHARGED FAITHFULLY?

Another standard of evaluation will be the faithfulness with which the believer has discharged the responsibility which has been entrusted to him by the Master. In 1 Corinthians 4:1, Paul portrays the minister of Christ as a steward of the mysteries of God. The next verse articulates an unchanging principle in the program of God: *"Moreover it is required in stewards [oikonomos], that one be found faithful."* The word *oikonomos* is derived from the two Greek words *oikos* (house) and *nemō* (to manage). It primarily denotes the manager of a household or estate.[4] A Christian steward is, therefore, one who manages a trust which is committed to him by God and who is responsible to render an account of his faithfulness to the heavenly Master.

Since the Christian is called to please God, Paul could boldly write in 1 Corinthians 4:3-4, *"But with me it is a very small thing that I should be judged by you or by a human court . . . . He who judges me is the Lord."* Because each believer is the Lord's steward, Paul warns Christians against judging one another. In Romans 14:10 he writes, *"But why do you judge your brother? Or why do you show contempt for your brother? For we shall all stand before the judgment seat of Christ."* In the following verses he specifically makes reference to each Christian as a steward who must give an account to God: *"So then each one of us shall give account of himself to God. Therefore let us not judge one another anymore"* (vv. 12-13). Walvoord comments on this passage:

> Inasmuch as each believer must give account to God, it is presumptive for a believer to attempt to judge his brother especially in areas where doubt exists as to what the will of God may be. This does not mean that the preacher of the Gospel is not called upon to rebuke sin or to reprove those who are outside the will of God, but it does require a recognition of the fact that our judgment is not the final one. Ultimately our main question is not whether someone else is serving the Lord, but whether we

---

[4] Vine, *An Expository Dictionary of New Testament Words with Their Precise Meanings for English Readers*, IV, 74.

ourselves are properly fulfilling God's stewardship as committed to us. The principle is plainly laid down, however, in verse 12, that everyone will have to account for his life at the judgment seat of Christ.[5]

Christians are not to usurp Christ's role as judge. Rather than examining another's faithfulness each believer should examine his own life in order to see if he is being faithful with the responsibilities, opportunities, abilities, and resources that God has uniquely entrusted to him.

Not only in the epistles does the Christian find instruction regarding stewardship, but also in the Gospels there are principles that apply. Even a cursory reading of the Gospels reveals that Christ Himself had much to say about stewardship and resultant rewards. The principle of faithfulness with the stewardship responsibility entrusted to a believer is illustrated in three major parables: the parable of laborers in the vineyard (Mt. 20:1-16), the parable of the talents (Mt. 25:14-30), and the parable of the pounds (Lk. 19:11-27). In each of these parables emphasis is placed on different truths.

Each of these parables deals explicitly or implicitly with some aspect of the kingdom of God. The kingdom can be viewed from the different vantage points mentioned below as well as from other perspectives. There is a mystery form of the kingdom which exists presently. There will be a literal millennial kingdom following the tribulational period. This aspect of the kingdom will be theocratic, mediatorial, and temporary in duration. There is also the eternal reign of God which is the universal aspect of the kingdom.

Although each has its own peculiarities, there are still broad principles which apply to the government of God regardless of the dispensation or period of time encompassed by that aspect of the kingdom. Each of these parables contextually has a primary interpretation and application, as well as secondary applications. Christians today are a part of the spiritual kingdom through faith in Jesus Christ. Paul writes of God's work on behalf of the believer in relation to the present spiritual aspect of the kingdom. He states, *"He has delivered us from the power of darkness and conveyed us into the kingdom of the Son of His love"*

---

[5] John F. Walvoord, *The Church in Prophecy* (Grand Rapids: Zondervan Publishing House, 1964), pp. 146-47.

(Col. 1:13). There are principles which are always true and relate to the broader aspect of the kingdom which includes the believers of this dispensation, namely, the members of the Body of Christ.

### The Parable of the Laborers in the Vineyard

The parable of the laborers in the vineyard (Mt. 20:1-16) in its context primarily refers to the millennial kingdom. Peter had just finished lamenting that he and the other disciples had left all to follow Christ (Mt. 19:27). Jesus responded, *"Assuredly I say to you, that in the regeneration, when the Son of Man sits on the throne of His glory, you who have followed Me will also sit on twelve thrones, judging the twelve tribes of Israel"* (Mt. 19:28). The obvious interpretation is that Christ is speaking of His millennial reign on earth. Yet in this parable He illustrates the principle of faithfulness which also has application to the universal aspect of God's kingdom.

In summary, this parable deals with individuals whom the householder hires to work in his vineyard. Some were commissioned to work in the morning, others he commissioned to work throughout the day at the third, sixth, ninth, and eleventh hours. That evening the lord of the vineyard called his laborers together to pay them beginning at the last one hired and ending with the first. Each was paid the same amount of money although each labored different amounts of time. Each did not have equal opportunity, but each received equal pay.

G. Campbell Morgan elaborates on this truth in his exposition of the parable. He insightfully writes:

> This parable is intended to teach one simple truth, that a man's reward will be, not according to the length of his service, not according to the notoriety of his service, but according to his fidelity to the opportunity which is given him. The men at the beginning of the day entered into a covenant and an agreement. The Master of the vineyard went out later in the day, saw others standing idle, and sent them in. When He said, "Why stand ye here all the day idle?" Their answer was, "Because no man hath hired us." That is why they had not been at work before, they had not had their opportunity. When He created opportunity by sending them in, then in that last hour they were true to the only opportunity they had,

and therefore their reward was as great as the reward of the men that had been at work twelve hours.[6]

Morgan guards this interpretation with the statement:

> The whole application of the parable is to service, and the reward of service for men in the Kingdom. . . . There is no thought about equal payment for unequal work. If we attempt to base upon this parable the teaching that if a man lives and loiters through ten hours, and comes in at the eleventh, he is on equal rights with the man who has worked from the beginning, we are absolutely unfair to the other parables of Jesus.[7]

The point of the parable is that of equal compensation for unequal *opportunity*, not equal compensation for unequal work. Being a faithful steward of the opportunity which has been entrusted to a believer is a Biblical standard for the believer's reward.

### The Parable of the Talents

The parable of the talents (Mt. 25:14-30) in its immediate context of the Olivet discourse has reference to the tribulation saints who will be judged at the time of Christ's return to earth just prior to the establishment of the millennial kingdom. The verse following this parable (v. 31) refers to Christ's return in glory to sit upon His throne. Christ was thus illustrating reward in the millennial kingdom.

This parable and the preceding one (the parable of the ten virgins) portray the responsibilities of the Lord's servants while He is bodily absent from them. Yet an unchanging principle is illustrated in this parable which applies to God's administration in all ages, namely, that reward is based on faithfulness.

The parable pictures the temporary departure of Christ as a man who went to a far country. He entrusted his goods to his servants according to their individual ability (*dynamis*). To one servant he

---

[6] G. Campbell Morgan, *Studies in the Four Gospels* (Old Tappan NJ: Fleming H. Revell Company, 1931), I, 243.

[7] Ibid.

gave five talents, to another two, and to another one.[8] The first two servants each doubled their original gift, and the third hid his talent in the ground. After a long time the lord of the vineyard returned to reckon with them. Unto each of the first two the lord said, *"Well done, good and faithful servant, you were faithful over a few things, I will make you ruler over many things. Enter into the joy of your lord"* (vv. 21, 23).

Homer Kent considers the problem which arises in this parable with regard to the unfaithful servant. He writes:

> The *weeping and gnashing of teeth* show clearly that this symbolizes eternal punishment (8:12; 13:42, 50; 22:13; 24:51). Herein is the crux of the interpretation. If this reckoning is the judgment of the believer's works, then we apparently have a true believer suffering the loss of his soul because of the barrenness of his works. But that interpretation would contradict Jn. 5:24. . . . The best solution applies the parable to the Tribulation saints (whether Jew or Gentile) because of the clear association with the preceding verses. This explanation agrees with other Scriptures that at the time of Christ's return, the believing remnant will be gathered to enjoy Millennial blessings, but those then living who have no real belief in their Messiah will be removed (Ezk. 20:37-42). Of course, the principle is true for men of all ages that God holds men responsible for their use of his gifts.[9]

These monetary talents represent that which God has entrusted to each believer in this life. Each must one day give an account to his Master of his stewardship. Those who have been faithful in this life will be given much more responsibility in the life to come. Revelation 22:3

---

[8] "The 'talent' was not a coin, but a unit of monetary reckoning. Its value was always high, though it varied with the different metals involved and the different monetary standards. . . . It was mentioned by Jesus. . . . In the parable of the talents in Mt. xxv. 15-28 it is referred to in verse 18 as *argyrion*, which may suggest that our Lord had the silver talent in mind." D. H. Wheaton, "Money," *The New Bible Dictionary*, ed. by J. D. Douglas (Grand Rapids: Wm. B. Eerdmans Publishing Co., 1962), p. 840 (ellipses added).

[9] Homer A. Kent, Jr., "The Gospel According to Matthew," *The Wycliffe Bible Commentary*, ed. by Charles F. Pfeiffer and Everett F. Harrison (Chicago: Moody Bible Institute, 1962), p. 975.

has reference to believers in the eternal state and says, *"His servants shall serve Him."* This life is a testing ground in order to be granted privileged service with the Lord as a reward for faithfulness now. This parable, therefore, teaches that where there are unequal abilities and differing capacities yet equal faithfulness, there will be equal reward.

### The Parable of the Pounds

The parable of the pounds (Lk. 19:11-27) has reference to the same eschatological setting as the parable of the talents in that it has primary application to the tribulation saints. Christ's audience *"thought the kingdom of God would appear immediately"* (v. 11). They thought Christ would establish His literal Davidic throne in Jerusalem from which He would reign as King, and would deliver the Jews from their Roman bondage. To answer this false assumption Christ presents a parable in which He portrays Himself as a certain nobleman who went into a far country *"to receive for himself a kingdom and to return"* (v. 12). During His absence He entrusted to each of his ten servants a pound[10] with which to trade and to engage in business. Verse fifteen states, *"And so it was that when he returned, having received the kingdom, he then commanded these servants, to whom he had given the money, to be called to him, that he might know how much every man had gained by trading."*

The questions which must be answered are: What Kingship is in view? What return of Christ is pictured? The obvious conclusion is that reference is made to Christ's millennial kingdom, and the return is His second advent, at which time He will execute judgment upon the faithless unregenerates and will usher the tribulation saints (both Jews and Gentiles) into millennial blessing.

Although this parable was not written primarily to describe believers of this dispensation, there are nonetheless principles for believers of all ages regarding faithful stewardship of that which the Lord has entrusted to them. The parable indicates that when these servants appeared before their lord to give an account of their stewardship, one servant had

---

[10] A pound or *mina* was a Greek coin which was used as currency. According to Merrill Tenney's comment in 1962, "A pound was worth 100 drachmas, about $16.50 in American money." Merrill C. Tenney, "The Gospel According to Luke," *The Wycliffe Bible Commentary*, ed. by Charles F. Pfeiffer (Chicago: Moody Bible Institute, 1962), p. 1060.

gained ten pounds from his single original pound. To him the lord graciously responded, *"Well done, good servant; because you were faithful in a very little, have authority over ten cities"* (v. 17).

Another servant gained five pounds from his original one and to him the lord said, *"You also be over five cities"* (v. 19). To each was given proportionately greater privileged service according to his faithfulness. The final servant who did nothing with his pound apparently represents an unregenerate man, perhaps a member of the Jewish nation to whom God had entrusted much. He is called a *"wicked servant"* (v. 22) and apparently is one of Christ's enemies who would not allow Him to reign over him and thus was to be slain (vv. 14, 27).

The principle which is illustrated in this parable is that where there is equal capability and opportunity but unequal faithfulness the reward will be varied.[11] Each servant was entrusted with the same amount, but each did not earn the same amount. To the one who earned more, proportionately more was given in reward. To the one who earned less, proportionately less was given to him. Morgan emphasizes the difference between this parable and the parable of the talents. He states:

> Here let us be careful not to confuse the parable of the pounds with the parable of the talents. They are entirely different. In the parable of the talents, the Lord gave to one ten [sic], and another five [sic], and to one one.[12] That was a parable dealing with variety of gifts. This is not that, and that is not this. In this case every servant had a like amount. If that was a parable showing variety of gifts, this is a parable stressing equal opportunity, during the Lord's absence. He has given to every one of His bond servants a pound. This marks common opportunity, and common responsibility.[13]

Scroggie similarly contrasts the parables of the talents and of the pounds. He pointedly states, "The former (Matt. xxv.) teaches that where there is unequal ability but equal faithfulness, the reward will be the same; and the latter (Luke xix) teaches that where there is equal ability

---

[11] W. Graham Scroggie, *What About Heaven? Comfort for Christians* (London: Pickering & Inglis, Ltd., n.d.), p. 109.

[12] It should read *"to one five, and another two"* (cf. Mt. 25:15).

[13] Morgan, *Studies in the Four Gospels*, III, 215-16.

but unequal faithfulness the reward will be graded."[14] In contrast to these two parables the parable of the vineyard taught the principle that unequal opportunity combined with equal faithfulness brings equal reward.

Each of these parables illustrates principles regarding the stewardship responsibility and accountability of believers. In the epistles, the principles of stewardship are stated explicitly in lucid propositions whereas in the Gospels these principles are illustrated implicitly in parables. In both it is required of stewards that a man be found faithful with the trust that has been deposited with him by the Lord. Faithfulness is one of God's unchanging standards for reward.

## THE SERVICE: WILL IT ABIDE?

Having examined the servant and the stewardship responsibilities, a third issue in regard to the standards of the believer's judgment needs to be briefly considered, namely, the work itself. Although this issue has been dealt with in an earlier section, in the interest of completeness it deserves mention here. In 1 Corinthians 3 it was noted that the fire, which metaphorically pictures God's holy evaluation, will test every man's work to determine its quality *"of what sort it is"* (v. 13). Is the work worthy of reward or unworthy of reward? Not only the results of one's work whether great or small, but such factors as motive and means, determine the quality of the work. Was it performed selfishly for self-glory, or selflessly for the glory of God? Was the work performed through the energizing of the flesh or through the energizing of the Holy Spirit? Was it done in accord with the will of God or did it arise from the schemes of man? Pentecost comments on these issues:

> That which *God* is permitted to do in and through the child of God is that which is the gold, silver, and costly stones, and that which the individual does by his own power, for his own glory, because it suits his own will, because it promotes his own purpose, is the wood and the hay and the stubble.[15]

The work which withstands this divine scrutiny will be graciously rewarded (v. 14), but the work which does not pass the test will be

---

[14] Scroggie, *What About Heaven? Comfort for Christians*, p. 109.
[15] Pentecost, *Prophecy for Today: An Exposition of Major Themes on Prophecy*, p. 158.

burned up, thus deserving no reward. Walvoord notes the thrust of the figure of the building which pictures the Christian's life:

> Taken as a whole, the figure of a building is a reminder, first, of the necessity of building upon Christ the foundation as the only true preparation for eternity. Second, our lives should be lived in such a way that they will have eternal value, and the time and effort extended will be worthy of reward by the Lord at the judgment seat of Christ. It is a reminder that the only real values in life are those which are eternal.[16]

DeHaan elaborates on the significance of the two classes of material representing the believer's works. He writes:

> The first are the fruits of the Spirit; the wood, hay, and stubble are the fruits of the flesh. One represents spiritual service; the other fleshly endeavor. Men are impressed with the bulk and the mass and the bigness of fleshly manifestations of carnal service, but God recognizes only the value of small but genuine service and when the books are opened by and by, the things we applaud as big, will vanish in smoke, while the little things we overlooked will mount and shine in the Kingdom of our Lord.[17]

The point is that the Lord is not only concerned with the quantity of the work (and He is interested in quantity as clearly illustrated in the parables), but He is also concerned with the quality of the work which is determined by why it is done and how it is done. He will *"bring to light the hidden things of darkness and reveal the counsels of the hearts"* (1 Cor. 4:5).

God has unchanging, uncompromising standards for the believer in regard to the servant himself, his faithfulness, and his work. Regarding the servant, was he disciplined? Regarding the stewardship, was it discharged faithfully? Regarding the service, will it abide? In light of clear Biblical principles and conflicting contemporary practices the believer must be continually on guard lest the world's

---

[16] Walvoord, *The Church in Prophecy*, p. 149.

[17] DeHaan, *The Judgment Seat of Christ: A Scriptural Examination of the Three Judgments of the Believer—Past, Present, Future*, p. 23.

philosophies and practices encroach into his life. DeHaan issues a needed warning for today:

> We are living in an age of mass worship. Things must be big. This indeed is the supercolossal age of history. Everything must be big, big in business, big in religion, big in church life. We worship bigness as though this were an end in itself. If a meeting is big, that is the yardstick by which we measure. We measure the success of a program by the crowd which attends, the number of people who came forward, and the amount of money we are able to throw around and spend. But I just wonder how God looks at all this and how it will stack up when Jesus comes.[18]

Virtue does not inherently reside in smallness, nor in bigness. Virtue resides in faithfulness with the abilities and opportunities uniquely entrusted to each believer by God when they are employed for His glory.

---

[18] Ibid., pp. 23-24.

# CHAPTER 8

# THE EXTENT OF THE CHRISTIAN'S JUDGMENT

In the preceding chapter the standards of the Christian's judgment were considered. The question remains regarding the extent to which these standards will be applied. Numerous passages of Scripture relate to the extent of this judgment even though the expression "judgment seat" does not appear. The writers of the sacred text, under the direction of the Holy Spirit, deemed these passages worthy of inclusion and, therefore, they are worthy of consideration in developing a more complete understanding of the *bēma* examination.

## THE SEEMINGLY INSIGNIFICANT

There are times in a Christian's life and service when one's labor seems insignificant as viewed separately against the backdrop of the whole plan or work of God. An act of love and sacrifice can be thoughtlessly regarded by the doer and the observer as inconsequential in comparison to the occasions of great advancement by the Christian community. Jesus spoke of the significance of the apparently insignificant when He instructed His disciples in Matthew 10:42. He said, *"And whoever gives one of these little ones only a cup of cold water in the name of a disciple, assuredly, I say to you, he shall by no means lose his reward."* In context this verse primarily applies to those that would contribute to meeting the needs of Christ's commissioned disciples. Such a one was promised a reward no matter how inconsequential the act might have seemed.

Within this teaching there is the principle that in the program of God nothing which is done to further God's purpose is too insignificant for reward. God is the God of detail. Christ told His disciples that God is concerned about the lowly sparrow (v. 29) and *"the very hairs of your head are all numbered. Do not fear therefore; you are of more value than many sparrows"* (vv. 30-31). Jesus showed His disciples not only that God was infinitely great enough to care for the universe, but that He was infinitely great enough to care for every detail of their existence. E. Schuyler English comments on this passage:

> No labor of love will be too insignificant for the Lord's notice, none will be too small to receive His commendation. *"Whosoever shall give to drink unto one of these little ones a cup of cold water only in the name of a disciple . . . shall in no wise lose his reward"* (Matt. 10:42). Nor will that reward be measured equal only to the work itself, but will be dealt out multiplied and running over.[1]

Haldeman expands the application when he writes, "The kindly smile, the cup of cold water in His name, the cheery word spoken in the fitting season, the clasp of hand by which you lifted another to firmer footing in the way of faith; all this will be remembered."[2]

The writer of Hebrews alludes to this same truth that God will not forget work that was done for Him: *"For God is not unjust to forget your work and labor of love which you have shown toward His name, in that you have ministered to the saints, and do minister"* (Heb. 6:10). Pache brings the two passages mentioned here together in his comment:

> And anyone at all has had a thousand opportunities to give a cup of cold water, a gesture, which, though cost nothing, is of value because of the love and the smile that accompany it. According to Hebrews 6:10, God is not unrighteous to forget one's work, his love, and his service rendered to the saints. The Lord who delighted in the gift of the widow's mite, something unnoticed or despised by men, will be able, in the most humble and modest of folk to find reasons for bestowing magnificent rewards.[3]

---

[1] E. Schuyler English, *Things Surely to Be Believed: A Primer of Bible Doctrine* (Neptune, NJ: Loizeaux Brothers, 1956), pp. 274-75.

[2] Haldemen, *Ten Sermons on the Second Coming of Our Lord Jesus Christ*, p. 342.

[3] Rene Pache, *The Future Life*, trans. by Helen I. Needham (Chicago: Moody Press, 1962) p. 241.

If God were to refrain from rewarding Christians for their work and loving service then He would be unrighteous. He would not be keeping the promise that He had made to them. What God has promised He will provide. He will faithfully reward believers for their faithful service.

God's awareness of the Christian's life and service extends to the seemingly insignificant. God remembers the unremembered acts of love that men have forgotten. All that is done for the Lord will be faithfully remembered and fully recompensed according to God's standard, not man's. The smallest service will be rewarded by the Lord.

## PERSONAL SACRIFICE

Jesus' account of the widow's mite illustrates the principle that God looks with favor upon those who are willing to sacrifice for Him. Mark 12:41-44 states:

> *Now Jesus sat opposite the treasury and saw how the people put money into the treasury. And many who were rich put in much. Then one poor widow came and threw in two mites, which make a quadrans [equivalent to a few cents]. So He called His disciples to Himself and said to them, "Assuredly, I say to you that this poor widow has put in more than all those who have given to the treasury; for they all put in out of their abundance, but she out of her poverty put in all that she had, her whole livelihood."*

Jesus used this real life incident to teach His disciples that sacrifice is not determined by how much one gives, but by how much he gives in proportion to what he has left. DeHaan gives a picturesque contemporary application:

> That poor widow who gave her dime out of her poverty will receive a greater reward than the rich man who donated one million dollars to the work but did it out of his abundance, and still had a million left for himself. The Lord will not only consider the amount on the face of the check, but especially the balance which was left on the stub, after the check was written.[4]

---

[4] DeHaan, *The Judgment Seat of Christ: A Scriptural Examination of the Three Judgments of the Believer—Past, Present, Future*, p. 29.

Jesus said of the widow that she had cast in more than all the others, yet in monetary value it is obvious that she had not. Gromacki explains:

> She did not put in more than the others, yet Jesus said that she did. In quantity or amount, she didn't; but in quality, she did. They put in the dividend check, the interest on the savings account, the profit from the sale of a property, and still, they had enough left over to maintain a very high standard of living. The widow put in her bread money, the rent allotment, the clothing allowance. She needed that money to live on, but she wanted God to have it. She was indeed a sacrificial giver; they were not.[5]

Although reward is not explicitly mentioned in this passage, it is clear that God graciously considers the sacrifice of those who desire to please Him. This truth is clearly stated in Jesus' response to Peter's complaint that he and the disciples had left all to follow Christ. Jesus responded, *"So He said to them, 'Assuredly, I say to you, there is no one who has left house or parents or brothers or wife or children, for the sake of the kingdom of God, who shall not receive many times more in this present time, and in the age to come eternal life'"* (Lk. 18:29-30). Thus it is apparent that the final evaluation of the believer's life at the judgment seat of Christ will encompass the issue of his loving sacrifice for the Lord.

### UNNOTICED SERVICE

In the Christian's life there are not only deeds that in themselves seem insignificant, but there are also those deeds which are done in seclusion which escape the public's view. While unregenerate and worldly individuals seek the plaudits of men, believers are encouraged to serve the Lord with the understanding that God notices even that which goes unnoticed by men. He will bestow rewards openly for faithful service. In contrast those who serve for the plaudits of men will lose their reward.

In the Sermon on the Mount in Matthew 6 this principle is illustrated by Christ through several examples. The first example which He uses considers the issue of giving:

---

[5] Gromacki, *Are These the Last Days?* pp. 165-66.

*Take heed that you do not do your charitable deeds before men, to be seen by them. Otherwise you have no reward from your Father in heaven. Therefore, when you do a charitable deed, do not sound a trumpet before you as the hypocrites do in the synagogues and in the streets, that they may have glory from men. Assuredly, I say to you, they have their reward. But when you do a charitable deed, do not let your left hand know what your right hand is doing, that your charitable deed may be in secret; and your Father who sees in secret will Himself reward you openly* (Mt. 6:1-4).

Although many Bible teachers differ concerning whether this passage is addressed to Christians, nevertheless, the principles found in the Sermon on the Mount certainly apply to all believers of all ages who are concerned about the true character of the kingdom of God.

In the same context Jesus restates the principle of the unimportance of notoriety in service through the illustration of prayer. Having condemned the hypocrites who love to pray publicly to be seen of men, Jesus instructs believers: *"But you, when you pray, go into your room, and when you have shut your door, pray to your Father who is in the secret place; and your Father who sees in secret will reward you openly"* (Mt. 6:6). Jesus concludes this specific thrust with a final illustration of fasting. He says, *"But you, when you fast, anoint your head and wash your face, so that you do not appear to men to be fasting, but to your Father who is in the secret place; and your Father who sees in secret will reward you openly"* (Mt. 6:17-18).

Those who serve in order to receive the applause and compliments of men in so doing receive their reward. Men's passing praise is their reward, and thus they receive none from God (Mt. 6:1-4). Gromacki provides the balance of this truth:

Jesus was not opposed to charity, prayer, or fasting. He was not opposed to these virtues being done in public either. He *was* opposed to religious works being done in public just for the sake of being seen. That type will not receive any reward in heaven. That spiritual exercise was only done for self-exaltation and for self-gratification; it was not performed for the honor and glory of God. True spiritual exercise is done toward God with no thought of human recognition.[6]

---

[6] Gromacki, *Are These the Last Days?* p. 167.

Notoriety in itself does not gain reward nor forfeit reward; but that which is done for the express purpose of receiving the plaudits of men is regarded as unworthy of reward by God. The believer's examination and reward will extend to that which escapes the notice of men.

### SUFFERING UNJUSTLY

The Sermon on the Mount extends this reward motif to those believers who suffer unjustly for righteousness' sake. Jesus concludes His beatitudes with these statements:

> *Blessed are those who are persecuted for righteousness' sake, for theirs is the kingdom of heaven. Blessed are you when they revile and persecute you, and say all kinds of evil against you falsely for My sake. Rejoice and be exceedingly glad, for great is your reward in heaven, for so they persecuted the prophets who were before you* (Mt. 5:10-12).

As believers live and serve in the world, opposition and suffering are inevitable. Paul spoke of the universal experience of suffering persecution within the lives of believers. He wrote, *"Yes, and all who desire to live godly in Christ Jesus will suffer persecution"* (2 Tim. 3:12). In the midst of such suffering the promise extends, *"Rejoice and be exceedingly glad, for great is your reward in heaven"* (Mt. 5:12; also cf. Lk. 6:22-23).

### SINCERITY

Another issue which will be considered at the examination is the believer's sincerity. Although this is an umbrella concept under which all deeds can be placed, it is nonetheless an important factor in the judgment. Sincerity connotes the genuineness of an act of which motive has a part. The term suggests that which is done without deceit or pretense. Sincerity in isolation is not inherently virtuous for many people are sincere, but wrong. However, sincerity in relationship to the Word and will of God is essential for an act to be worthy of reward.

Jesus illustrated this principle in Luke 14:12-14 as He revealed the hidden motives for invitations which were extended to particular individuals. In these verses Christ instructs:

> *When you give a dinner or a supper, do not ask your friends, your brothers, your relatives, nor rich neighbors, lest they also invite you back, and you be repaid. But when you give a feast, invite the poor, the maimed, the lame, the blind. And you will be blessed, because they cannot repay you; for you shall be repaid at the resurrection of the just.*

The primary application of this passage is to the resurrection of the Old Testament saints at the commencement of the millennial kingdom. Jesus' conversation took place under the Old Testament economy and was addressed to a Jew, specifically a Pharisee, who had invited Him to dinner. He warned this man that there is a danger in social dealings which could sap the virtue from a good act. If one were to invite rich people in order that they may reciprocate and return the invitation, what virtue would there be in that act? That would not be genuine hospitality or love, but rather a calculated selfishness which would eventually benefit the host.

Jesus suggested a revolutionary strategy to test the sincerity of one's motives. Rather than always to invite those who are willing and able to reciprocate, Jesus suggested that this Pharisee invite those who were entirely unable to return the favor. This done according to the will of God would be worthy of reward, not necessarily in one's present life but in eternity. The reward motif throughout Scripture indicates that the dividends of the Christian life are often postponed, with great returns reserved for the life to come. Sincerity of heart is essential in service for the Lord. Gromacki says, "God is a spiritual cardiologist; He is interested in the condition of your heart."[7]

## INTENTIONS

The Bible suggests that another area of life to which the judgment seat of Christ will extend is to the believer's intentions. An Old Testament passage clearly illustrates that this is a factor in the righteous judgment of God upon the life of one of His saints. This Old Testament example is found in 1 Kings 8:17-19. David had longed to build a house in which God could dwell among His people, but because he was a man of war God had passed on this privilege to David's son,

---

[7] Gromacki, *Are These the Last Days?* p. 165.

Solomon. After the temple was completed, during his dedicatory message Solomon reminded the people of David's original intention and of God's response:

> *Now it was in the heart of my father David to build a temple[a] for the name of the Lord God of Israel. 18 But the Lord said to my father David, 'Whereas it was in your heart to build a temple for My name, you did well that it was in your heart* (1 Ki. 8:17-18).

Three times David's heart is mentioned in these two verses. God was pleased with David's attitude and the intention of his heart. Although this particular project was not a part of God's purpose for David, nevertheless, God commended David for his good intention.[8] C. Ernest Tatham comments on this principle:

> A beautiful illustration of this is found in 1 Kings 8:17-19 where we learn that; although David was deprived the honor of building the Lord's house, he was given credit for the *desire* to do so. Observe especially the words, "thou didst well that it was in thine heart."[9]

Gromacki applies this principle to the lives of believers today:

> Within local churches scattered throughout our country, there are men and women who would like to do more for God and His work, but they are unable to do so. Here is a cripple who would love to walk from house to house in order to carry on personal evangelism, but he can't. Here is an elderly gentleman, just saved, who wishes that he could have been converted when he was a young man in order that he might give his life for missionary service, but he can't. Here is a widow who desires to give more money to the work of the ministry, but she can't. God knows this. He will not hold you responsible for what you cannot do; however, He is interested in your heart.[10]

Another Old Testament example of intentions which please God is found in the account of Abraham and Isaac (Gen. 22). God tested

---

[8] Ibid., p. 164.

[9] C. Ernest Tatham, "Three Bible Judgments," *Our Hope* 63 (October 1956): 239.

[10] Gromacki, *Are These the Last Days?* pp. 164-65.

Abraham through His command to offer up Isaac, his only son, as an offering to the Lord. Abraham had made the necessary preparations to fully obey God. By faith he intended to take his own son's life, but God intervened and provided a substitutionary ram which was providentially caught in a thicket.

The writer of Hebrews, under the directing of the Holy Spirit, explains Abraham's actions and indicates that in the mind of God Abraham's intention was regarded as the act itself: *"By faith Abraham, when he was tested, offered up Isaac"* (Heb. 11:17). The word translated "offer" (*prosenēnochen*) is the perfect active indicative of *prospherō*. The perfect tense[11] is the tense which views the action as complete. God thus regarded Abraham's intention as the completed act itself. His intention was regarded as a righteous deed.

In this chapter, consideration has been given to some of the issues which extend the scope of the believer's judgment far beyond the obvious issues. That which is perhaps regarded as insignificant may well be worthy of reward. God, likewise, will consider the personal sacrifice involved; those deeds done for the glory of God but unseen by the human eye; suffering unjustly for righteousness' sake; sincerity within the will of God; and one's righteous intentions.

At this final examination, the Lord will evaluate every area of life and service with a righteous standard. To each believer God has entrusted various resources and responsibilities which will be evaluated. The stewardship of one's mental resources, one's physical resources, one's financial resources, one's social responsibilities, one's family responsibilities, and all other resources and responsibilities will be brought under examination.

---

[11] Dana and Mantey write, "Its basal significance is the progress of an act or state to the point of culmination and the existence of its finished results. That is, it views action as a finished product." H. E. Dana and Julius R. Mantey, *A Manual Grammar of the Greek New Testament* (Toronto: Macmillan Company, 1955) p. 200.

# CHAPTER 9

# THE NEGATIVE ASPECTS OF THE CHRISTIAN'S JUDGMENT

The nature of the negative aspects of the judgment seat of Christ is an issue which is subject to a measure of disagreement among Bible scholars. Previously it has been shown that full atonement has been made for all of the believer's sins, and all of the judicial penalty for sin has been removed through the all-sufficient, substitutionary death of Jesus Christ. Any negative aspects of the evaluation, therefore, are not forensically punitive in nature. In light of this great truth these questions remain: Will the Christian who has been unfaithful and who has lived carnally experience any loss, grief, or shame at the judgment seat of Christ? Will heaven be a joyous place for the unfaithful? Will the unfaithful believer be ashamed when he meets the Lord at the judgment seat? These questions need to be considered within the prescribed limits of Biblical revelation.

## SUFFER LOSS

Scripture clearly indicates that rewards can be received and that rewards can be lost. In 1 Corinthians 3:15 Paul writes, *"If anyone's work is burned, he will suffer loss [of reward]; but he himself will be saved, yet so as through fire."* This passage does not teach the fallacious notion of loss of salvation, but rather it teaches the possibility of loss of rewards. Unfaithfulness is an issue not treated lightly in the Word of God. Sin in the believer's life brings real and experiential temporal loss and real eternal loss. Sale-Harrison writes of this dual loss:

The seriousness of a Christian's life of failure is clearly outlined in many portions of God's Word, for the life lived outside God's will suffers a dual loss. It has a serious effect on his earthly life in loss of power, joy and communion with God; but the loss revealed at the Judgment Seat of Christ is even more tragic.[1]

The loss of rewards which could have been received at the judgment seat of Christ will be a real and noticeable loss. This loss will be as real as Lot's physical loss when he escaped Sodom's judgment. Concerning this, Pache writes:

> Imagine the consternation of the one who in an instant will see the disappearance of all his works, since they had been inspired by self-seeking, and who will lose everything except his life. Does he not resemble Lot, the carnal believer, settled down in Sodom in the midst of the world and its compromises? In the day when judgment fell, Lot did indeed escape the fire; but he lost his goods, his wife, and even his honor (Gen. 19).[2]

The term *zēmioō* is translated "suffer loss" in 1 Corinthians 3:15. In its passive form it means to experience forfeiture or to suffer loss. This word is derived from *zēmia* which appears with its antonym in Philippians 3:7: *"But what things were gain [kerdē] to me, those I have counted loss [zēmian] for Christ."* No judicial punishment for sin in terms of satisfying God's justice is involved.

Arndt and Gingrich are wrong and do violence to the analogy of faith when they indicate *zēmioō* in 1 Corinthians 3:15 means to "be punished."[3] They are reading more into this verse than what Paul carefully intended. Vine states that *zēmioō* in the active voice can and does signify to damage. However, he says to the contrary of Arndt and Gingrich that in the passive voice it means "to suffer loss" or "to forfeit."[4]

---

[1] Sale-Harrison, *The Judgment-Seat of Christ: Incentive and a Warning*, p. 42.

[2] Pache, *The Future Life*, p. 237.

[3] Arndt and Gingrich, *A Greek-English Lexicon of the New Testament and Other Earl Christian Literature*, p. 339.

[4] Vine, *An Expository Dictionary of New Testament Words with Their Precise Meanings for English Readers*, II, 121.

Robertson and Plummer suggest that the verb, *zēmiōthēsetai*, be regarded as indefinite with the understood subject being "it." This has reference to the "reward" mentioned in verse fourteen rather than the definite subject "he."[5] Thus, these two verses would read, *"If anyone's work which he has built on it endures, he will receive a reward. If anyone's work is burned, it [the reward] shall be forfeited; but he himself [autos] shall be saved."*

Robertson and Plummer state that the *autos* supports this interpretation. They write, "The *autos* is in contrast to the *misthos*: the reward will be lost, but the worker himself will be saved."[6] This translation is a legitimate usage of the passive voice of *zēmioō*, specifically meaning to be forfeited. This conclusion is also supported by Paul's contrast between *autos* and *misthos*. If the translation should read, *"If anyone's work is burned, it [the reward] shall be forfeited,"* then this would coincide with the analogy of faith and clear Scriptural statements that Christ took all of the believer's punishment for sin.

The question here is therefore not punishment, but rather loss of reward. There is no inherent idea of physical or mental suffering here. The basic idea is loss or forfeiture of reward which one could have received. For each Christian there is potential reward. However, if the believer is not faithful, he will lose that reward, not in the sense that he once had it, but he will lose it in the sense that he could have had it.

In 2 John 8 the apostle John writes: *"Look to yourselves, that we do not lose those things we worked for, but that we may receive a full reward."* The question which this verse poses is whether it is possible for a believer to lose rewards which would be bestowed because of past faithfulness in the light of present or future unfaithfulness.

In context, John had just warned his readers of many deceivers who had entered into the world. Likewise, in the discussion which follows this verse the apostle continues his warning against false doctrine. John warns his readers, "Look to yourselves," or "Take heed to yourselves." The importance of such care and watchfulness is given in the light of the impending opposition. The reason for caution is presented by the apostle both negatively and positively.

---

[5] Robertson and Plummer, *A Critical and Exegetical Commentary on the First Epistle of St. Paul to the Corinthians*, p. 65.
[6] Ibid.

First he says, *"Look to yourselves, that we [you][7] do not lose those things we[8] worked for."* The "you" refers to the readers and the "we" refers to the apostle John and others who had brought them the gospel and had taught them.

John's desire was that his labor be not lost through the advances of false teachers. Thus, if *apolesēte* is the correct reading, there is no thought that the believers who are addressed would lose rewards which they would have otherwise received. John rather did not want *his* investment of time and energy to be lost and wasted because of *their* deception and *their* defection. Therefore he wrote, *"Look to yourselves, that we do not lose those things we worked for."* His further and perhaps greater concern was that they might receive (*apolabēte*) a full reward, that is, that they might receive all that would be eternally theirs through continued faithfulness.

In Revelation 3:11, the apostle John's statement again raises the question of loss of reward. He writes, *"Behold, I come quickly! Hold fast what you have, that no one may take your crown."* The believers in the church in Philadelphia would not be assured of their crown by simply having begun to run the race well. The importance of holding fast in their stance against their opposition was considered essential if they were to receive the reward for faithfulness. The Greek text says "that no one" (*mēdeis*) take their crown whether it be human foes or supernatural foes (cf. 3:9). The exhortation implies that these believers needed to remain faithful and not transgress by yielding to the opponents' temptations. Through neglect and yielding to the tempter these Philadelphian believers could forfeit the reward which they could have received had they been faithful.

Paul also writes of the need for righteous living in order to receive a reward. In 2 Timothy 2:5 he states, *"And also if anyone competes in athletics, he is not crowned unless he competes according to the rules."*

---

[7] This verse presents a textual problem. The editors of the United Bible Societies' Greek New Testament prefer *apolesēte* rather than *apolesōmen*. They give the former a B rating. A. T. Robertson concurs with their decision. See *Word Pictures in the New Testament*, Vol. VI: *The General Epistles and the Revelation of John* (Nashville: Broadman Press, 1931), p. 253.

[8] Again this presents a problem. The editors here prefer *eirgasametha* over *eirgasasthe* and give it a very speculative C rating. See Bruce M. Metzger, *A Textual Commentary on the Greek New Testament* (London: United Bible Societies, 1971), p. 721. This was also Robertson's conclusion. See *The General Epistles and the Revelation of John*, p. 253.

Ezekiel 18:24 also raises the question concerning whether God will forget the righteous deeds of a believer who later strays away from the Lord. The verse asks the question:

> But when the righteous turneth away from his righteousness, and committeth iniquity, and doeth according to all the abominations that the wicked man doeth, shall he live? All his righteousness that he hath done shall not be mentioned: in his trespass that he hath trespassed, and in his sin that he hath sinned, in them shall he die.

This is indeed somewhat of a problem verse. However, a verse in the New Testament clearly states, *"For God is not unjust to forget your work and labor of love which you have shown toward His name, in that you have ministered to the saints, and do minister"* (Heb. 6:10). Feinberg suggests that this one in Ezekiel who did righteous deeds was merely outwardly righteous. He had *"hand righteousness"* without *"heart righteousness."* Feinberg writes, "But when one who was formerly outwardly conforming to the statutes of the Lord commits apostasy, not merely backsliding or occasional offenses, he must die in his sinful condition."[9] Similarly, Fausset writes:

> "Righteous"—one *apparently* such; as in Matt. ix.13, "I came not to call the righteous" . . . [they are those] who are so apparently and outwardly before men. Those alone are true saints who by the grace of God persevere.[10]

This writer concurs with Feinberg and Fausset that these whose righteous deeds will be forgotten are not true believers but those who merely outwardly conformed to the law. Hebrews 6:10 clearly teaches that God is not unjust to forget the believer's service which was done for Him even though he strays away for a time.

Another passage which relates to loss and the judgment seat of Christ is 1 Corinthians 9:24-27. Although this expression does not appear here, the idea of striving for a prize and an incorruptible crown

---

[9] Charles Lee Feinberg, *The Prophecy of Ezekiel: The Glory of the Lord* (Chicago: Moody Press, 1969), p. 103.

[10] A. R. Fausset, "Jeremiah—Malachi," in Vol. II of *A Commentary, Critical, Experimental, and Practical on the Old and New Testaments*, by Robert Jamieson, A. R. Fausset, and David Brown (3 vols.; Grand Rapids: Wm. B. Eerdmans Publishing Co., n.d.), p. 267.

relates directly to the rewards of believers. Also, in this passage Paul states that he severely disciplines his body and makes it his slave *"lest, when I have preached to others, I myself should become disqualified"* (v. 27). The word *adokimos* ("a castaway," KJV) means disqualified, not passing the test or worthless.[11] Paul is not making reference to loss of salvation but rather to loss of reward. Paul's concern is that he do nothing which would disqualify him or render him unworthy of reward in the race of life. Mason explains:

> The bema was a stand on which the judges stood to observe and evaluate the actions of the contestants. If any athlete broke a rule, one or more of the judges (referees or umpires) would point to him and cry, "*Adokimos!*" (that is, "Disqualified!"). And thus he missed the prize (victor's wreath—*stephanos*) regardless of the place he finished in the race or contest. Likewise, when an event was completed, the contestants stood before the *bema* to hear the judges' announcement of the results, and to receive such reward as might properly be theirs. This is a uniquely fitting illustration to make clear to us the fact that service and life are to be evaluated by our Lord, with possible reward or disqualification.[12]

Although the *bēma* evaluation is for the purpose of bestowing rewards for faithful service, it is also true that a Christian will go unrewarded or lose potential rewards for unfaithfulness.

In 2 Corinthians 5:10, Paul indicates that every one will receive back (*komisētai*) the things done in his body whether good or bad (*phaulos*). The question this verse raises is how does one "receive back" that which Paul calls bad (*phaulos*). The things which a believer receives back for his good works are obviously rewards, but how can one receive back for sinful works without it involving some sort of punishment? The answer rests in the fact that unworthy, sinful deeds merit no reward. An unfaithful Christian receives the appropriate recompense for that which is worthless, namely, no recompense at all. For example, a student who turns in a worthless assignment receives a failing grade. He receives what

---

[11] Arndt and Gingrich, *A Greek-English Lexicon of the New Testament and Other Early Christian Literature*, p. 18.
[12] Mason, "A Study of Pauline Motives as Revealed in 2 Corinthians 4:16-6:4a," pp. 219-20.

he deserves. His poor work results in just recompense, a loss of the grade that could have been his if his work had measured up to the established academic standards. Likewise, an unfaithful Christian will receive the commensurate recompense for his worthless works. He will receive zero, or no reward at all.

Reward will only be granted for righteous deeds. All sinful deeds, thoughts, and motives will be consumed instantaneously as works of the flesh which are unworthy of reward. Some Christians will stand empty-handed, without excuse, having had much of their work and service rendered unworthy of reward. They will experience a real and eternal loss of reward, but they themselves shall be saved, yet so as through fire.

## EXPERIENCE SHAME

The question which remains is: Will there be grief, sorrow, and shame at the judgment seat of Christ because of unfaithfulness and carnal living in this life and the resultant loss of rewards in the life to come?

Some conservative Christian spokesmen teach affirmatively that there will indeed be tears, sorrow, and shame at the *bēma* evaluation. For example, Savage asks, "Tears at the judgment seat of Christ? Tears of regret that we did so little to merit a great reward? Yes, tears of remorse when we realize for the first time just how much it cost Him to provide for our salvation!"[13] Dollar again states, "He's going to send all of the wicked, lazy, unprofitable Christians . . . to outer darkness for one thousand years and they shall weep and there shall be gnashing of teeth."[14] John R. Rice warns:

> If you do not want to be "ashamed before Him at His coming;"
> if you do not want to face the "terror of the Lord," and suffer
> loss, seeing your works all burned up, then, dear Christian,
> WATCH NOW, labor, win souls, abide in Christ, live a holy
> life. There will be tears in Heaven for your sin and failure
> here.[15]

---

[13] Savage, *The Heavenlies: Purified Places, Perfected Peoples, Perpetual Plans*, p. 143.

[14] Dollar, "Rewards."

[15] John R. Rice, *Tears in Heaven* (Murfreesboro, TN: Sword of the Lord Publishers, 1941), p. 11.

M. R. DeHaan more generally comments:

> I confess I do not know all that is implied in this verse by the expressions, "man's work shall be burned," and "suffer loss," and "saved . . . so as by fire." But even though we may not know fully what these figures actually represent, one thing is crystal clear—it will be a terrible calamity for believers to suffer loss when they might have had something that would abide at the Judgment Seat of Christ. It certainly will not be a pleasant experience to "suffer" loss.[16]

Finally, P. W. Philpott spoke of tears at the judgment seat of Christ: "I can imagine there may be some tears at that time, for we not only shall face the good things that we have done, but also the things that have been evil in our lives."[17] Each of the men quoted above speaks of sorrow and remorse at the judgment seat of Christ.

Other conservative Bible teachers emphasize the aspects of anticipation and joy at the *bēma* evaluation. For example, Merrill Unger writes:

> Two major events, which every child of God may joyfully anticipate, are outlined in the prophetic Word and will occur in the celestial realms after the rapture. The first is the judgment of the believer's works with the dispensing of rewards. The second is the public identification of Christ with His glorified people, prefigured as His marriage to them.[18]

In another work he elucidates the fact of joyful anticipation of the *bēma*:

> For the believer the judgment seat of Christ holds no terrors, but rather happy anticipation. Conscious that the guilt of his sin has been removed once-for-all and forever, the Christian's heart is filled with joyful desire to serve Him who loosed him from his sins by His own blood, and to achieve for His glory.[19]

---

[16] M. R. DeHaan, *Studies in First Corinthians: Messages on Practical Christian Living* (Grand Rapids: Zondervan Publishing Rouse, 1956), p. 46.

[17] P. W. Philpott, "Will There Be Any Tears in Heaven, and Why?" in *Light on Prophecy: A Coordinated, Constructive Teaching: Being the Proceedings and Addresses at the Philadelphia Prophetic Conference, May 28-30, 1918* (New York: Christian Herald Bible House, 1918), p. 235.

[18] Merrill F. Unger, *Beyond the Crystal Ball* (Chicago: Moody Press, 1973), p. 55.

[19] Unger, *Great Neglected Bible Prophecies*, p. 120.

Similarly, Stewart Custer in commenting on the nature of the *bēma* evaluation states, "Some preachers paint this scene as though believers will be shedding bitter tears at that day. But Scripture does not say that. There is instead a boundless joy, a comfort beyond words."[20] In the light of these divergent opinions a question remains: Who is right? In order to determine which view most satisfactorily represents the teaching of the writers of the Sacred Writ, one must ask, What saith the Scriptures?

The apostle John provides some helpful light in solving this controversial issue. In 1 John 2:28 he writes, *"And now, little children, abide in Him, that, when He appears, we may have confidence, and not be ashamed before Him at His coming."* In this verse John speaks of Christ's appearing (*hina ean phanerōthē*) for those whom he calls his "little children" (*teknia*). The apostle is doubtless referring to the rapture of the church. Here *ean* is used with the aorist subjective, *phanerōthē*. This term in the subjunctive mood views Christ's coming with a measure of uncertainty in regard to its time, rather than with uncertainty in regard to the fact of its occurrence. Kenneth Wuest explains:

> "When" is *ean*, "if," used with the subjunctive mode, the mode of future probability. The doubt is here, not as to the *fact* of our Lord's coming for His Church, He promised that, but as to the time of that coming. One could translate, "whenever He shall appear." The exhortation, "Be constantly abiding in Him" is given in view of the uncertainty of the time of His coming. The believer must live in close fellowship with His Lord that he may be ready for that coming.[21]

One purpose for continual abiding in Christ in this life is explained by the apostle who in essence writes, "that whenever He shall appear, we may have boldness and not be ashamed from Him at His coming." This statement apparently has reference to the judgment seat of Christ when each believer is in the presence of Christ Himself. The verse suggests that those who have faithfully abided in Christ will have boldness (*parrēsia*) at His appearing. The term *parrēsia* denotes courage,

---

[20] Stewart Custer, "The Power of the Unseen (II Cor. 4:16-5:10)," *Biblical Viewpoint* 8 (April 1974): 29.

[21] Kenneth S. Wuest, *Wuest's Word Studies from the Greek New Testament for the English Reader*, Vol. IV: *Golden Nuggets, Untranslatable Riches, Bypaths in These Last Days* (Grand Rapids: Wm. B. Eerdmans Publishing Co., 1966) pp. 138-39.

confidence, boldness, fearlessness especially in the presence of persons of high rank.[22]

In contrast to boldness there will be those who experience shame (*aischynō*) in the presence of the Lord Jesus. Although the term *aischynthōmen* is clearly a first aorist passive subjunctive, its meaning is ambiguous. In the passive voice, *aischynō* can either mean to be ashamed or to be put to shame.[23] The main problem is not in defining shame, but in determining what *causes* the shame. Does the believer produce the response of shame through his own reflection upon his unfaithfulness while on earth? Or does Christ put the believer to shame through rebukes for unfaithfulness, thus bringing shame upon the unfaithful believer?

The passive voice coupled with the expression *ap' autou* suggests that a believer withdraws in shame from the Lord's presence. It suggests a shrinking back from Him, perhaps from a sense of guilt,[24] with the believer producing the action. Another possible interpretation is to understand Christ as putting the believer to shame. Coupled with the passive voice, *ap' autou* could suggest that Christ is driving the unfaithful Christian away from Him in shame. This seems contrary to the tenor of New Testament Scripture which pictures the church as the bride of Christ who will be ushered into His presence to enjoy His presence throughout eternity. Such action would also imply that there is an unsatisfied offense between the Lord and the believer.

Peter serves as an illustration of how Jesus graciously responded to unfaithfulness in the life of one of His followers. After Jesus had been arrested and was being taken to the high priest's house, Peter followed afar off. When Peter arrived at the hall, a series of three denials began which was climaxed by the cock crowing. Then Luke writes, *"And the Lord turned, and looked at Peter. Then Peter remembered the word of the Lord, how He had said to him, 'Before the rooster crows, you will deny Me three times.' So Peter went out and wept bitterly"* (Lk. 22:61-62). Peter's memory was jolted by Christ's glance, but it was Peter's reflection upon

---

[22] Arndt and Gingrich, *A Greek-English Lexicon of the New Testament and Other Early Christian Literature,* p. 636.

[23] Ibid., p. 25.

[24] A. E. Brooke, *A Critical and Exegetical Commentary on the Johannine Epistles,* in the *International Critical Commentary*, ed. by C. A. Briggs, et al. (Edinburgh: T. & T. Clark, 1912) p. 66.

the past that caused his deep sorrow. In heaven, as well as in hell, saints and sinners respectively will apparently retain their memory of life on earth in some measure. Luke writes of the memory of Abraham in paradise and of the memory of the rich man in hades: *"But Abraham said, 'Son, remember that in your lifetime you received your good things, and likewise Lazarus evil things; but now he is comforted and you are tormented'"* (Lk. 16:25).

The cause of shame at the judgment seat of Christ apparently arises from one's own realization of sin, unfaithfulness, and neglected opportunities rather than from receiving shame from Christ. Plummer concurs with this conclusion:

> This cannot well be improved, but it is very inadequate: the Greek is "be ashamed *from* Him," or "be shamed *away from* Him"; strikingly indicating the averted face and shrinking form which are the results of the shame. "Turn with shame" or "shrink with shame from Him" have been suggested as renderings. . . . The interpretation "receive shame from Him" is probably not right.[25]

Robert Candlish likewise concurs that reflection rather than rebuke is the cause of the shame at the *bēma*. He writes:

> And what a thought! What a contingency or possibility to be imagined! "To be ashamed before him at his coming!" It is a very strong expression. It carries us back to that old scene in Paradise when it was lost. The guilty pair "hear the voice of the Lord God walking in the garden, in the cool of the day." And they shrink with shame from him "at his coming." Is it thus that we should shrink at his coming now? Were he at this moment to appear, how would we feel? What would be our first impulse, or instinct? To run to meet him, or to shrink from him in shame?[26]

---

[25] A. Plummer, *The Epistles of St. John with Notes, Introduction and Appendices*, in the *Cambridge Bible for Schools and Colleges*, ed. by J. J. S. Perowne (Cambridge: University Press, 1884; London: C. J. Clay, M. A. & Son, 1884) p. 117.

[26] Robert S. Candlish, *The First Epistle of John* (Grand Rapids: Zondervan Publishing House, n.d.), pp. 211-12.

In conclusion the Bible suggests that there will be shame at the judgment seat of Christ to a greater or lesser degree, depending upon the measure of unfaithfulness of each individual believer. Therefore, it should be each believer's impelling desire to be well-pleasing to the Lord in all things. Although there apparently will be reflection upon this earthly life with some regret, there will also be the realization of what is ahead for the believer in the heavenly life. This latter realization will be the source of boundless joy.[27]

E. Schuyler English seems to best strike a proper balance when he writes:

> Joy will indeed be the predominant emotion of life with the Lord; but I suspect that, when our works are made manifest at the tribunal, some grief will be mixed with the joy, and we shall know shame as we suffer loss. But we shall rejoice also as we realize that the rewards given will be another example of the grace of our Lord; for at best we are unprofitable servants.[28]

The elements of remorse, regret, and shame cannot be avoided in an examination of the judgment seat of Christ. But this sorrow must be somewhat relative because even for the finest of Christians there will be some measure of failure, and the smallest sin would be worthy of unceasing remorse in the light of God's unapproachable holiness. This would mean that the finest of Christians could sorrow throughout

---

[27] Revelation 21:4 says, *"And God will wipe away every tear from their eyes; there shall be no more death, nor sorrow, nor crying. There shall be no more pain, for the former things have passed away."* The question this verse raises is whether there will be any tears of remorse, or perhaps tears of remorse for a short period of time in heaven. The answer must be that *this* verse is not referring to tears of remorse, but tears and sorrow that came *on earth* during the time of the believer's present sojourn. The writer is simply contrasting life on earth and life in heaven. Walvoord states, "There is no just ground for imagining from this text that saints will shed tears in heaven concerning the failures of their former life on earth. The emphasis here is on the comfort of God, not on the remorse of the saints. The tears seem to refer to tears shed on earth as the saints endured suffering for Christ's sake, rather than tears shed in heaven because of human failure. This is in keeping with the rest of the passage which goes on to say that sorrow, crying, or pain will also be no more in existence." John F. Walvoord, *The Revelation of Jesus Christ* (Chicago: Moody Press, 1966), p. 315.

[28] English, "The Church at the Tribunal," p. 29.

eternity. However, this is not the picture that the New Testament gives of heaven. The overwhelming emotion is joyfulness and gratefulness. Although there is undeniably some measure of remorse or regret, this is not the overriding emotion to be experienced throughout the eternal state. Hoyt concludes:

> The emotional condition of the redeemed is that of complete and unending happiness. Emotion proceeds from the realization of facts in personal experience. Hope will at last become reality for all those who are delivered from the bondage of corruption into the glorious liberty of the children of God (Rom. 8:18-25). Elimination of the curse, pain and death will also remove sorrow, tears and crying (Rev. 21:4).[29]

The glorified bride, the church, has been redeemed and will be changed to enjoy unhindered fellowship with her Lord throughout eternity. Peter encourages the suffering believers: *"but rejoice to the extent that you partake of Christ's sufferings, that when His glory is revealed, you may also be glad with exceeding joy"* (1 Pet. 4:13). Jude's benediction expresses the fact that God's intention is that believers experience exceeding joy in Christ's presence. He writes:

> *Now to Him who is able to keep you from stumbling, and to present you faultless before the presence of His glory with exceeding joy, to God our Savior, who alone is wise, be glory and majesty, dominion and power, both now and forever. Amen* (Jude 24-25).

The judgment seat of Christ might be compared to a commencement ceremony. At graduation there is some measure of disappointment and remorse that one did not do better and work harder. However, at such an event the overwhelming emotion is joy, not remorse. The graduates do not leave the auditorium weeping because they did not earn better grades. The overwhelming emotion is gratefulness because they were graduated and gratefulness for what they did achieve. To overdo the sorrow aspect of the judgment seat of Christ is to make heaven hell. To underdo the sorrow aspect is to make faithfulness inconsequential.

---

[29] Hoyt, *The End Times*, pp. 231-32.

# CHAPTER 10

# THE POSITIVE RESULTS OF THE CHRISTIAN'S JUDGMENT: GENERAL REWARDS

The judgment seat of Christ will be a serious occasion for evaluation, and it will also be a celebrated occasion for commendation. The *bēma* evaluation and the reward motif stand side by side, the latter being the direct result of the former. That which the believer has done faithfully for the glory of God in his earthly sojourn will be graciously rewarded in heaven. A person enters God's kingdom through faith but will enjoy rewards in the kingdom because of faithfulness.

The New Testament contains many allusions and explicit references to the nature of the Christian's eschatological rewards. Although there are no protracted passages dealing with this subject, taken together they provide glimpses of the rewards that are in store for faithful Christians. The New Testament writers were suggestive rather than exhaustive in their individual contributions to the reward motif.

The rewards referred to in Scripture which apply to Christians will be considered under two broad divisions. First, this chapter will examine the numerous general rewards which are found in the New Testament. Along with this there will be an examination of the fact that there will be different degrees of reward. Then in the following chapter the special "crown" rewards, which will be granted for special service, will be discussed.

## VARYING DEGREES OF REWARDS

The fact that there will be varying degrees of rewards has already been suggested in the section dealing with the parables. However, other significant passages help establish and expound this truth. The parables which were considered earlier suggest that Christians' rewards will differ according to the degree of faithfulness with one's unique resources, opportunities, and abilities. Other passages suggest the nature of these proportionate rewards.

Paul states in 1 Corinthians 15:40-42 that there will be varying degrees of glory at the resurrection:

> There are also celestial bodies and terrestrial bodies: but the glory of the celestial is one, and the glory of the terrestrial is another. There is one glory of the sun, another glory of the moon, and another glory of the stars; for one star differs from another star in glory. So also is the resurrection of the dead.

These verses indicate that believers will possess differing degrees of glory after the resurrection. Just as the stars, planets, moon, and sun vary in their luminescence, so also will glorified Christians differ in their glory. Although in this passage Paul is primarily discussing the resurrection, there is a clear statement here of the manner in which believers will appear after the resurrection in the eternal state. He does not give the reason here for the varying degrees of glory for he is not discussing rewards. Rather he is content within his purpose to state the fact of differences in degrees of splendor. However, the subject of rewards is not altogether absent in the immediate context for in verse fifty-eight Paul states, *"Therefore, my beloved brethren, be steadfast, immovable, always abounding in the work of the Lord, knowing that your labor is not in vain in the Lord."*

Paul further indicates that there are even in some sense varying degrees of manifested glory in this life. He writes, *"But we all, with unveiled face, beholding as in a mirror the glory of the Lord, are being transformed into the same image from glory to glory, just as by the Spirit of the Lord"* (2 Cor. 3:18). Since there is a relative mutable glory in this life, it is not difficult to accept the fact of relative immutable glory in the eternal state, especially in the light of explicit Biblical revelation.

Another passage, although referring to resurrected Old Testament saints, teaches this same truth of differing degrees of post-resurrection glory. Daniel 12:3 states, *"Those who are wise shall shine like the brightness of the firmament, and those who turn many to righteousness like the stars forever and ever."* If both the Old Testament and the New Testament apply this truth to Old Testament saints and New Testament saints respectively, it would appear that varying degrees of splendor, and thus varying degrees of reward, are changeless divine principles in God's dealings with His people. A. H. Strong elaborates upon this truth:

> Although there will be degrees of blessedness and honor, proportioned to the capacity and fidelity of each soul (Luke 19:17,19; 1 Cor. 3:14,15), each will receive as great a measure of reward as it can contain (1 Cor. 2:9), and this final state, once entered upon, will be unchanging in kind and endless in duration (Rev. 3:12; 22:15).[1]

The judgment seat of Christ will determine the degree of glory, privilege, and honor which each believer will receive. Pentecost suggests that at least in part "our reward in eternity will be a capacity to manifest and radiate forth the glory of God."[2] This seems to be true since even in this life the measure of glory the believer manifests is a derived glory from beholding Christ in the Word of God. God manifests Himself in the believer to produce glory in this life. It would seem that the glory which the believer radiates in the eternal state is the derived glory of God. Thus, part of the Christian's reward is apparently the privilege of manifesting forth the glory of the Lord in the eternal state. Pentecost gives a helpful illustration of this truth:

> You perhaps have gone into some fine home or public hall where they had a beautiful, crystal chandelier. When it was lit up, the whole chandelier sparkled with beautiful radiance. If you were to examine that chandelier, you would find that it is made up of a number of small bulbs; there might be some 25 watt, some 50 watt, some 100 watt, perchance some 500 watt bulbs. Each one had a different capacity but each one was shining to the limit of its capacity. That chandelier was beautiful because of

---

[1] Strong, *Systematic Theology*, p. 1030.
[2] Pentecost, *Prophecy for Today: An Exposition of Major Themes on Prophecy*, p. 160.

the total capacity of all that was within it. In eternity, some of us are going to shine to the glory of God with a 25 watt capacity, and some with a capacity of 50 watts, some with 100 watts, and some with 500 watts. All will contribute to the glory of God according to the capacity that has been given us at the bema of Christ. Won't we be unhappy when we get up there and find we have only a 25 watt capacity in the midst of all those with 100 watt capacity? No, because each will be shining to the limit of his capacity. And through the shining of all believers there will be a full and brilliant manifestation of the glory of God.[3]

In heaven no one will be discontent and envy someone else's reward. First, no believer will receive less reward than is due him; nor will anyone receive more. Second, envy and jealousy, which are regrettably part of the believer's experience in this life, will not be found in heaven for Paul says of the glorified church *"that He might present her to Himself a glorious church, not having spot or wrinkle or any such thing, but that she should be holy and without blemish"* (Eph. 5:27). Similarly, Jude writes that Christ will *"present you faultless before the presence of His glory with exceeding joy"* (Jude 24). Heaven will not be a place of discontentment and jealousy but a place of satisfaction and exceeding joy. However, each believer is determining in this life his capacity to receive and to reflect God's glory throughout eternity. God is only limited in what He can give by what each Christian can receive. One's degree of faithfulness on earth determines one's capacity for reward in heaven.

Although glory is one aspect of the believer's reward, there are other aspects which deserve consideration. The Scriptures present both temporal and eternal rewards. Temporal blessings and rewards which God bestows on the righteous include such things as health, food, shelter, raiment, long life, riches, honor, etc. Since the thrust of this examination is to consider rewards bestowed at the judgment seat of Christ, only eschatological rewards will be considered in the following sections.

## PRAISE

A verse which has been considered previously indicates that one aspect of the faithful believer's reward will be praise (*epainos*) or

---

[3] Ibid.

commendation from God. In 1 Corinthians 4:5 Paul states, *"Therefore judge nothing before the time, until the Lord comes . . . then each one's praise will come from God."* As suggested earlier this statement literally means that the praise which is due or belongs to each one shall be given from God.[4] This passage indicates that the reward of praise will be bestowed upon those to whom it is due in proportion to each one's faithfulness. To hear, *"Well done, good and faithful servant,"* from the lips of the Savior will be a joyous occasion and a gracious reward indeed. The praise of men, or lack of it, in this life will seem inconsequential in light of the praise of God.

## HONOR

Honor (*timē*) is another aspect of the believer's reward in the eternal state. Peter writes of this in light of trials which Christians experience in this life: *"That the genuineness of your faith, being much more precious than gold that perishes, though it is tested by fire, may be found to praise, honor, and glory at the revelation of Jesus Christ"* (1 Pet. 1:7). Vine indicates that honor is "to be the reward hereafter of 'the proof of faith' on the part of tried saints."[5] Thayer concurs that honor will appear in the rewards of the future life.[6] Paul writes of future honor as a reward of patient welldoing in Romans 2:7: *"Eternal life to those who by patient continuance in doing good seek for glory, honor, and immortality."* Then in verse ten he writes, *"but glory, honor, and peace to everyone who works what is good, to the Jew first and also to the Greek."*

The exact form which this honor will take is not explicitly revealed. For the disciples who desired privileged positions, honor was to reign with Christ in the millennial kingdom (Mt. 20:20-24). Jesus spoke of the honor which the Father would bestow upon those that serve Him: *"If anyone serves Me, let him follow Me; and where I am, there My servant will be also. If anyone serves Me, him My Father will honor"* (Jn. 12:26). Again Jesus suggested that believers will be granted honor by God when He said, *"How can you believe, who receive honor from one another, and*

---

[4] Arndt and Gingrich, *A Greek-English Lexicon of the New Testament and Other Early Christian Literature*, p. 159.

[5] Vine, *An Expository Dictionary of New Testament Words with Their Precise Meanings for English Readers*, II, 230.

[6] Thayer, *Greek-English Lexicon of the New Testament*, p. 624.

*do not seek the honor that comes from the only God?"* (Jn. 5:44). Honor is apparently public acknowledgment in contrast to praise which can be public or private in nature. Honor suggests a recipient and an audience, whereas praise needs only a recipient. Honor will be bestowed upon those who have been found worthy of public esteem through faithfulness in their earthly sojourn.

## GLORY

Glory (*doxa*) is one aspect of the reward motif which was mentioned in the section which dealt with the degrees of rewards. Several passages other than those mentioned earlier reveal this aspect of the believer's reward. In Colossians 3:4 Paul writes, *"When Christ who is our life appears, then you also will appear with Him in glory."* Again in Romans 8:18 he states, *"For I consider that the sufferings of this present time are not worthy to be compared with the glory which shall be revealed in us."* This state of eternal blessedness is associated with a brilliancy of appearance. Jesus says of the righteous, *"Then the righteous will shine forth as the sun in the kingdom of their Father. He who has ears to hear, let him hear!"* (Mt. 13:43). This reward will perhaps involve the capacity of the believer to manifest or reflect the glory of Christ throughout the eternal state, with the greater reward being the greater capacity to manifest God's glory. Christ will be the One Who is ultimately glorified through His manifested glory in the saints.[7]

Another verse which refers to this anticipated glory is Romans 9:23: *"and that He might make known the riches of His glory on the vessels of mercy, which He had prepared beforehand for glory."* Also, in 2 Corinthians 4:17 Paul says, *"For our light affliction, which is but for a moment, is working for us a far more exceeding and eternal weight of glory."*[8] A part of the blessedness of heaven will be the glory which a believer will manifest throughout eternity.

## ABUNDANT ENTRANCE

Peter exhorts the Christians to give diligence to make their calling and election sure so that they might stand firmly. He adds this explanation: *"For so an entrance will be supplied to you abundantly*

---

[7] Pentecost, *Things to Come*, p. 226.
[8] For further reference to future glory see Philippians 3:21; Colossians 1:27; 1 Corinthians 15:43; 2 Timothy 2:10; Hebrews 2:10; 1 Peter 5:1.

*[plousiōs]* into the everlasting kingdom of our Lord and Savior Jesus Christ" (2 Pet. 1:11). Peter's use of the adverb *plousiōs*, which means richly or abundantly,[9] no doubt encompasses the other aspects of the believer's gracious commendation and generous rewards.

## TREASURE

Jesus expounded a principle which pictured this life as a time of making eternal investments and the future life as a time of enjoying the dividends. In Matthew 6:19-21 Jesus said:

> *Do not lay up for yourselves treasures on earth, where moth and rust destroy and where thieves break in and steal; but lay up for yourselves treasures in heaven, where neither moth nor rust destroys and where thieves do not break in and steal. For where your treasure is, there your heart will be also.*

Christ indicated that the believer's reward can be compared to heavenly treasure which is accumulating for enjoyment in the eternal state. The nature of this treasure is not described within the limits of Biblical revelation. The suggestion is, however, that the believer can make an eternal investment in heaven through his life on earth and that the dividends will be rewards which are significant and desirous.

## INHERITANCE

Several passages in the New Testament teach that the believer will one day inherit the things which God has made available to him. Entrance into the kingdom of God is not earned but is a gift through faith in Jesus Christ. The believer's inheritance is one aspect of his eternal reward for his faith in Christ in his present existence. In Colossians 3:24 the expression *"the reward of the inheritance"* appears: *"Knowing that from the Lord you will receive the reward of the inheritance; for you serve the Lord Christ."* Notice that in this context Paul had just told Christian slaves to completely obey their masters: *"Bondservants, obey in all things your masters according to the flesh, not with eyeservice, as men-pleasers, but in sincerity of heart, fearing God.*

---

[9] Arndt and Gingrich, *A Greek-English Lexicon of the New Testament and Other Early Christian Literature*, p. 679.

*And whatever you do, do it heartily, as to the Lord and not to men"* (3:22-23).

After giving the command, which in itself seems very difficult to obey, especially if the slave owner was an unbeliever, Paul then gave the underlying reason and further motivation for complete obedience. He told these Christian slaves something that they needed to know and never forget: *"knowing that from the Lord you will receive the reward of the inheritance; for you serve the Lord Christ"* (v. 24). He was telling them to take the far look, to focus on what is ahead for all believers after the unfairness and injustice of this life is over. Paul here emphasized the positive aspect of obedience. Servants were to seek to please God, and not obey just to avoid being punished. They were to look ahead and be reminded of the eternal inheritance that awaits all believers.

In Colossians 1:12-14 Paul writes of this inheritance for *all* believers:

> *Giving thanks to the Father who has qualified us to be partakers of the inheritance of the saints in the light. He has delivered us from the power of darkness and conveyed us into the kingdom of the Son of His love, in whom we have redemption through His blood, the forgiveness of sins.*

In Romans 8:16-17a Paul teaches that *all* believers are heirs of God because of their position as sons: *"The Spirit Himself bears witness with our spirit that we are children of God, and if children, then heirs—heirs of God and joint heirs with Christ."* Paul reminded these believers that they are God's children. What a privileged position! Because believers are God's children, we share in the inheritance that God gives. He has already given believers the best gifts of His Son, forgiveness, salvation, the indwelling Holy Spirit, and eternal life.

Next, Paul suggests that not only can we all enjoy God's treasures as heirs of God, but we must also endure life's trials because we are the children of God: *"if children, then heirs—heirs of God and joint heirs with Christ, if* (or "since" [see Rom. 3:30]; *eiper* in Greek—used of a thing which is assumed to be) *we suffer with Him, that we may also be glorified together"* (8:17). Paul told the Romans that now that they were in God's family by faith, suffering should be expected (Acts 14:22; Rom. 8:36; Phil. 1:29; 1 Pet. 2:21).

This suffering is not the suffering that accomplished reconciliation and redemption. The believer can never share in this redemptive suffering which Christ alone took upon Himself. Rather, this is the suffering that naturally arises in a hostile world towards believers in Christ, especially those who faithfully follow Him. Jesus alluded to this when He said to His disciples:

> *If the world hates you, you know that it hated Me before it hated you. If you were of the world, the world would love its own. Yet because you are not of the world, but I chose you out of the world, therefore the world hates you. Remember the word that I said to you, "A servant is not greater than his master." If they persecuted Me, they will also persecute you. If they kept My word, they will keep yours also* (Jn. 15:18-20).

Similarly, Paul wrote to Timothy, *"Yes, and all who desire to live godly in Christ Jesus will suffer persecution"* (2 Tim. 3:12). In this life the faithful believer encounters opposition from the world which hates Christ. Suffering is the seed that is sown in the present that will produce the fruit of glory in the future when all believers enjoy their complete and full inheritance in the very presence of God (Rom. 8:18).

Another verse that speaks of the believer's inheritance is James 2:5: *"Listen, my beloved brethren: Has God not chosen the poor of this world to be rich in faith and heirs of the kingdom which He promised to those who love Him?"* James makes it clear that the only condition for being heirs of the kingdom is to have genuine faith. It is possible to be very poor in this life and very rich in the next life. God's ways are not man's ways. In 1 Corinthians 1:26-28 Paul reminded the Corinthian believers of God's standards for His choosing them: *"For you see your calling, brethren, that not many wise according to the flesh, not many mighty, not many noble, are called. But God has chosen the foolish things of the world to put to shame the wise, and God has chosen the weak things of the world to put to shame the things which are mighty; and the base things of the world and the things which are despised God has chosen, and the things which are not, to bring to nothing the things that are, that no flesh should glory in His presence."*

The poor of this world who are rich in faith can look forward to a great future which lies ahead for all believers. All believers as children of God are heirs of God's kingdom which He has promised to those who believe in Him and love Him. James reminds these suffering Christians that even though they may be poor in this world, they can look forward to being rich heirs in God's eternal kingdom. What a great reward for their faith!

The gospel seems to have more appeal to the poor than to the wealthy. Wealth can tend to make a person think that he can get along by himself without any need for God. James reminded these believers that material poverty is not a barrier to real, lasting, eternal wealth. They could look forward to enjoying their inheritance in God's eternal kingdom as children of God.

God's message to the poor of this world, as well as to everyone else, is that if they will believe in the Lord Jesus Christ they will be heirs of God and His kingdom and joint heirs with Jesus Christ. This true spiritual wealth will not fade away. It is available to the rich on the very same basis as it is to the poor. Thus, the inheritance of the kingdom of God is an unfathomable reward for those who simply put their faith in the Lord Jesus Christ.[10]

## REIGN

Another aspect of the believer's reward in the eternal state is the degree to which he will share in Christ's rule and reign during the future millennial kingdom. The judgment seat of Christ will be the doorway to rulership in the millennium. At this time the particular position of each Christian will be determined on the basis of his life on earth. Jesus told His disciples that they would participate with Him in His rule over the twelve tribes of Israel. Christ said, *"Assuredly I say to you, that in the regeneration, when the Son of Man sits on the throne of His glory, you who have followed Me will also sit on twelve thrones, judging the twelve tribes of Israel"* (Mt. 19:28). The rule of the millennial kingdom will be administered by Christ through the apostles who will share His throne. Paul indicates that members of the Church, the body of Christ, will also reign with Him. He states, *"If we endure, we shall also reign with Him"* (2 Tim. 2:12). Walvoord comments on the significance of these two passages:

> The fact that Christ promised His disciples that they would rule over the twelve tribes of Israel and promised to faithful

---

[10] Other passages that refer directly or indirectly to the believer as an heir and to his inheritance are the following: Mt. 5:5; Acts 20:32; 26:18; 1 Cor. 6:9-10; 15:50; 2 Cor. 6:10; Gal. 4:7; 5:21; Eph. 3:6; 5:5; Ti. 3:7; Heb. 1:14; 1 Pet. 3:7, 9; Rev. 21:7.

members of the body of Christ a similar position of honor of reigning with Him, constitutes a confirmation of the premillennial concept that there will be an earthly kingdom between His second advent and the inauguration of the eternal state. These predictions imply a mediatorial kingdom in which Christ is the ruler and in which His followers will share responsibility.[11]

Second Timothy 2:11-13 give the necessary condition for reigning with Christ:

> *This is a faithful saying: For if we died with Him, we shall also live with Him. If we endure, we shall also reign with Him. If we deny Him, He also will deny us. If we are faithless, He remains faithful; He cannot deny Himself.*

This passage suggests that before the believer receives his crown he must bear his cross. Kent writes, "Hardship, struggle, discipline, labor—all must precede the enjoyment of reward."[12] In this passage there are four first-class conditions which means that the statements are assumed to be true. The second and third conditional statements are relevant to this discussion: *"If we endure, we shall also reign with Him. If we deny Him, He also will deny us."* The first of these two statements is very plain. The subject here is reward. The condition for reward is suffering or perhaps more accurately endurance (*hypomenō*) in afflictions that naturally arise. The believer who faithfully endures afflictions that come from a hostile, unbelieving world has the glorious promise of reigning with Christ.

The next statement, *"If we deny Him, He also will deny us,"* is a little more difficult to understand. The term used for "deny" is *arneomai*. It can mean to refuse, to deny, to disdain, or to disown.[13] Bible teachers differ in their interpretation of this passage. For example, Kent writes:

> If we deny Him, we may expect Him to deny us (Matt. 10:33). The same particle "if" (*ei*) is employed, assuming the condition to be true. However, the verb is a future tense, and thus Paul

---

[11] Walvoord, *The Church in Prophecy*, p. 155.

[12] Homer A. Kent, Jr., *The Pastoral Epistles: Studies in I and II Timothy and Titus* (Chicago: Moody Press, 1958), p. 271.

[13] Arndt and Gingrich, *A Greek-English Lexicon of the New Testament and Other Early Christian Literature*, p. 107.

is not stating that which was presently the case. He does not mean, "since we are denying him," but "if we shall deny him in the future (and some may)," the consequence is clear.[14]

Another interpretation is suggested by Epp. He writes:

> The promise, however, is that if we suffer with Him we shall reign with Him, but if we deny Him at the time of test or trial and do not suffer, *then He will deny us reigning.* We are not denied heaven, for the very next verse says, "If we believe not, yet he abideth faithful: he cannot deny himself." *But He will deny us our place in the kingdom.*[15]

This latter interpretation contextually commends itself since Paul is speaking about reward rather than salvation. The second and third conditional statements seem to go together. The second unquestionably deals with the concept of reward (if we endure suffering, we shall reign). Then the third naturally follows (if we deny or refuse, he will deny or refuse us). The question is, What can the believer refuse or deny? The word "Him" in the English text is absent in the Greek text of verses 11-12. The reader must supply the object of the denial. In light of the preceding statement it would seem that Paul is implying that if the believer should refuse the opportunity of suffering which God permits to come his way, then God will deny that believer the privilege of reigning with Christ. The final statement (*"If we are faithless, He remains faithful; He cannot deny Himself"*) emphasizes that nothing can reverse the believer's eternal position in Christ. The thrust of this passage, however, is faithfulness and reward. That which a believer will do in the area of service throughout eternity is entirely dependent upon and determined by what he has done in this life.

Revelation 20, likewise, supports the fact that the saints will share with Christ in His literal one thousand year reign over the earth. Church-age saints will enjoy this high privilege as well as the tribulation saints who were martyred because of their unwavering faith in Christ. Verse four asserts:

---

[14] Kent, *The Pastoral Epistles: Studies in I and II Timothy and Titus*, p. 272.
[15] Theodore H. Epp, *Present Labor and Future Rewards: The Believer, His Sin, Conduct, and Rewards* (Lincoln, NE: Back to the Bible Broadcast, 1960), pp. 81-82 (italics added).

> *And I saw thrones, and they sat on them, and judgment was committed to them. Then I saw the souls of those who had been beheaded for their witness to Jesus and for the word of God, who had not worshiped the beast or his image, and had not received his mark on their foreheads or on their hands. And they lived and reigned with Christ for a thousand years.*

Verse six of the same chapter seems to go beyond the previous statement concerning the future reign of tribulation saints and includes all those who will be involved in the first resurrection, that is, the resurrection unto life. Revelation 20:6 reads, *"Blessed and holy is he who has part in the first resurrection. Over such the second death has no power, but they shall be priests of God and of Christ, and shall reign with Him a thousand years."* Walvoord again comments on this passage:

> Some dispensationalists have interpreted these passages as teaching that only the church, the body of Christ, has part in the millennial reign and that other resurrected saints will not have this privilege. This conclusion seems to be contradicted by Revelation 20:4-6. It is probably more accurate to say that the church will reign with Christ in a different sense than saints of other ages. An illustration is afforded in the book of Esther in the relationship of Esther and Mordecai to Ahasuerus. Esther, the queen, reigned with Ahasuerus as his wife and queen while Mordecai reigned with Ahasuerus as his prime minister and chief administrative officer. Both Mordecai and Esther reigned with Ahasuerus but in different senses. It is possible that there may be a similar distinction observed in the millennial reign of Christ in that the church will follow her typical position as the bride of Christ while other saints will have other responsibility in the government of the millennium. There is no real need, however, for a sharp distinction between the church and saints of other ages in the eternal state, though the Scriptures seem to indicate clearly that each group of saints will retain its identity throughout eternity.[16]

There will be at least three classifications of responsibilities for believers in their exercise of rule with Christ. These duties will include

---

[16] Walvoord, *The Church in Prophecy*, pp. 156-57.

judicial, executive, and administrative responsibilities. Regarding the judicial aspect of reigning with Christ Paul writes:

> *Do you not know that the saints will judge the world? And if the world will be judged by you, are you unworthy to judge the smallest matters? Do you not know that we shall judge angels? How much more, things that pertain to this life?* (1 Cor. 6:2-3).

The executive aspect of the church's reign is based upon her relationship to Christ as His bride. The church, the bride of the King, will be a co-sharer in His reign. Chafer says, "As the bride of a king is not a subject of the king, but a consort with the king in his reign, so the Church will share the reign of Christ."[17] Although the millennial kingdom will terminate after the completion of the one thousand years, Christ will continue to reign forever. The Scripture teaches that the Church, Christ's bride, will continue to reign with Him eternally. Revelation 22:5 speaks of the believers' eternal reign: *"And they shall reign forever and ever."*

In Luke 19 it is suggested that believers will be graciously given administrative and managerial duties. In the parable of the pounds one servant was faithful with the one pound which had been entrusted to him and had gained ten pounds. To him was granted authority and rulership over ten cities. Similarly, the servant which had been faithful and had gained five pounds, was granted rulership over five cities. From this illustration it can be concluded that the degree of administrative privilege which will be given in the millennial kingdom will be in direct proportion to each believer's faithfulness in this life.

The fact that church-age saints will rule is specifically mentioned in God's message to the church in Thyatira. Revelation 2:26-27 states, *"And he who overcomes, and keeps My works until the end, to him I will give power over the nations—'He shall rule them with a rod of iron; they shall be dashed to pieces like the potter's vessels' —as I also have received from My Father."* Unger comments on this passage:

> Overcomers of matured and ripened (rotten) Balaamism and Nicolaitanism in the orgy of Romish corruption in the church

---

[17] Chafer, *Ecclesiology-Eschatology*, p. 378.

of Thyatira are promised the reward of the gift of "authority over the nations," millennial nations, to rule them with a rod of iron, with Christ, as the vessels of a potter are broken to shivers.[18]

When Christ returns to earth to establish His millennial kingdom, Christians who have been faithful in this life will share in His reign with Him and will be given positions of authority in the kingdom. Their reign will not be terminal but rather eternal, although the nature of the responsibilities will doubtless change at the conclusion of the millennial kingdom.[19]

## PRIVILEGED SERVICE

An aspect of the Christian's reward granted at the judgment seat of Christ and related to the foregoing is privileged service in the eternal state. Revelation 22:3 simply says, *"And His servants shall serve Him."* The nature of this service is not expressly revealed. It will be the privilege of those who have faithfully served the Lord on earth to serve Him in heaven. Doubtless, this service will include the judicial, executive, and administrative duties involved in co-ruling with Christ.

In his examination of the believer's rewards, Waldor Thalleen suggests that faithful service in this life will increase the capability of service, joy, and blessedness in eternity. He comments:

> This principle is set forth in the parable of the pounds, where the servant who gained ten pounds was given authority over ten cities, and the servant who gained five pounds was given authority over five cities. Those who are faithful in serving the Lord during this life increase their capability for rendering service and will be used by Him to the full extent of their capability throughout all eternity. The Christian will not just lay back and rest on flowery beds of ease throughout eternity, for it is written: *"and his servants shall serve him"* (Rev. 22:3).[20]

---

[18] Unger, *Great Neglected Bible Prophecies*, p. 117.

[19] For other passages not mentioned above dealing with the believer's reign, see 1 Pet. 2:9; Rev. 1:6; 3:21.

[20] Waldor Edward Thalleen, "The Christian Doctrine of Rewards" (unpublished Th.M. thesis, Dallas Theological Seminary, 1950), p. 30.

F. J. Horsefield offers additional light concerning the believer's increased capabilities in the eternal state. He writes:

> It would rather seem to indicate that some of the redeemed will be capable of greater joy, and blessing, and service, than others. . . . It is simply a question of capacity—a capacity that will have been, to a larger or smaller extent, developed by the employment of our talents here; by the opportunities of service of which we have availed ourselves; by the cultivation of the Christ-like spirit. The man who, in this life, has yielded himself unreservedly to the control of the Holy Spirit, living in the very atmosphere of fellowship with Christ, and seeking in every possible way the extension of the Kingdom of God, will thus have enlarged his capacity for the enjoyment of the yet more perfect communion of the life to come, and will doubtless be given some form of service in the Church triumphant that none other could undertake.[21]

Although Scripture does not explicitly describe the nature of this future service, it is clear from Biblical revelation that privileged service will be one aspect of the believer's reward. These assignments will be dispensed at the judgment seat of Christ. Keith Brooks aptly writes:

> We believe we have abundant Scripture reason for believing that going to be with Christ means something more than playing harps and singing psalms. There is sublime work to be done. Christ's prepared appointees, clothed in immortality, will be empowered as benefactors of the nations, shepherds of millions yet to live, eternal workers in God's great laboratory of the universe.[22]

Heaven will be a place of joyful activity and privileged service as the eternal reward of those joyfully serving the Lord now.

---

[21] F. J. Horsefield, *The Church and the Coming King* (London: Marshall Brothers, Ltd., 1926), p. 72.

[22] Keith L. Brooks, *Prophecy Text Book for Reference and for Classes* (Los Angeles: n.p., 1933), p. 44.

## OTHER REWARDS

There are several other rewards or spiritual blessings that appear in Scripture, but some are rather obscure with regard to what they actually represent. These are promised to "the overcomers" (*ho nikōn*).[23] From 1 John 5:4-5 it is clear that all Christians are overcomers positionally: *"For whatever is born of God overcomes the world. And this is the victory that has overcome the world—our faith. Who is he who overcomes the world, but he who believes that Jesus is the Son of God?"* The Apostle John, who also penned the book of Revelation, made it clear that when he was talking about "overcomers" he was referring to all of those who have placed their faith in the Lord Jesus Christ. When the various passages of Scripture in Revelation 2 and 3 are examined in light of how the Apostle John had already defined "overcomers," then it becomes abundantly clear that the biblical view is that all believers are indeed overcomers who will enjoy the spiritual blessings associated with being an overcomer by faith.

First John 5:4-5 is the only place in Scripture where this question is both asked and answered: Who is an overcomer? John clearly says, *"Who is he who overcomes the world, but he who believes that Jesus is the Son of God?"* Every person who believes in Jesus Christ as his or her personal Savior is an overcomer and can look forward to the blessings designated for overcomers in Revelation 2 and 3. This fact is made a reality because in John 16:33c Jesus said, *"I have overcome the world."* Jesus Christ is the ultimate Overcomer Who has made it possible for every believer who has trusted in His completed victory on the cross to be an overcomer too.

The promises to the overcomers in Revelation 2 and 3 are the following: to eat of the tree of life (Rev. 2:7); not to be hurt by the second death (Rev. 2:11); to eat of the hidden manna; to receive a white stone with a new name written in it (Rev. 2:17); to exercise power over the nations and to be given the morning star (Rev. 2:28); to be clothed in white raiment (Rev. 3:4-5); to be a pillar in the temple of God and to have written on him the name of God and the name of the city of God (Rev. 3:12); and to sit with Christ on His throne (Rev. 3:21).

The key factor in being an overcomer according to the Apostle John is saving faith in Jesus Christ. Being an overcomer is not because the

---

[23] For an in-depth discussion of the meaning of "overcomer," see the appendix in this book, "Who Are the Overcomers?"

believer achieves that position by what he does, but because by God's grace through faith he is in Christ, the Ultimate Overcomer.

In His address to each of the seven churches in Revelation 2 and 3, Christ promises a special blessing to every believer who overcomes. All Christians are overcomers, even though some may be more faithful in their daily walk than others. As a result some may receive a greater degree of blessing or reward than others, but all believers are overcomers and will receive the blessings promised to the overcomers. The Apostle John writes in Revelation 21:7 the promise that is clearly given to all overcomers: *"He who overcomes shall inherit all things, and I will be his God and he shall be My son."* All believers can claim that promise. (For a more complete discussion of this subject, see Appendix B.)

Even though the exact nature and full significance of these promised blessings may not be completely understood, the truth remains that God truly desires to reward those who belong to Him. Faith has its own reward in this life as well as in the life to come. What makes a person an overcomer? It is simply exercising faith in the Lord Jesus for one's eternal salvation. Genuine faith should move the believer to faithful living, experiencing the joy of being an overcomer in this life as he lives in light of the life to come.

The general and specific rewards that God has prepared for believers are beyond total understanding in this life, though they are real. God will create a new heaven and a new earth for these blessings to be experienced throughout eternity. This earthly existence is not all that there is. In fact, the best is yet to come! For the unbeliever, this life is as good as it gets, but for the believer this life is as bad as it gets. The Apostle Paul wrote to the Romans, *"For I consider that the sufferings of this present time are not worthy to be compared with the glory which shall be revealed in us"* (Rom. 8:18).

Knowing what an incredible, eternal future is ahead, every believer should have faith and courage to press on, facing temptations confidently in the power of the risen Christ and enduring hardship for the glory of God. The purpose of Bible prophecy is not to scare us, but to prepare us for what God has promised to those who trust in Him.

# CHAPTER 11

# THE POSITIVE RESULTS OF THE CHRISTIAN'S JUDGMENT: SPECIAL "CROWN" REWARDS

The New Testament mentions four or perhaps five rewards which are symbolically spoken of as crowns. They will be bestowed upon certain believers at the judgment seat of Christ for some specialized service or specific achievement. The crowns which are specifically mentioned are the incorruptible crown, the crown of rejoicing, the crown of righteousness, the crown of glory, and the crown of life. Biblical revelation does not indicate whether these are all of the crown rewards which will be bestowed upon Christians. Perhaps these crowns are only a representative sample of the special rewards which will be given.

These crowns which are mentioned in Scripture are related to certain facets of Christian achievement. It is conceivable that there are aspects of Christian service which are not specifically listed by these writers within the purpose of their epistle but which will be the basis of a similar reward. Otherwise, only four or five very specific areas of Christian endeavor would qualify as the exclusive basis of crown rewards. From the previous investigation it was shown that all areas of life and service will be taken into consideration for rewards.

In this chapter, an examination will be made of the two Greek words which are used for crowns in the New Testament, along with the probable figurative significance of the crowns, and the nature of each of the crowns which are specifically mentioned in relation to the believer's reward. Taken together with the general rewards previously discussed, these rewards are tokens of the grace of God which will be lavishly bestowed upon His children.

## THE MEANING OF CROWNS

In the Greek New Testament two words, *stephanos* and *diadēma* appear which are translated in the English text by the word "crown." The word *stephanos* is derived from the verb *stephō* which means to encircle or to put around.[1] It designates a woven wreath or garland which encircles the head. The words *stephanos* and *stephanoō* occur in the New Testament eighteen times and three times respectively. In New Testament times a *stephanos* was used for marriage and for festive occasions; as a means of expressing public recognition to the victor in an athletic contest; for heroic deeds in battle; or for distinguished service of some kind. In the reward motif of Scripture it is used of certain eschatological rewards granted to believers.[2]

The word *stephanos* was generally used to denote a victor's or conqueror's crown (wreath) rather than a kingly crown or crown of royalty. For the latter usage the word *diadēma* was employed. Although *stephanos* was occasionally used to denote a crown of royalty (as in the Septuagint in 2 Samuel 12:30 and Zechariah 6:11), it was generally used for a wreath awarded to a victor at the athletic contests or to a conqueror in battle or used as a garland at festive occasions. Whenever Paul used the term in his writings, he made reference to the wreath which was given to a victor.

In contrast to *stephanos*, the term *diadēma* is found in the New Testament only three times (Rev. 12:3; 13:1; 19:12). It is derived from the verb, *diadeō*, which means to bind around.[3] The term *diadēma* is always used to denote royalty, power to rule, or imperial sovereignty. Thayer indicates that *stephanos* was a crown in the sense of a chaplet, wreath, or garland which was a badge of victory in the games, of public worth, of military accomplishment, of marriage or festival occasions, while *diadēma* was used as a badge of royalty or kingly honor.[4]

In the Gospels, *stephanos* is used four times (Mt. 27:29; Mk. 15:17; Jn. 19:2, 5) of the crown (wreath) of thorns which Christ wore at the

---

[1] Thayer, *Greek-English Lexicon of the New Testament*, p. 587.
[2] William Edward Raffety, "Crown," *The International Standard Bible Encyclopedia*, ed. by James Orr (5 vols. Grand Rapids: Wm. B. Eerdmans Publishing Co., 1955), 762.
[3] Thayer, *A Greek-English Lexicon of the New Testament*, p. 136.
[4] Ibid.

time of his trial. Trench suggests an explanation for the use of *stephanos* on this occasion. He writes:

> The only occasion on which *stephanos* might seem to be used of a kingly crown is Matt. xxvii.29; cf. Mark xv.17; John xix.2; where the weaving of the crown of thorns (*stephanos akanthinos*), and placing it on the Saviour's head, is evidently a part of that blasphemous masquerade of royalty which the Roman soldiers would fain compel Him to enact. But woven of such materials as it was . . . it is evident that *diadēma* could not be applied to it; and the word, therefore, which was fittest in respect of the material whereof it was composed, takes the place of that which would have been the fittest in respect of the purpose for which it was intended.[5]

Every time Scripture refers to the believer's crowns, the word *stephanos* is used. This suggests that before Christians could receive their victors' wreaths, Christ first had to win the victory by wearing a wreath of thorns on His brow to conquer sin and death.

The figure of the victor's wreath which Paul uses to denote the believer's reward has significance against the backdrop of the Isthmian games. The winner of each event was given a wreath woven from evergreen sprays. The wreath had no intrinsic worth, but its value was based exclusively upon the honor which was bestowed upon the champion who was proven worthy to wear it. The wreath was merely symbolic of the honor and praise bestowed upon the victor for his outstanding accomplishment.

In Revelation 4:4 the twenty-four elders, who are apparently representative of the church, are pictured as wearing golden wreaths upon their heads. In verse ten, these are cast before the throne. This is an act of worship and of bestowing honor upon the One through Whose strength they were able to serve faithfully while on earth. Thalleen suggests that this act does not mean "that the Christian's reward terminates at this point, for rewards are eternal in their nature. He receives an incorruptible crown and glory that fadeth not away."[6] This event, however, does picture the way in which the believer will

---

[5] Trench, *Synonyms of the New Testament*, pp. 76-77.
[6] Thalleen, "The Christian Doctrine of Rewards," pp. 37-38.

respond with the rewards bestowed upon him. He will reciprocate and glorify God with them and praise God for them. Pentecost concludes, "It is made clear that the crowns will not be for the eternal glory of the recipient, but for the glory of the Giver."[7]

## THE NATURE OF THE CROWNS

Scripture suggests that these eschatological rewards will not be literal crowns as will be demonstrated under the discussion of the individual crowns. They rather seem to be symbolic of special honor bestowed for distinctive Christian service and living. Thayer suggests that these crowns are used metaphorically for "the eternal blessedness which will be given as a prize to the genuine servants of God and Christ."[8] Walvoord says, "The various crowns mentioned in Scripture taken together are a symbolic representation of the recognition by Christ of the faithful service of those who put their trust in Him."[9] Hogg and Watson likewise conclude, "Several passages speak of the rewards granted in that day under the simile of 'crowns,' surely a figure of the dignity of spiritual status conferred on approved character."[10] English concurs with the preceding men: "These rewards are symbolically referred to in many instances as crowns (1 Cor. 9:25; 1 Thess. 2:19; 1 Pet. 5:4; etc.)."[11] An examination of the crowns mentioned in the New Testament will support the conclusion that these crowns are indeed figures or symbols of some divine recognition.

### The Incorruptible Crown

In 1 Corinthians 9:25, Paul compares the Christian's life to that of an athlete. He writes, *"And everyone who competes for the prize is temperate in all things. Now they do it to obtain a perishable crown, but we for an imperishable crown."* The Greek word *stephanos* is used to denote the nature of the believer's wreath. This wreath will be by its very nature

---

[7] Pentecost, *Things to Come*, pp. 225-26.

[8] Thayer, *Greek-English Lexicon of the New Testament*, p. 587.

[9] Walvoord, *The Church in Prophecy*, p. 152.

[10] C. F. Hogg and J. B. Watson, *The Promise of His Coming: Chapters an the Second Advent* (London: Pickering & Inglis Ltd., n.d.), p. 46.

[11] E. Schuyler English, *Re-Thinking the Rapture* (Neptune, NJ: Loizeaux Brothers, 1954), p. 83.

imperishable.[12] The apostle Paul uses this term to contrast the eternal reward with that of the perishable wreath (*phthartos stephanos*), which is subject to decay, that is awarded to the victorious athlete.

Paul's readers were very familiar with the Isthmian games which required an athlete to endure the most rigid training for ten months in order to qualify for the games. He brought his body and life under the strictest discipline and temperance in order to obtain a laurel wreath which would begin to wither the moment its sprays were plucked from the tree. In contrast to the Greek athlete, the challenge issues forth to the Christian who runs to obtain an incorruptible prize to keep his body and life under the strictest discipline. He is challenged to forsake the allurements of the flesh that would hinder him in his spiritual race of life. Self-discipline and self-control are necessary to resist fleshly lusts so that the Christian can serve Christ to the fullest extent. Through discipline and diligence he can have a significant part in augmenting God's work and obtain for himself an eternal reward which will never fade away or perish.

There is some question as to whether this incorruptible wreath is a separate reward for certain Christians who keep a tight rein on their lives or whether it simply connotes the nature of the other four crowns. Thalleen is perhaps correct in his suggestion:

> It may be that reference is being made here to the nature of the other four crowns, rather than to a separate crown called the "incorruptible crown." The exhortation would then be one to diligence on the part of the Christian because of the incorruptible nature of the crowns bestowed at the end of his race.[13]

If Thalleen is right, then there are only four crowns (wreaths) mentioned specifically in the New Testament as rewards for believers. If it is a separate reward, it is for those Christians who have lived triumphantly. Gromacki writes:

> This is given to the Christian who practices self control or discipline in his spiritual life and service. It is given to the believer who excels in spiritual dedication. It is given to the triumphant

---

[12] Arndt and Gingrich, *A Greek-English Lexicon of the New Testament and Other Early Christian Literature*, p. 125.

[13] Thalleen, "The Christian Doctrine of Rewards," p. 34.

one, not to the also-ran or mediocre believer. Carnal, immature, backslidden church members have no chance for this award. It is given to the one who has endured hardness as a good soldier of Jesus Christ, who has not entangled himself with the affairs of this life, who has striven for mastery (2 Timothy 2:3-5).[14]

If the incorruptible crown is indeed a special crown, a Christian needs to exercise keen discernment and careful self-discipline if he is to measure up to the stringent requirements of this crown reward.

### *The Crown of Rejoicing*

In 1 Thessalonians Paul writes that the Thessalonian believers will be his crown of rejoicing when Christ appears. He states, *"For what is our hope, or joy, or crown of rejoicing (stephanos kauchēseōs)? Is it not even you in the presence of our Lord Jesus Christ at His coming?"* (1 Thess. 2:19). In Philippians 4:1, Paul probably alludes to this same crown when he indicates that the Philippian believers who are his converts also are his crown. He writes, *"Therefore, my beloved and longed-for brethren, my joy and crown (stephanos), so stand fast in the Lord, beloved."* The crown is obviously figurative, thus not referring to a literal wreath, for Paul states that believers are figuratively his wreath of rejoicing.

The expression *stephanos kauchēseōs* is probably best understood with *kauchēseōs* being a genitive of apposition. Dana and Mantey describe this usage by saying, "A noun which designates an object in an individual or particular sense may be used in the genitive with another noun which designates the same thing in a general sense."[15] In this case the expression would mean "the crown which consists of rejoicing or glorying." Paul's reward would, therefore, be the eternal joy that he would experience because these believers who were his converts would be with him forever in heaven, rather than a literal wreath which he would wear.

This reward of rejoicing has been called the soul-winner's crown by many because of the great joy which will be experienced by those who have introduced others to the Savior. Paul writes in 2 Corinthians 11:2 of the event: *"For I am jealous for you with godly jealousy. For I have*

---

[14] Gromacki, *Are These the Last Days?* p. 169.
[15] Dana and Mantey, *A Manual Grammar of the Greek New Testament*, p. 79.

*betrothed you to one husband, that I may present you as a chaste virgin to Christ. "* Probably not only those who have led individuals to Christ, but also those who were instrumental in their salvation through prayer or through sowing the seed of the Gospel will share in this reward of joy.

For such individuals heaven will be an occasion of increased jubilation. The judgment seat of Christ will be a joyous place for those who have been faithful in praying for and witnessing to those who need the Savior.

### The Crown of Righteousness

Another reward which is available for those who meet the requirements is the crown of righteousness. Paul writes of this crown in his final epistle just prior to his martyrdom:

> *I have fought a good fight, I have finished the race, I have kept the faith. Finally, there is laid up for me the crown of righteousness [ho tēs dikaiosynēs stephanos], which the Lord, the righteous Judge, will give to me on that Day, and not to me only but also to all who have loved His appearing* (2 Tim. 4:7-8).

A. T. Robertson explains Paul's usage of the expression "crown of righteousness." He calls this expression a genitive of apposition and says it metaphorically refers to "the crown that consists in righteousness and is also the reward for righteousness."[16]

This is not, however, the same as *"the gift of righteousness"* which is the positional righteousness that is imputed to each Christian the moment he believes in Jesus Christ. It is rather some special eschatological reward *"laid up"* for those who have lived according to God's will in the light of Christ's imminent return. Paul says this reward will be bestowed upon *"all who have loved His appearing."* This reward is for those who are *"looking for the blessed hope and glorious appearing of our great God and our Savior Jesus Christ"* (Ti. 2:13) and who recognize that their *"citizenship is in heaven, from which we also eagerly wait for the Savior, the Lord Jesus Christ"* (Phil. 3:20). These live their lives in light of eternity, following the admonition of Colossians 3:1-4:

---

[16] Robertson, *The Epistles of Paul*, p. 631.

*If then you were raised with Christ, seek those things which are above, where Christ is, sitting at the right hand of God. Set your mind on things above, not on things on the earth. For you died, and your life is hidden with Christ in God. When Christ who is our life appears, then you also will appear with Him in glory.*

Unger says, "The perpetual attitude of advent-expectancy produces practical and experimental righteousness, in right and holy living, which has a reward, just as positional righteousness in Christ accompanies salvation."[17] Although the conditions for this reward are relatively clear, the exact form that this reward will take in the eternal state is obscure. Perhaps, as Betz suggests:

The crown of righteousness is a crown which consists of righteousness. It involves the capacity to reflect the very righteousness of Christ (cf. Rev. 3:5; 19:7-8). It is possible to be saved and yet fail to receive this reward.[18]

Some believers perhaps will regrettably be like Demas described in the same context as this crown: *"For Demas has forsaken me, having loved this present world"* (2 Tim. 4:10). A Christian cannot love the Savior and His appearing as well as love this present world and its allurements. For those who expectantly and eagerly await the Lord with godly living, there is laid up for them the crown of righteousness.

### The Crown of Glory

Peter lists another reward which is symbolized by a crown and is described as the unfading crown of glory. He writes to undershepherds, *"And when the chief Shepherd appears, you will receive the crown of glory [tēs doxēs stephanos] that does not fade away [amarantinos]"* (1 Pet. 5:4). Again, the noun in the genitive *doxēs* is probably best understood as the genitive of apposition. Therefore, the wreath of glory metaphorically would be the wreath that consists of glory. The use of the article with this expression seems to imply some definite

---

[17] Merrill F. Unger, "The Doctrine of the Believer's Judgment," *Our Hope* 58 (February 1952): 506.

[18] Harlan D. Betz, "The Nature of Rewards at the Judgment Seat of Christ" (unpublished Th.M. thesis, Dallas Theological Seminary, 1974), pp. 33-34.

reward consisting of glory rather than just the glory considered earlier under the discussion of general rewards. Apparently this reward will be some special portion of glory which will be the eternal possession of the faithful undershepherd.

The adjective *amarantinos* further describes this crown as unfading, similar to the previously considered imperishable crown. This term literally means "composed of amaranth" which is a flower so named because it never withers or fades, and when plucked off revives if moistened with water. Hence it is a symbol of perpetuity and aptly describes this specific reward.[19]

The qualifications for this wreath of glory are expressed in I Peter 5:2-3: *"Shepherd the flock of God which is among you, serving as overseers, not by compulsion but willingly, not for dishonest gain but eagerly; nor as being lords over those entrusted to you, but being examples to the flock."* The pastor's or undershepherd's reward is for those who have been faithful to their divine appointment to feed and lead the flock of God. The faithful undershepherd is one who does not perform the responsibilities by constraint, but willingly, sacrificially, and eagerly. He directs the flock, but he does not stand as a dictator over the flock. In all areas of life he leads by a godly example and with a humble spirit. To such a faithful undershepherd the Lord will grant glory, praise, and honor at the judgment seat of Christ. Although he is often misunderstood, evil spoken of, and unappreciated, the undershepherd can be assured that God has reserved a special reward for those who are faithful to their divine calling.

This wreath of glory mentioned by Peter is not to be confused with the wreath of glorying (rejoicing) which is mentioned by Paul in 1 Thessalonians 2:19. The reward which Peter mentions is described by the word *doxa* and suggests praise and honor. The reward which Paul mentions is described by the word *kauchēsis* which suggests boasting and glorying. The latter is granted to individuals because of their faithfulness to their soul-winning responsibilities, while the former is granted to undershepherds because of their faithfulness to their shepherding responsibilities, specifically to teaching the Word of God.[20]

---

[19] Thayer, *Greek-English Lexicon of the New Testament*, p. 30.

[20] Renfer, "The Judgment-Seat of Christ," pp. 46-47.

### The Crown of Life

This final special reward is the only one which is specifically mentioned twice in the New Testament. This crown is first mentioned in James 1:12: *"Blessed is the man who endures temptation; for when he has been approved, he will receive the crown of life [ton stephanon tēs zōēs], which the Lord has promised to those who love Him."* Again in Revelation 2:10 it appears: *"Do not fear any of those things which you are about to suffer. Indeed, the devil is about to throw some of you into prison, that you may be tested, and you will have tribulation ten days. Be faithful until death, and I will give you the crown of life [ton stephanon tēs zōēs]."*

In both occurrences, the word in the genitive should probably be understood as a genitive of apposition. Metaphorically it denotes "the wreath that consists of life." The definite article in both occurrences seems to suggest some definite quality or aspect of life. Unger writes, "The genitive seems to be that of quality, and would seem to speak of a 'reward which consists of life,' a fuller entrance into the glory and exaltation of Him, who is 'the Life' (Jn. 14:6)."[21]

The condition for this reward is faithfulness to the Lord through enduring trials and suffering (Jas. 1:12), even to the point of death (Rev. 2:10). This is sometimes called the martyr's or sufferer's crown, although martyrdom is not the only condition for it. God has prepared a special aspect of life in the eternal state as a reward for those who have suffered for the Lord in this life. Matthew 5:10-12 speaks of this same truth regarding special reward for those who suffer for the cause of Christ:

> Blessed are those who are persecuted for righteousness' sake, for theirs is the kingdom of heaven. Blessed are you when they revile and persecute you, and say all kinds of evil against you falsely for My name sake. Rejoice and be exceedingly glad, for great is your reward in heaven, for so they persecuted the prophets who were before you.

Enduring trials in this life brings eternal enrichment in the next life. The crown of life mentioned above is not the same as the gift of life

---

[21] Unger, "The Doctrine of the Believer's Judgment," *Our Hope* 58 (February 1952), p. 504.

which is received the moment one believes, as recorded in Romans 6:23: *"For the wages of sin is death; but the gift of God is eternal life through Jesus Christ our Lord."* The crown of life is a reward bestowed because of faithfulness to Christ in suffering, while the gift of life is a gift which is given because of faith alone in Christ unto salvation. The gift of life is the necessary condition to qualify for the crown of life.

In light of the prospect of receiving one or several of these special rewards at the judgment seat of Christ, there is a sobering admonition and final reminder in Scripture. The apostle John, in the concluding chapter of Biblical revelation writes:

> *And he said to me, "Do not seal the words of the prophecy of this book, for the time is at hand. . . . he who is righteous, let him be righteous still; he who is holy, let him be holy still." And behold, I am coming quickly, and My reward is with Me, to give to every one according to his work"* (Rev. 22:10-12).

# CHAPTER 12

# CONCLUSION

This study of the judgment seat of Christ has been presented in an effort to meet the need for a systematic and comprehensive examination of this vital doctrine. The task has been to glean insights from the broader fields of doctrine, specifically, Christology, soteriology, ecclesiology, and eschatology in order to understand the nature, purpose, and significance of the eschatological *bēma*. This treatise has brought two great doctrinal divisions into juxtaposition, namely, ecclesiology and eschatology, for this awesome event involves the future evaluation of the church.

The specific purpose of this study has been to carefully establish the limits of this judgment in regard to its nature and results. The basic thesis has been that the judgment seat of Christ is a most solemn evaluation at which there will be no judicial condemnation, nor will there be any judicial punishment for the believer's sins, whether confessed or unconfessed. Rather there will be commendation or loss of reward according to the faithfulness of the Christian's life. There also may be some measure of shame and remorse which will arise from seeing one's fleshly works rendered unworthy of reward, but there will be no judicial punishment for unfaithfulness since Christ has borne all the penalty for the believer's sins.

The general judgment theory, which has been traditionally and tenaciously espoused by Christendom at large, rejects the idea of a unique and separate judgment for church-age saints. The proponents of the general judgment theory believe that there will be one final judgment at the consummation of the world. At this time all people of all ages, both believers and unbelievers, will be simultaneously resurrected and judged. At this event the righteous will receive reward, and the unrighteous will be condemned to eternal punishment. Many of the major Protestant creeds and confessions and many of the major writers of systematic theologies have, likewise, espoused and taught the general judgment theory.

This theory, however, was proven to be fallacious. Its proponents employ a spiritualizing method of interpretation of prophetic passages rather than a literal method which takes into account figures of speech; they confuse Israel and the church; they fail to recognize the irreconcilable differences between Biblical judgments with regard to time, place, purpose, and participants; and they misinterpret crucial passages such as Daniel 12:2; John 5:28-29; and Matthew 25:31-46. It was concluded that because of the progressive nature of revelation, there are passages which if considered in isolation would seem to teach a general judgment. However, when these are considered in light of the whole counsel of God and understood literally, they do not support a general judgment. Rather than finding in these passages of Scripture the doctrine of a *general judgment*, it should be recognized that they are *general statements* of the doctrine of judgment. Considered together these passages clearly teach that there will be a series of eschatological judgments of which the judgment seat of Christ for church-age saints is a unique part.

Having established that the judgment seat of Christ will be a unique eschatological judgment, the etymological and cultural backgrounds of the *bēma* were considered. Etymologically, *bēma* comes from the Greek verb *bainō* which simply means to go up or to ascend. The primary meaning of *bēma* was a step or a raised place, and later it was used of a platform which was reached by steps. In the New Testament this term appears twelve times with only two of these occurrences referring to the eschatological *bēma*, namely, in Romans 14:10 and 2 Corinthians 5:10.

Culturally, the term had its roots in the Grecian games and the Roman law court. In the Panhellenic games, the *bēma* was the seat upon which the appointed judges sat as they observed the athletic contests and awarded prizes to the winning contestants. Paul's reference to the *bēma* in his second epistle to the Corinthians was cast against the background of the familiar biennial Isthmian games. The victor of each event was awarded a victor's wreath. Although it had no intrinsic worth, consisting only of woven sprays of celery or laurel which soon withered, the wreath signified the worth and achievement of its wearer.

Paul compared the believer's prospect of an imperishable reward at the judgment seat of Christ with this perishable wreath in 1 Corinthians 9:25: *"And everyone who competes for the prize is temperate in all things. Now they do it to obtain a perishable crown, but we for an imperishable crown."*

The Romans likewise had their *bēma*, although it primarily involved the Roman legal system in contrast to the Grecians and their athletic games. The term was applied to the official seat or tribunal of a Roman magistrate. This tribunal of the Roman magistrate was the most awesome representation of jurisprudence in existence at that time. In both the Roman and the Grecian usage, *bēma* referred to the physical character of a place ("a raised place") and conveyed the concepts of prominence, dignity, and authority.

The period, place, and participants of the judgment seat of Christ were considered next. The temporal boundaries of this future event can be Scripturally established. This evaluation will occur subsequent to the pretribulational rapture of the church and prior to the second advent of Christ to establish the millennial kingdom. First Corinthians 4:5 indicates that the evaluation will occur after the rapture: *"Therefore judge nothing before the time, until the Lord comes, who will both bring to light the hidden things of darkness and reveal the counsels of the hearts. Then each one's praise will come from God."* Revelation 19:7-8 establishes the *terminus ad quem* of this event. These verses indicate that at the second advent the glorified saints will already have been clothed in white raiment which is the righteous deeds of the saints. The actual duration of this evaluation is open to much speculation ranging from instantaneous to seven years. The place where the *bēma* evaluation will occur is in the sphere of the heavenlies, probably in heaven itself before the throne of Christ.

The participants in the judgment are Christ, Who will righteously and infallibly examine the believers, and Christians who will be examined. The general judgment theory proponents teach that all peoples of all ages, believers and unbelievers, will be present at this final assize. However, this conclusion is erroneous. Only the church-age believers from Pentecost to the rapture of the church will be present. Unbelievers will appear before the Great White Throne after the millennium according to Revelation 20:5, 11-15. All believers of this dispensation will be present at the judgment seat of Christ. None will be exempt from appearing at this adjudication whether spiritual or carnal, faithful or unfaithful; each and every Christian will be summoned to appear before the *bēma*. Thus the judgment seat of Christ is all-inclusive—including all church-age saints, and at the same time all-exclusive—excluding all unbelievers and saints from other dispensations.

The nature of the Christian's judgment was determined to be individual rather than corporate. Second Corinthians 5:10 indicates this: *"For we must all appear before the judgment seat of Christ, that each one may receive the things done in the body."*

This judgment was also considered in relation to the other judgments which affect Christians. First, the significance of Christ's judgment for sin on the cross was considered. The question which needed to be answered was: To what extent did the work of Christ on the cross relate to sins in the Christian's life?

Scripture teaches that Christ's death was all-sufficient, completely satisfying God's wrath toward sin in the believer. The question of sin in regard to God's justice has been forever satisfied in the mind of God by the all-sufficient sacrifice of His Son. The penalty for the believer's sins has been fully paid in the Person of his substitute. The Christian has been in court, condemned, sentenced, and executed in his substitute, Jesus Christ. God cannot exact payment for sins twice since payment has been fully and forever paid. The believer is seen by the Father as clothed in the righteousness of Christ. He can find no more to judicially accuse in the Christian than He can find to accuse in Jesus Christ. Therefore, at the judgment seat of Christ forensic punishment will not be meted out for the believer's sins.

The two contemporary judgments of the Christian are, first, his self-judgment and second, his disciplinary judgment. Each Christian is called upon to examine himself to see if there is any unconfessed sin in his life. If there is, he is to confess and forsake it. This action avoids the second present judgment, namely, the disciplinary judgment of the Christian. Failure to judge oneself invites God's disciplinary judgment for the purpose of restoring the wayward believer to fellowship with the Father. This judgment is not punitive in the sense of forensically satisfying God's righteous demands, but rather instructive. To the erring believer it may well seem like punishment, but it stems from God's love rather than His wrath.

Punishment is a judicial act whereby a person must render personal payment for his sins by suffering in some way. Retribution rather than correction is primarily in view. Chastisement is a family act between a father and a son, not between a judge and a criminal. A son is dealt with in order to correct his waywardness. Discipline is primarily an act of restoration rather than an act of retribution. Punishment and chastisement view an act from different perspectives. Chastisement does not primarily look back at the sin, but rather forward to restoration and growth. Punishment looks back at the offense and cries out that the demands of the law be satisfied by future suffering. Punishment stems from the realm of law. Chastisement stems from the relationship of love.

Although the believer is not forensically punished for his sins, nevertheless, there will be temporal consequences as well as eternal consequences for sin. Present unconfessed sin results in a loss of desire for service because one is out of experiential fellowship with God. Unconfessed sin also results in loss of power in the believer's life since the sin grieves the Holy Spirit. Furthermore, unconfessed sin results in loss of opportunity since the sinning believer is not living according to the will of God. Although these are three present consequences of unconfessed sin, similarly, there will be future consequences. When a believer is not walking in experiential fellowship with God, he is passing up opportunities for reward which he will never have again. As a result he will lose the reward that God would have so lavishly bestowed upon him had he been faithful. This will be a real and eternal loss indeed.

In light of what is accomplished in these three judgments, it must be concluded that at the *bēma* evaluation God will not mete out punishment for sins in the believer's life. That was settled at the cross. The only question which will remain concerns the faithfulness of each believer as a member of the body of Christ. The result of this examination will be the reception or the loss of rewards.

Several erroneous suggestions concerning the purpose of the *bēma* evaluation have been advocated by some. There are those who believe that salvation will be an issue there. This view is generally espoused by those of the general judgment persuasion. It was shown that this view is wrong since the judgment seat of Christ is only for Christians. Others believe it will be a place where punishment or chastisement will be meted out. However, as stated earlier, Scripture teaches that God's justice has been fully satisfied at the cross on behalf of the believer. Chastisement will likewise have no purpose there, for God's purpose in discipline is to foster holy living in this life. At the judgment seat the believer will already be in his glorified body, without the old sin nature, and without the capability of moral improvement. Any development in the believer's experiential sanctification is limited to the Christian's life on earth.

Unconfessed sins, as such, will not be an issue at the *bēma*. Unconfessed sins relate to fellowship in this life, standing as a barrier to fellowship and growth. Confession brings "family" forgiveness and restored fellowship. Forensic forgiveness has, however, been granted once for all. Colossians 2:13 states, *"And you, being dead in your trespasses and the uncircumcision of your flesh, He has made alive together with Him, having forgiven you all trespasses."*

The primary purpose of the judgment seat of Christ is to reveal and review the Christian's life and service, and then to reward him for what God deems worthy of reward. Also, the present purpose of the *bēma* evaluation is to serve as a source of motivation for contemporary godly living. Paul writes in 2 Corinthians 5:9 against the backdrop of the *bēma*: *"Therefore we make it our aim, whether present or absent, to be well pleasing to Him."*

Not only is the purpose of this event to serve as present motivation for the believer, it will also be the place of future manifestation of one's life and service. Second Corinthians 5:10 literally states, *"For we must all be made manifest at the judgment seat of Christ."* One's actions as well as motives must be revealed for what they are. Not only will these be exposed, but they will be evaluated in order to determine what is worthy of reward and what is unworthy of reward. First Corinthians 3:13 says, *"Each one's work will become clear; for the Day will declare it, because it will be revealed by fire; and the fire will test each one's work, of what sort it is."* After the evaluation, rewards will be bestowed for faithful living and sacrificial service. For unfaithfulness, one will forfeit the reward that he could have received. Paul writes, *"If anyone's work which he has built on it endures, he will receive a reward. If anyone's work is burned, he will suffer loss; but he himself will be saved, yet so as through fire"* (1 Cor. 3:14-15).

In order for the believer to qualify for rewards God has revealed the nature of His basic standards. In regard to the servant the question is, was he disciplined? First Corinthians 9:25 states, *"And everyone who competes for the prize is temperate in all things. Now they do it to obtain a perishable crown, but we for an imperishable crown."* The apostle compares the rigid discipline that an athlete needs to win a perishable reward with that which a Christian needs to obtain an imperishable reward.

A second standard relates to one's stewardship responsibility: Was it discharged faithfully? First Corinthians 4:2 states, *"Moreover it is required in stewards that one be found faithful."* Each believer has been entrusted with abilities, opportunities, responsibilities, and resources which God has uniquely provided. For these each believer is accountable as a steward. Three parables teach principles which apply to a believer's stewardship. The parable of the laborers in the vineyard (Mt. 20:1-16) teaches that God will give equal compensation for faithfulness in spite of unequal opportunity, not equal compensation for unequal work. The parable of the talents (Mt. 25:14-30) teaches that where there are unequal abilities and differing capacities, yet equal faithfulness, there will be equal reward. The parable of the pounds (Lk. 19:11-26) teaches that where there is equal capability and opportunity, yet unequal faithfulness, the reward will be graded.

Another basic standard of evaluation at the *bēma* is in relationship to the service: Will it abide? Only that which was done for the glory of God, according to His will, and through the energizing of the Holy Spirit will be regarded worthy of reward. This evaluation is concerned with the quality, not just the quantity, of the service. Man's standard for success is often bigness, while God's standard is faithfulness, using the abilities and opportunities uniquely entrusted to each believer for the glory of God.

The judgment seat evaluation will be a comprehensive examination extending to all areas of life and service. The seemingly insignificant acts of love will not go unnoticed nor unrewarded. Matthew 10:42 teaches that even the giving of a cup of cold water can be worthy of reward. Personal sacrifice will be considered in the bestowal of rewards. Mark 12:41-44 illustrates how Jesus took note of the sacrifice involved when the poor widow put all that she had into the treasury, in comparison to those who gave out of their abundance. God also considers those acts which escape the public's view. Such deeds as giving, prayers, and fasting are not to be done for the praise of men, lest selfish and proud motives spoil the worth of the act.

Suffering unjustly for the cause of Christ will also bring reward from God as indicated in Matthew 5:10-12. Sincerity is another factor which will be taken into consideration by the Lord in His future evaluation as seen in Luke 14:12-14. Finally, God will even consider the righteous intentions of a believer who truly desires to serve God in a greater way but is restricted by some unalterable limitations. First Kings 8:17-19 indicates that David longed to build a house in which God could dwell among His people, but because he was a man of war God had passed this privilege to David's son, Solomon. Yet God praised David for his worthy intentions. From the preceding it is clear that God's evaluation of the believer's life will be thoroughly comprehensive, extending to all areas of life and service.

Although all of the believer's sins have been atoned for and all of sin's penalty has been paid, there will still be two negative factors involved at the judgment seat of Christ. First, the unfaithful believer will suffer loss of reward for works unworthy of reward (cf. 1 Cor. 3:15). To lose some future blessedness which one might have received will be a real loss indeed. A second negative aspect will be that of shame and remorse from the realization that one could have been more faithful but instead was negligent and unfaithful (cf. 1 Jn. 2:28). This shame will not be imposed by Christ at the *bēma* but will be self-imposed through the realization of the potential rewards one forfeited and one's sense of unworthiness in the presence of the holy Christ. This element of remorse and sorrow must be somewhat relative and temporary, for heaven will be a place for the redeemed and glorified church to enjoy unhindered communion with her Lord throughout eternity. Peter and Jude speak of the exceeding joy that is to be the believer's portion in heaven (cf. 1 Pet. 4:13; Jude 24-25).

The positive aspects of the judgment seat of Christ involve the bestowal and reception of both general and special rewards. Rewards will be granted in varying degrees depending upon the faithfulness of each believer. The parables, as considered previously, help establish this fact. Likewise, 1 Corinthians 15:40-42 suggest that there will be varying degrees of glory for the saints in heaven. Yet in heaven there will be no discontent with one's own reward or envy for another's reward for the old nature will no longer be present in the believer. Each believer is determining in this life his capacity to receive and reflect God's glory throughout all eternity.

Some of the general rewards mentioned in Scripture are such things as the following: praise from God (1 Cor. 4:5); honor (1 Pet. 1:7; Rom. 2:7); glory (Rom. 8:18; 2 Cor. 4:17); abundant entrance into the eternal state (2 Pet. 1:11); treasure in heaven (Mt. 6:19-21); an eternal inheritance (Col. 1:12-14; 3:24); sharers in Christ's reign (2 Tim. 2:12; Rev. 20:4, 6); and privileged service (Rev. 22:3). Taken together these general rewards indicate something of the blessedness which is in store for believers in the eternal state.

The special rewards which were considered in this book were the crown rewards which will be granted to individual believers for some specialized service or specific achievement. The word which the Biblical writers use to describe these crowns is *stephanos*, which generally denotes a victor's wreath rather than the term *diadēma*, which generally denotes the crown of royalty and kingship. These crowns seem to be symbolic of some special honor or eternal blessedness rather than literal wreaths to be worn during the eternal state.

The incorruptible crown (1 Cor. 9:25) is conferred upon those believers who keep their body and life in subjection, forsaking the allurements of the world and the satisfaction of fleshly desires which would hinder them in the spiritual race of life. Some suggest that perhaps this is not a specific crown but rather it connotes the nature of the other four crowns, namely, that they are imperishable.

The crown of rejoicing (1 Thess. 2:19; Phil. 4:1), as well as the other three crowns, is probably best understood appositionally as the crown (reward) that consists of rejoicing, etc. This crown denotes the glorying or rejoicing that the believer, who has been faithful in witnessing for Christ, will have in heaven. The presence of his spiritual children in heaven will be cause for eternal jubilation.

The crown of righteousness (2 Tim. 4:7-8) will be granted to those who are eagerly awaiting the Lord's return, accompanied by godly living. This reward perhaps involves the capacity to reflect the very righteousness of Christ in greater measure. The crown of glory (1 Pet. 5:4) will be bestowed upon undershepherds who have been faithful in leading and feeding that portion of the flock allotted to them by God. Finally, the crown of life (Jas. 1:12; Rev. 2:10) will be granted to those who are faithful to the Lord in the midst of trials and suffering, even to the point of death. Perhaps this reward involves some fuller entrance into the glory and bliss of the eternal state.

Few doctrines found in the Word of God have greater significance to the believer's life today than the doctrine of the judgment seat of Christ. The degree to which the Christian allows the Holy Spirit to direct and empower his life determines the degree of heavenly glory which he will experience. Walvoord challengingly writes:

> The knowledge of this coming judgment drove Paul on through defamation, prisons, stripes, shipwrecks, stoning, perils, weariness, pain, and burden of the churches. It was not the fear of hell; it was not to keep his hands from sin alone; it was the fear of facing the Saviour, the one who had suffered the penalty for all sin, who had bled and died for him, facing Him with empty hands, with wasted life.[1]

This doctrine spotlights the principles of human responsibility and the grace of God. God holds each believer accountable for that which He has entrusted to him and He will graciously reward faithfulness.

The judgment seat of Christ is an exceedingly solemn and sobering portion of prophetic truth, bringing Biblical ethics and Biblical eschatology into juxtaposition. The apostle John provides an appropriate parting challenge:

> *Behold what manner of love the Father has bestowed on us, that we should be called children of God! Therefore the world does not know us, because it did not know Him. Beloved, now we are children of God; and it has not yet been revealed what we shall be, but we know that when He is revealed, we shall be like Him, for we shall see Him as He is. And everyone who has this hope in Him purifies himself, just as He is pure* (1 Jn. 3:1-3).

And again he writes of Christ, *"And behold, I am coming quickly, and My reward is with Me, to give to every one according to his work"* (Rev. 22:12). The appearance of each believer before the judgment seat of Christ could be only a tissue paper's breadth away.

---

[1] John F. Walvoord, "Judgments and Rewards to Christians, to Gentiles, and to Jews," in *Light for the World's Darkness*, comp. and ed. by John W. Bradbury (New York: Loizeaux Brothers, 1944), p. 74.

# APPENDIX A

# THE OLD TESTAMENT SAINTS' JUDGMENT

The foregoing treatise has been limited to a consideration of the nature of the church-age saints' judgment. These believers constitute only a part of the redeemed who have or who will have espoused saving faith in God, and who will thus enjoy God's presence forever. Since the church-age saints have an evaluation of their lives at the judgment seat of Christ, it would seem likely that the Old Testament saints, tribulation saints, and millennial saints must also have some sort of final evaluation in order to receive some measure of reward for faithfulness in this life. The evaluation of each of these three groups will be considered with regard to the time, the nature, and the results of each.

The Old Testament saints occupy a unique position in God's program and must not be confused with the church-age saints.[1] They occupy unique positions in the program of God, receive unique promises, and experience separate judgments.

### *The Time of the Old Testament Saints' Judgment*

The time of the Old Testament saints' judgment can be determined with a good measure of certainty by a consideration of several key passages of Scripture. Daniel 11 describes some of the major events which will occur during the seventieth week of Daniel. Chapter twelve

---

[1] Chafer lists twenty-four contrasts between Israel and the church which demonstrate that these two groups are separate entities which must be distinguished in God's program. Chafer, *Ecclesiology—Eschatology*, pp. 47-53.

begins with a description of events which will occur at the close of the seventieth week of Daniel:

> *At that time Michael shall stand up, the great prince who stands watch over the sons of your people; and there shall be a time of trouble, such as never was since there was a nation, even to that time. And at that time your people shall be delivered, every one who is found written in the book. And many of those who sleep in the dust of the earth shall awake, some to everlasting life, some to shame and everlasting contempt* (Dan. 12:1-2).

Pentecost comments on the significance of these verses in relation to the time of the Old Testament saints' resurrection:

> In Daniel 12:1-2 the resurrection is said to take place "at that time," which must be the time previously described, or at the time of the closing events of the seventieth week, when the end comes to the Beast. "At that time" there will be both a deliverance (v. 1) and a resurrection (v. 2). This passage seems to indicate that the resurrection is associated with the act of deliverance from the Beast at the second advent.[2]

Isaiah 26:19-21 gives further support that the resurrection of Old Testament saints will occur at the close of the great tribulation. These verses show that the deliverance which comes with the resurrection does not occur *"until the indignation is past"* (v. 20). These verses state:

> *Your dead shall live; Together with my dead body they shall arise. Awake and sing, you who dwell in dust; For your dew is like the dew of herbs, And the earth shall cast out the dead. Come, my people, enter your chambers, And shut your doors behind you; Hide yourself, as it were, for a little moment, Until the indignation is past. For behold, the LORD comes out of His place To punish the inhabitants of the earth for their iniquity; The earth will also disclose her blood, And will no more cover her slain* (Isa. 26:19-21).

Again, Pentecost aptly comments:

> This indignation is none other than the tribulation period and the resurrection of Israel is said to take place at the termination

---

[2] Pentecost, *Things to Come*, pp. 410-11.

of that period. It seems to be an error to affirm that the church and Israel are both resurrected at the rapture. Scripture shows that Israel will be resurrected at the close of the tribulation period, while the church will be resurrected prior to it.[3]

In Daniel 12:3, immediately following the reference to the resurrection of the Old Testament saints at the close of the tribulation period, Daniel writes, *"Those who are wise shall shine like the brightness of the firmament, and those who turn many to righteousness like the stars forever and ever."* Although somewhat obscure, this is a probable reference to the results of a judgment that is conducted for resurrected Old Testament saints. If this is the case, then it seems probable to conclude that some sort of evaluation of these saints will occur just subsequent to their resurrection. Hoyt gives support to this conclusion. Having just stated that tribulation saints will be raised and judged at the close of the tribulation, he writes:

> At this same time, there is reason to believe, there will occur the resurrection of the Old Testament saints (Dan. 12:1-2; Isa. 26:19-21). They too belong to the first resurrection and will therefore take their place with that host of resurrected saints in reigning with Christ (Rev. 20:4-6). Such distinguished characters as Abraham, Isaac and Jacob shall assemble (Matt. 8:11). David too will be there and be king over them and shall be their prince forever (Ezek. 37:24-25). Without a doubt a special judgment will be conducted for these saints to determine the place and position they will occupy in the kingdom (Dan. 12:3; Mal. 3:16-17).[4]

It seems reasonable to assume, therefore, that resurrected Old Testament saints will experience a judgment just prior to Christ's establishment of the millennial kingdom.

### The Nature of the Old Testament Saints' Judgment

The nature of the Old Testament saints' judgment following the tribulation is a subject that is obscure in Biblical revelation. Scripture reveals that a judgment upon all living Israelites who survive the tribula-

---

[3] Ibid., p. 411.
[4] Hoyt, *The End Times*, p. 219.

tion will occur just prior to Christ's establishment of His millennial rule. However, this judgment is to determine who among living Israelites at the end of the tribulation will enter into the kingdom (Ezek. 20:34-38), rather than being a judgment of the resurrected Old Testament saints. It can only be conjectured that the Old Testament saints' lives will be examined with regard to obedience to the Law and faithfulness in serving God since Scripture does not describe this evaluation.

### The Results of the Old Testament Saints' Judgment

Daniel 12:3 suggests the nature of part of the reward which the Old Testament saints will receive. This verse states, *"Those who are wise shall shine like the brightness of the firmament, and those who turn many to righteousness like the stars forever and ever."* Hoyt again comments, "Without doubt a special judgment will be conducted for these saints to determine the place and position they will occupy in the kingdom (Dan. 12:3; Mal. 3:16-17)."[5] Scripture indicates that saved Israel (resurrected Old Testament saints and the righteous remnant from the tribulation period) will be ushered into the millennial kingdom to enjoy fulfillment of all of God's promises to her. It is conceivable, though not revealed, that as Hoyt suggests this judgment will determine the specific position and place of privileged service that each will have in the millennial kingdom.

## THE TRIBULATION SAINTS' JUDGMENT

There is more explicit Biblical revelation concerning the judgment of tribulation saints than there is concerning the judgment of resurrected Old Testament saints. Revelation 6 and 7 describe the saints who will be martyred during the tribulation. Revelation 6:9 reads, *"When He opened the fifth seal, I saw under the altar the souls of those who had been slain for the word of God and for the testimony which they held."* These martyrs will be both believing Jews and believing Gentiles. Revelation 7:9 states, *"After these things I looked, and behold, a great multitude which no one could number, of all nations, tribes, peoples, and tongues, standing before the throne and before the Lamb, clothed with white robes, with palm branches in their hands."*

---

[5] Ibid.

### The Time of the Tribulation Saints' Judgment

The time of the tribulation saints' judgment is clearly established in Revelation 20:4-6. This passage speaks specifically of their resurrection:

> *And I saw thrones, and they sat on them, and judgment was committed to them. Then I saw the souls of those who had been beheaded for their witness to Jesus and for the word of God, who had not worshiped the beast or his image, and had not received his mark on their foreheads or on their hands. And they lived and reigned with Christ for a thousand years* (Rev. 20:4).

This resurrection occurs at the conclusion of the tribulation just prior to Christ's establishment of His earthly kingdom. Since Scripture also indicates that these saints are to reign with Christ a thousand years, it would be safe to conclude that their judgment would occur at this time also. Hoyt comments on this issue:

> At the end of the tribulation period when persecution has ceased because the Antichrist and his legions have been destroyed, the closing events of the first resurrection occur. The tribulation martyrs are raised (Rev. 20:4-6) and judged. This conclusion is based on the fact that they are given positions of honor and responsibility.[6]

Unger concurs:

> The resurrection of the tribulation saints likely takes place at the end of the tribulation period (Rev. 6:9-11; 20:4). Since this group is not in the Church, the Body of Christ, it will not likely be judged for works at the same time and scene with [Church] believers, but will certainly appear for adjudication before entering the marriage feast (Rev. 19:7-9).[7]

### The Nature of the Tribulation Saints' Judgment

The parable of the talents (Mt. 25:14-30) and the parable of the pounds (Lk. 19:11-27) contextually refer to tribulation saints. These

---

[6] Ibid.

[7] Unger, *Great Neglected Bible Prophecies*, p. 108 (brackets added).

parables have been shown to deal with the principle of faithfulness with the abilities and opportunities which the Lord has provided. From this it can be concluded that the Lord will examine the life of each tribulation saint in much the same way that He will examine the lives of church-age saints. Details of this evaluation are not included in Biblical revelation.

### The Results of the Tribulation Saints' Judgment

As mentioned earlier, Revelation 20:4 indicates that these saints will have the privilege of sharing in Christ's millennial reign. Matthew 25:21, 23 reveal that positions of joyous rulership and authority will be granted for faithful service in this life. Verse twenty-one states, *"His lord said to him, 'Well done, good and faithful servant; you were faithful over a few things, I will make you ruler over many things. Enter into the joy of your lord.'"* Luke 19:17, 19 similarly reveal the privileged service that is in store for resurrected and rewarded tribulation saints. Each saint's authority in the millennial kingdom will be dependent upon the degree of faithfulness in his earthly life. Luke 19:16-19 express this principle:

> *Then came the first, saying, "Master, your mina has earned ten minas. And he said to him, "Well done, good servant; because you were faithful in a very little, have authority over ten cities." And the second came, saying, "Master, your mina has earned five minas." Likewise he said to him, "You also be over five cities."*

Again in Matthew there is a reference to the reward of the tribulation saints: *"Then the King will say to those on His right hand, 'Come, you blessed of My Father, inherit the kingdom prepared for you from the foundation of the world.'"* (Mt. 25:34). Although these rewards are specifically limited to the millennial kingdom, the tribulation saints' rewards will doubtless extend to the eternal state.

## THE MILLENNIAL SAINTS' JUDGMENT

At the close of the tribulation period the righteous who are living will be ushered into the millennial kingdom in their natural bodies. Therefore, in the millennial kingdom there will be saints who have not been resurrected or raptured, and whose earthly lives have not been judged since their lives will not have been completed. Whether these millennial saints will have some sort of evaluative judgment is not revealed. The Scriptures are completely silent concerning this issue.

It could be conjectured that these saints will need to undergo a bodily change similar to the Christians' rapture to fit them for the eternal state. First Corinthians 15:50 states, *"Now this I say, brethren, that flesh and blood cannot inherit the kingdom of God; nor does corruption inherit incorruption."* It could also be conjectured that since all other saints will have an evaluative judgment, it would therefore seem logical that millennial saints would require an examination. Although such an event seems possible and even probable, such an assumption of course goes beyond the bounds of explicit Biblical revelation. Deuteronomy 29:29 states, *"The secret things belong to the LORD our God, but those things which are revealed belong to us and to our children forever, that we may do all the words of this law."* The silence of the Scriptures at this point accents the fact that Biblical revelation was not given to satisfy all of the believer's curiosity. God did not deem it necessary for believers today and saints of preceding ages to have all the facts and information concerning life in the millennial kingdom. Rather, Biblical revelation was given to provide the information necessary for believers to live godly lives and have a blessed hope prior to the personal return of Christ, the living Word.

# APPENDIX B

# WHO ARE THE OVERCOMERS?

B ible prophecy was not written to *scare* us, but to *prepare* us. Some speakers and writers are using Bible prophecy as a weapon to *scare* believers, rather than a tool to *prepare* believers.

There has been an ongoing debate about the identity of the overcomers referred to in the book of Revelation. Some have divided believers into two groups: those who are saved, but living carnal lives, and those who are saved and are "overcomers" living a more victorious life. Those believers are the "saved plus." However, the biblical evidence supports another view, namely, that *all* genuine believers are "overcomers."

Those who put believers in Christ into two different categories teach that believers who live victorious lives will reign with Christ during the Millennium. The rest, who are carnal, non-victorious believers will fail the victory test at the judgment seat of Christ. As a result, these who fail to be victorious Christians will experience weeping, wailing, and gnashing of teeth in outer darkness.

George Zeller, who refutes this skewed position, has written two outstanding articles addressing this subject, titled, "Weeping and Gnashing of Teeth: Will This Be the Fate of True Christians?"[1] and "Who Is the Overcomer of Revelation 2–3?"[2] In each article Zeller summarizes the position of those who teach this view and uses Scripture to refute this errant view.

---

[1] www.middletownbiblechurch.org/doctrine/hodgesgn.htm
[2] www.middletownbiblechurch.org/doctrine/hodgesov.htm

### History and Prevalence of the Two-Believer View

This position originated in the nineteenth-century with the writings of men like Robert Govett, D. M. Panton, G. H. Pember, and G. H. Lang. A more modern writer who has influenced evangelical dispensational circles is a former Dallas Theological Seminary professor, Zane Hodges. He has written a number of books and commentaries which set forth this theological position.[3]

The teachings and writings of Zane Hodges have influenced other Bible teachers and writers who now embrace this view, like Joseph Dillow,[4] author of *The Reign of the Servant Kings* and the greatly expanded version of the same book, *Final Destiny*. Dillow's original book, *The Reign of the Servant Kings*, has become the standard-bearer and most dominant apologetic for this position. Another writer, Robert Wilkin,[5] and his organization, the Grace Evangelical Society, also hold to this view[6] and heartily recommend the works of both Dillow and Hodges. Others influenced by Hodges and Dillow and who advocate this view include Chuck and Nancy Missler,[7] Paul Benware,[8] Tony Evans,[9] and

---

[3] Zane C. Hodges, *The Gospel Under Siege: Faith and Works in Tension* (Dallas: Redención Viva, 1981), 127-41; *Grace in Eclipse: A Study on Eternal Rewards* (Dallas: Redención Viva, 1985), 83-111; "Hebrews" in *The Bible Knowledge Commentary: New Testament*, ed. John F. Walvoord and Roy B. Zuck (Wheaton, IL: Victor, 1983; reprint, Colorado Springs: Cook, 1996), 787; *Hebrews: The Journey of Faith* (Dallas: Victor Street Bible Chapel, 2010), 25-26; and *The Hungry Inherit: Refreshing Insights on Salvation, Discipleship, and Rewards* (Chicago: Moody Press, 1972), 113-14, 119.

[4] Joseph C. Dillow, *Final Destiny: The Future Reign of the Servant Kings* (Monument, CO: Paniym Group, 2012), esp. 229-41, 661-76, 764-95, 868-94; *The Reign of the Servant Kings: A Study of Eternal Security and the Final Significance of Man* (Miami Springs, FL: Schoettle, 1992), 344-48; 469-87, 534-49, 554-59. Dillow credits Hodges's influence in his acknowledgements in *Reign of the Servant Kings*, xx.

[5] Robert N. Wilkin, *The Road to Reward: Living Today in Light of Tomorrow* (Irving, TX: Grace Evangelical Society, 2003), 51-60; *The Ten Most Misunderstood Words of the Bible* (Denton, TX: Grace Evangelical Society, 2012), 179-81.

[6] Robert Vacendak, "Revelation" in *The Grace New Testament Commentary*, ed. Robert N. Wilkin (Denton, TX: Grace Evangelical Society, 2010), 1260.

[7] Chuck and Nancy Missler, *Kingdom, Power, & Glory: The Overcomer's Handbook* (Coeur d'Alene, ID: King's High Way, 2008).

[8] Paul N. Benware, *The Believer's Payday* (Chattanooga, TN: AMG, 2002), 26-40, 92, 99; "Notes on the Book of Revelation," 30 (http://paulbenware.com/ministries/writings-2/).

[9] Tony Evans, "The Overcomers of the Kingdom," Tape LK104B (Dallas: The Urban

Charles Stanley.[10] These writers divide the church of Jesus Christ into two groups who have very different millennial destinies. The victorious overcomers rule and reign with Christ in the Millennial Kingdom while the many barren or carnal believers suffer some measure of punishment or separation during the millennial reign of Christ. Hodges, Dillow, and others who embrace this view teach that being an overcomer is a status that must be earned by victorious, faithful living.

This writer and others, such as George Zeller and James E. Rosscup,[11] hold to the view that *all* genuine believers are overcomers and will receive the rewards that Christ has promised them. When the various passages of Scripture are properly understood, it becomes clear that this is the biblical view.

### SUPPORT FOR ALL BELIEVERS BEING OVERCOMERS

One of the clearest portions of Scripture on this subject is 1 John 5:4-5. The Apostle John clearly declares who the overcomers are: *"For whatever is born of God overcomes the world. And this is the victory that has overcome the world—our faith. Who is he who overcomes the world, but he who believes that Jesus is the Son of God?"*

Nothing could be clearer about who the Apostle John was referring to in these verses when he refers to *all* those who have espoused faith in Jesus Christ as overcomers. This is the only place in the entire Bible where the question is both asked and answered: Who is an overcomer? John is referring to *all* believers who by definition have placed their faith in Jesus Christ: *"Who is he who overcomes the world, but he who believes that Jesus is the Son of God?"* Every person who believes in Jesus Christ as his or her personal Savior is an overcomer!

This fact is made a reality because in John 16:33c Jesus said, *"I have overcome the world."* Jesus Christ is the ultimate Overcomer whose completed victory provides the basis on which all believers are also considered overcomers in Him.

---

Alternative); "Rewards for Christians," in *The Tim LaHaye Prophecy Study Bible*, ed. Tim LaHaye, Edward Hindson, Thomas Ice, and James Combs (Chattanooga, TN: AMG, 2000), 1234.

[10] Charles Stanley, *Eternal Security: Can You Be Sure?* (Nashville: Oliver-Nelson, 1990), 124-28. Stanley also wrote the foreword to Hodges's book, *Grace in Eclipse*.

[11] James E. Rosscup, "The Overcomer of the Apocalypse," *Grace Theological Journal* 3 (Fall 1982): 261-86.

Next, it should be noted that the Apostle John is the same person who wrote the epistle of 1 John as well as the book of Revelation. When John uses the word *overcomer* in Revelation 2 and 3, it must be assumed that he is using the word to mean the very same people who he referred to in 1 John 5:4-5, which are *all* believers in Christ. When John says in Revelation 2 and 3, *"he who overcomes,"* he is essentially saying, *"he who believes."* First John 5:1 states, *"Whoever believes* (present tense) *that Jesus is the Christ is born of God."* John again uses the present tense in Revelation 2 and 3 in reference to overcomers, describing all believers as having an ongoing status as overcomers because of their unchanging position in Christ, the ultimate Overcomer. Since *all* believers are declared to be overcomers, it makes good sense to say that all of the promises given in Revelation 2 and 3 also apply to *all* believers, not just to those who live more victoriously than others. Even the Apostle Peter had a number of incredible failures.

When Scripture is properly understood in its full context, this view that *all* believers are overcomers is clearly taught. In 1 John 4:4, the Apostle John once again clarifies who the overcomers are: *"You are of God, little children, and have overcome them, because He who is in you is greater than he who is in the world."*

Being an overcomer is not determined by what a believer has earned or achieved in his daily life but is based on Who dwells within the believer. God's presence and power within *every* believer makes *every* believer an overcomer. *"You"* refers to believers, in contrast to those of the world.

The key element in being an overcomer according to the Apostle John is saving faith. All Christians will sin from time to time, some more than others. The Apostle John understood that when he wrote this epistle. In 1 John 1:8 he writes to believers (*"My little children"*), stating clearly, *"If we say that we have no sin, we deceive ourselves, and the truth is not in us."* John tells us God's solution for sin in the Christian's life: *"If we confess our sins, He is faithful and just to forgive us our sins and to cleanse us from all unrighteousness"* (1 John 1:9). Being an overcomer is not because we achieve that position by merit, but because we are in that position in Christ by grace!

*All* Christians are overcomers, even though some may be more faithful in living out their Christian lives than others. As a result, some believers may receive more rewards than others. Rewards are based on faithfulness, while being an overcomer according to the Apostle John is based on genuine faith in Christ. There are not two classes of Christians: overcomers and non-overcomers. There are not two destinations for believers: the Millennial Kingdom and outer darkness.

The same Apostle John, who also wrote 1 John, refers to believers as overcomers on several occasions in Revelation 2 and 3. In these two chapters Christ addresses the seven churches of Asia Minor as He evaluates their spiritual conditions. Scholars have noted that similar spiritual conditions have characterized churches down through the ages. In his address to each of these seven churches, Christ promises a special blessing to *every* believer who overcomes. It should also be noted that the Apostle John wraps up his letter by referring to *all* believers again in Revelation 21:7: *"He who overcomes shall inherit all things, and I will be his God and he shall be My son."*

In the context of Revelation 21, the writer is referring to *all* believers. God will dwell with them (v. 3); He will wipe away every tear from their eyes (v. 4a); there shall be no more death, nor sorrow, nor crying (v. 4b); and He will make all things new (v. 5). This passage distinguishes between just two classes of people (saved vs. unsaved), not two kinds of saved people (overcoming believers vs. non-overcoming believers). Verse 7 makes it clear that the overcomer is a son of God, which is the position of every believer. Then John makes a contrast with unbelievers in verse 8: *"But the cowardly, unbelieving, abominable, murderers, sexually immoral, sorcerers, idolaters, and all liars shall have their part in the lake which burns with fire and brimstone, which is the second death."* These are not carnal, sinning believers. The distinction made here is between two groups of people, believers and unbelievers, not two kinds of Christians.

In Revelation 21:27 John summarizes what he has been saying: *"But there shall by no means enter it anything that defiles, or causes an abomination or a lie, but only those who are written in the Lamb's Book of Life."* Again, John is making a clear distinction between the saved and the unsaved. He is not distinguishing a special class of believers who are spiritual victors from those who are saved but not spiritual victors. In Revelation 21 and 22 *every* believer partakes in *every* blessing described in these two chapters.

## PROMISES TO OVERCOMERS IN REVELATION 2–3

Returning to Revelation 2 and 3, we see that the blessings Christ promised to the overcomers apply to *all* believers. In Revelation 2:7 Christ promised, *"To him who overcomes I will give to eat from the tree of life, which is in the midst of the Paradise of God."* Whether the eating from the tree of life is a picture of living forever or whether it represents enjoying some aspects of heaven, the promised blessing is for *all* true believers. In Revelation 22:14 we are told, *"Blessed are those who wash their robes, that they may have the right to the tree of life, and may enter through the gates into the city"* (NASB). The very next verse then contrasts the plight of unbelievers: *"But outside are dogs and sorcerers and sexually immoral and murderers and idolaters, and who loves and practices a lie"* (v. 15). Who has the right to the tree of life? *All* believers. God will admit *all* believers into heaven for all eternity.

To the persecuted church of Smyrna, Christ said in Revelation 2:11, *"He who overcomes shall not be hurt by the second death."* This refers to the eternal blessing of *all* believers, whether or not they are martyred. Paul wrote in 1 Corinthians 15:54b-57, *"Death is swallowed up in victory. 'O Death, where is your sting? O Hades, where is your victory?' The sting of death is sin, and the strength of sin is the law. But thanks be to God, who gives us the victory through our Lord Jesus Christ."* Once again we see that *all* Christians experience this victory through Christ. *All* believers will escape the second death. Later in Revelation the Apostle John described the second death: *"Then Death and Hades were cast into the lake of fire. This is the second death. And anyone not found written in the Book of Life was cast into the lake of fire"* (Rev. 20:14-15). *All* believers will escape the second death, which is being cast into the lake of fire.

In Revelation 2:17 Christ promises, *"To him who overcomes I will give some of the hidden manna to eat. And I will give him a white stone, and on the stone a new name written which no one knows except him who receives it."* This expression of hidden manna could be a symbol of Christ just as the bread and cup were symbols of his body and blood in the Gospels. Such a reference would apply to *every* believer because we are considered overcomers by faith in Christ. If eating the hidden manna refers to the future activity of *every* believer, then the white stone would likely refer to *every* believer as well. For a further explanation of what the white stone might represent, see James Rosscup's excellent article, *"The Overcomer of the Apocalypse."*

In Revelation 2:26 Jesus promises, *"And he who overcomes, and keeps My works until the end, to him I will give power over the nations."* This applies to *all* believers. Revelation 5:9-10 refer to the twenty-four elders who represent the church whom Christ has redeemed by his own blood. These verses state, *"You are worthy to take the scroll, and to open its seals; for You were slain, and have redeemed us to God by Your blood out of every tribe and tongue and people and nation, and have made us kings and priests to our God; and we shall reign on the earth."* This is referring to *all* believers who are redeemed by Christ. *Every* believer will reign with Christ on earth, not just a select few. In Revelation 20:4-6 we are told that *all* who belong to the first resurrection will reign on earth with Christ for a thousand years. Also, Revelation 22:5 refers to the ultimate eternal reign of *all* believers with Christ: *"There shall be no night there: They need no lamp nor light of the sun, for the Lord God gives them light. And they shall reign forever and ever."*

Next, in Revelation 3:5-6 Christ promises, *"He who overcomes shall be clothed in white garments, and I will not blot out his name from the Book of Life; but I will confess his name before My Father and before His angels."* In Revelation 19:7 we see a word picture of the glorified church consisting of *all* believers from Pentecost to the rapture of the church in heaven. They will be clothed in clean and bright garments: *"Let us be glad and rejoice and give Him glory, for the marriage of the Lamb has come, and His wife (the church) has made herself ready. And to her it was granted to be arrayed in fine linen, clean and bright, for the fine linen is the righteous acts of the saints."* This blessing is for *all* believers (the bride of Christ), not just a group or class of more victorious or more fruitful believers. Again, the Apostle John who penned these words describes the overcomer in 1 John 5:4-5 as anyone who believes in Jesus Christ as his or her Savior: *"For whatever is born of God overcomes the world. And this is the victory that has overcome the world—our faith. Who is he who overcomes the world, but he who believes that Jesus is the Son of God?"*

In Revelation 3:5-6 Christ also promises to the overcomers, *"I will not blot out his name from the Book of Life; but I will confess his name before My Father and before His angels."* Clearly, this applies to each and every believer, for no believer's name will ever be blotted out of the Book of Life, AND each and every believer will be confessed as a believer before our heavenly Father and His angels. There is no way around this conclusion by using hermeneutical gymnastics to say that this passage applies only to a certain class of victorious Christians rather than *all* Christians.

In speaking to the church at Philadelphia, Christ promises in Revelation 3:12, *"He who overcomes, I will make him a pillar in the temple of My God, and he shall go out no more. I will write on him the name of My God and the name of the city of My God, the New Jerusalem, which comes down out of heaven from My God. And I will write on him My new name."* Christ is speaking of the believer's secure position in heaven when he is called a *"pillar in the temple of My God."* The entirety of the heavenly city is referenced by the word *"temple."* To go along with this picture, the Christian, like a pillar, will have permanency in God's temple. This is true of *every* believer. Also, *every* believer will bear God's name in heaven as a *"child of God."* *All* believers are assured of eternity in the presence of God because of their faith in Christ who has qualified them to be overcomers.

Lastly, Christ speaks to the overcomers of the Laodicean church in Revelation 3:21: *"To him who overcomes I will grant to sit with Me on My throne, as I also overcame and sat down with My Father on His throne."* This promise is not given to some select group of super spiritual believers within the church. It is a promise to all genuine believers who have overcome sin and the world by faith in Jesus Christ. The promise is that *all* believers will sit with Christ on His throne in glory. They will share in Christ's glory and eternal reign. Again, Revelation 22:5 assures *every* believer that *"they shall reign forever and ever."* Sitting with Christ on His throne implies reigning with Christ forever. This will be the future privilege of *every* believer because each has been made worthy by his faith in the Lord Jesus Christ.

The clear conclusion for this writer is that the overcomers referred to in 1 John and the book of Revelation are *all* believers who make up the church of Jesus Christ. The spiritual blessings cataloged in Revelation 2 and 3 for the overcomers clearly apply to *all* believers, not a select group of believers. There is no evidence that these blessings will be given to certain believers who achieve or earn a certain level of victory, while being denied to underachieving believers. *All* believers in Christ are overcomers according to the definition and description articulated by the Apostle John. Each believer will receive the blessings designated by Christ for *all* believers. These passages do not contain two classes of Christians: those believers who overcome and those believers who do not overcome.

## ALL BELIEVERS ARE SUPER-OVERCOMERS

In Romans 8:37 Paul makes this declaration of *all* believers, *"Yet in all these things we* (all Christians) *are more than conquerors* (*hypernikōmen*) *through Him who loved us."* The root word for *conquerors* (*nikōn*) is the same word used in 1 John 5 and Revelation 2 and 3. However, in this verse there the Greek word *hyper* is used as a prefix to the word *conqueror* or *overcomer*. From the Greek preposition *hyper* we get the idea of *"super."* To express it in our modern terminology: *"supersize"*! Paul says that in the middle of all our challenges and trials we are (right now) *"more than conquerors through Him who loved us."* We are not merely overcomers, but literally *super*-conquerors, or *super-sized* overcomers! In Christ we have already gained a super-sized victory.

The expression *hypernikōmen* refers to *every* believer, whether or not we as believers in Christ understand and believe that truth, or "feel" that truth in our life, or experience practical victory each day. As believers, we are in Christ, and because of that, we share His super-sized victory. This is who we are, and our identity as overcomers is not based on what we have done or what we are doing. Super-overcomers are who we are in Christ right now! How can this be true? Because Christ has overcome the world Himself (John 16:33c). We find our true identity in our relationship by faith with Christ! It is victory based on our position, not on our performance. It is rooted in God's grace, not our merit.

# BIBLIOGRAPHY

Abbott-Smith, G. *A Manual Greek Lexicon of the New Testament.* 3rd ed. Edinburgh: T. & T. Clark, 1937.

Abendroth, Dallas. "The Work of I Corinthians 3:13." Unpublished B.D. monograph, Grace Theological Seminary, 1966.

Aland, Kurt; Black, Matthew; Martini, Carlo M.; Metzger, Bruce M.; and Wikgren, Allen, eds. *The Greek New Testament.* 2nd ed. Stuttgart: United Bible Societies, 1968.

Alford, Henry. *Acts, Romans, Corinthians.* Vol. II of *The Greek Testament.* Revised by Everett F. Harrison. 4 vols. Chicago: Moody Press, 1968.

"Archaeology and Christian Beginnings." *The Biblical Archaeologist* 2 (September 1939): 25-36.

Armerding, Carl. "The Four and Twenty Elders." *Our Hope* 50 (July 1943): 29-33.

Arndt, William F., and Gingrich, F. Wilbur, trans. *A Greek-English Lexicon of the New Testament and Other Early Christian Literature.* By Walter Bauer. 4th ed. Chicago: University of Chicago Press, 1957. Cambridge: Syndics of the Cambridge University Press, n.d.

Bancroft, Emery H. *Christian Theology, Systematic and Biblical.* Bible School Park, NY: Echoes Publishing Company, 1925.

Barclay, William. *The Gospel of Matthew: Volume 2 (Chapters 11 to 28).* The Daily Study Bible. 2nd ed. Philadelphia: Westminster Press, 1958.

_____. *The Letter to the Romans.* The Daily Study Bible. 2nd ed. Philadelphia: Westminster Press, 1957.

_____. *The Letters to the Corinthians.* The Daily Study Bible. 2nd ed. Philadelphia: Westminster Press, 1956.

Barnhouse, Donald Grey. *God's Discipline: Exposition of Bible Doctrines, taking the Epistle to the Romans as a Point of Departure.* Vol. IX: *Romans.* Grand Rapids: Wm. B. Eerdmans Publishing Company, 1964.

Barrett, C. K. *A Commentary on the First Epistle to the Corinthians.* 2nd ed. London: Adam & Charles Black, 1971.

Bates, William H. "Judgment or Judgments? A Study in Biblical Eschatology." *Our Hope* 20 (October 1913): 218-27.

Baughman, Ray E. *The Kingdom of God Visualized.* Illustrated by Gerald Schmoyer. Chicago: Moody Press, 1972.

Baxter, J. Sidlow. *His Part and Ours: God's Promises and Our Responsibilities in the Christian Life.* Grand Rapids: Zondervan Publishing House, 1960.

Bedford, Dean S. "The Return of Our Lord an Incentive to Soul-winning." *The Sure Word of Prophecy.* Compiled and edited by John W. Bradbury. New York: Fleming H. Revell Company, 1943.

Bellshaw, William Gilbert. "The General Judgment Theory." Unpublished Th.M. thesis, Dallas Theological Seminary, 1955.

Benware, Paul N. *The Believer's Payday.* Chattanooga, TN: AMG, 2002.

Berkhof, L. *Systematic Theology.* 4th ed. Grand Rapids: Wm. B. Eerdmans Publishing Company, 1941.

Bernard, J. H. "The Second Epistle to the Corinthians." In Vol. III of *Expositor's Greek Testament.* Edited by W. Robertson Nicoll. 5 vols., reprinted. Grand Rapids: Wm. B. Eerdmans Publishing Company, 1970.

Betz, Harlan D. "The Nature of Rewards at the Judgment Seat of Christ." Unpublished Th.M. thesis, Dallas Theological Seminary, 1974.

Beyler, Clayton. "The Judgment." *Prophecy Conference: Report of Conference Held at Elkhart, Indiana, April 3-5, 1952,* Scottdale, PA: Mennonite Publishing House, 1953.

Blackstone, William Eugene. *Jesus Is Coming.* New York: Fleming H. Revell, 1908.

Boice, James Montgomery. *The Last and Future World.* Grand Rapids: Zondervan Publishing House, 1974.

Bolton, Samuel. *The True Bounds of Christian Freedom.* London: Banner of Truth Trust, 1964.

Boyer, James L. *An Exposition of I Corinthians.* Winona Lake, IN: Grace Theological Seminary, n.d.

_____. *For a World Like Ours: Studies in I Corinthians.* Winona Lake, IN: BMH Books, 1971.

_____. *Johannine Epistles.* Winona Lake, IN: Grace Theological Seminary, 1965.

_____. *Prophecy: Things to Come: A Study Guide.* Winona Lake, IN: BMH Books, 1973.

Brandon, S. G. F. *The Judgment of the Dead: The Idea of Life after Death in the Major Religions.* New York: Charles Scribner's Sons, 1967.

Braune, Karl. "The Epistles General of John." Translated by J. Isidor Mombert. In Vol. IX of *Commentary on the Holy Scriptures.* Edited by John Peter Lange. New York: Charles Scribner's Sons, 1915.

Broderick, Robert C. "Judgment, General." *The Catholic Encyclopedia.* 1976.

Broneer, Oscar. "The Apostle Paul and the Isthmian Games." *The Biblical Archaeologist* 25 (1962): 2-31.

_____. "Corinth: Center of St. Paul's Missionary Work in Greece." *The Biblical Archaeologist* 14 (December 1951): 78-96.

_____. "The Isthmian Victory Crown." *American Journal of Archaeology* 64 (1962): 259-63.

_____. "Paul and the Pagan Cults at Isthmia." *Harvard Theological Review* 64 (April-July 1971): 169-87.

Brooke, A. E. *A Critical and Exegetical Commentary on the Johannine Epistles.* In *The International Critical Commentary.* Edited by C. A. Briggs, *et al.* Edinburgh: T. & T. Clark, 1912.

Brooks, Keith L. "The Practical Aspect of the Blessed Hope." *Unveiling the Future: Twelve Prophetic Messages.* Compiled and edited by T. Richard Dunham. Findlay, OH: Fundamental Truth Publishers, 1934.

_____. *Prophecy Text Book for Reference and for Classes.* Los Angeles: n.p., 1933.

_____. *Prophetic Questions Answered: Questions that Have Been Submitted to the American Prophetic League, Inc., and Answered by its President.* Grand Rapids: Zondervan Publishing House, 1941.

Brown, Francis; Driver, S. R.; and Briggs, Charles A., eds. *A Hebrew and English Lexicon of the Old Testament with an Appendix Containing the Biblical Aramaic.* Oxford: Clarendon Press, 1907.

Bruce, F. F. *Commentary on the Book of the Acts: The English Text with Introduction, Exposition, and Notes.* In *The New International Commentary on the New Testament.* Edited by F. F. Bruce. Grand Rapids: Wm. B. Eerdmans Publishing Company, 1954.

_____, "First Epistle to the Corinthians." *The Zondervan Pictorial Encyclopedia of the Bible.* 1975. Vol. I.

Bullinger, E. W. *Figures of Speech Used in the Bible Explained and Illustrated.* London: Eyre and Spottiswoode, 1898. Reprint ed. Grand Rapids: Baker Book House, 1968.

Camp, Norman H. "Rewards." *A Brief Outline of Things to Come.* Compiled by Theodore H. Epp. Chicago: Moody Press, 1952.

Candlish, Robert S. *The First Epistle of John.* Grand Rapids: Zondervan Publishing House, n.d.

Cevetello, J. F. X. "Purgatory." *New Catholic Encyclopedia.* 1967. Vol. XI.

Chafer, Lewis Sperry. *Grace.* Findlay, OH: Dunham Publishing Company, 1922.

_____. *Major Bible Themes.* Findlay, OH: Dunham Publishing Company, 1926.

_____. *Major Bible Themes: 52 Vital Doctrines of the Scripture Simplified and Explained.* Revised by John F. Walvoord. Revised ed. Grand Rapids: Zondervan Publishing House, 1974.

_____. *Salvation*. Grand Rapids: Dunham Publication of Zondervan Publishing House, 1917.

_____ . *Systematic Theology*. Vol. VII: *Doctrinal Summarization*. Dallas: Dallas Seminary Press, 1948.

_____. *Systematic Theology*. Vol. IV: *Ecclesiology—Eschatology*. Dallas: Dallas Seminary Press, 1948.

_____. *Systematic Theology*. Vol. VI: *Pneumatology*. Dallas: Dallas Seminary Press, 1948.

Clark, H. David. "The First and the Last." *The Baptist Bulletin,* March, 1975, pp. 12-13.

Clark, Rufus W. "Hope of Christ's Coming as a Motive to Holy Living and Active Labor." *Second Coming of Christ: Premillennial Essays of the Prophetic Conference, Held in the Church of the Holy Trinity, New York City*. Chicago: F. H. Revell, 1879.

Cleveland, Howard Z. "Reward." *Baker's Dictionary of Theology*. Edited by Everett F. Harrison. Grand Rapids: Baker Book House, 1960.

Clouse, Robert G. "Judgment." *The New International Dictionary of the Christian Church*. Edited by J. D. Douglas. Grand Rapids: Zondervan Publishing House, 1974.

Conybeare, W. J., and Howson, J. S. *The Life and Epistles of St. Paul*. New ed. Grand Rapids: Wm. B. Eerdmans Publishing Company, 1966.

Cook, William Robert. "The Judgment-Seat of Christ as Related to the Believer's Walk." Paper presented to the professor of Systematic Theology, Dallas Theological Seminary, May 1953.

Cooper, David L. *Future Events Revealed: According to Matthew 24 and 25*. Los Angeles: David L. Cooper, 1935.

Cooper, J. T. "The Judgment, or Judgments." *Second Coming of Christ: Premillennial Essays of the Prophetic Conference, Held in the Church of the Holy Trinity, New York City*. Chicago: F. H. Revell, 1879.

Cremer, Hermann. *Biblico-Theological Lexicon of New Testament Greek*. Translated by William Urwick. 4th ed. Edinburgh: T. & T. Clark, 1895.

Culver, Robert D. *Daniel and the Latter Days*. Chicago: Moody Press, 1954.

Custer, Stewart. "The Power of the Unseen (II Cor. 4:16-5:10)." *Biblical Viewpoint* 8 (April 1974): 24-31.

Dabney, Robert L. *Lectures in Systematic Theology*. Reprinted. Grand Rapids: Zondervan Publishing House, 1972.

Dana, H. E., and Mantey, Julius R. *A Manual Grammar of the Greek New Testament*. Toronto: Macmillan Company, 1955.

DeHaan, M. R. *The Believer's Judgments*. Grand Rapids: Radio Bible Class, 1963.

_____. *The Judgment Seat of Christ: A Scriptural Examination of the Three Judgments of the Believer—Past, Present, Future*. Grand Rapids: Radio Bible Class, n.d.

_____. *Studies in First Corinthians: Messages on Practical Christian Living.* Grand Rapids: Zondervan Publishing House, 1956.

Dennett, E. *The Blessed Hope: Being Papers on the Lord's Coming and Connected Events.* Denver: Wilson Foundation, 1873.

Denney, James. *The Second Epistle to the Corinthians.* In *The Expositor's Bible.* Edited by W. Robertson Nicoll. Cincinnati: Jennings & Graham, n.d. New York: Eaton & Mains, n.d.

DeRu, G. "The Conception of Reward in the Teaching of Jesus." *Novum Testamentum* 8 (1966): 202-22.

Dilling, John Robert. "A Critical Treatment of I Corinthians 9:27." Unpublished B.D. monograph, Grace Theological Seminary, 1952.

Dillow, Joseph C. *Final Destiny: The Future Reign of the Servant Kings.* Monument, CO: Paniym Group, 2012.

_____. *The Reign of the Servant Kings: A Study of Eternal Security and the Final Significance of Man.* Miami Springs, FL: Schoettle, 1992.

Dobbs, W. C. "The Concept of Reward in the Teaching of Jesus." Unpublished Th.D. dissertation, Southern Baptist Theological Seminary, 1954.

Dodson, Kenneth F. *The Prize of the Up-Calling or Paul's Secrets of Victory.* Grand Rapids: Baker Book House, 1969.

Dollar, George W. *A History of Fundamentalism in America.* Greenville, SC: Bob Jones University Press, 1973.

_____. "Rewards." Sermon preached at Faith Baptist Church, LaCrosse, WI, n.d. (Taped.)

Dunham, T. Richard. "The Fallacy of the General Judgment Theory." *Unveiling the Future: Twelve Prophetic Messages.* Compiled and edited by T. Richard Dunham. Findlay, OH: Fundamental Truth Publishers, 1934.

Earle, Ralph. "Crown." *Baker's Dictionary of Theology.* Edited by Everett F. Harrison. Grand Rapids: Baker Book House, 1960.

Edson, Frank F. "Spiritual Gifts and the Judgment Seat of Christ." Unpublished Th.M. thesis, Dallas Theological Seminary, 1969.

Edwards, Thomas Charles. *A Commentary on the First Epistle to the Corinthians.* 2nd ed. New York: A. C. Armstrong & Son, 1886.

Emmerson, George J. *The End in View.* London: Marshall Brothers, Limited, n.d.

English, E. Schuyler. "The Church at the Tribunal." *Prophetic Truth Unfolding Today.* Edited by Charles Lee Feinberg. Old Tappan, NJ: Fleming H. Revell Company, 1968.

_____. *Re-Thinking the Rapture.* Neptune, NJ: Loizeaux Brothers, 1954.

_____. *Things Surely to Be Believed: A Primer of Bible Doctrine.* Neptune, NJ: Loizeaux Brothers, 1956.

Epp, Theodore H. *Present Labor and Future Rewards: The Believer, His Sin, Conduct and Rewards.* Lincoln, NE: Back to the Bible Broadcast, 1960.

_____. *The Sinning Christian and His Judgment.* Lincoln, NE: Back to the Bible Publishers, n.d.

Evans, Tony. "Rewards for Christians." In *The Tim LaHaye Prophecy Study Bible.* Edited by Tim LaHaye, Edward Hindson, Thomas Ice, and James Combs. Chattanooga, TN: AMG, 2000.

Evans, William. *The Great Doctrines of the Bible.* Chicago: Moody Press, 1949.

Farrar, Frederic W. *History of Interpretation: Bampton Lectures, 1885.* New York: E. P. Dutton, 1886. Reprint ed. Grand Rapids: Baker Book House, 1961.

Fausset, A. R. "I Corinthians-Revelation." In vol. III of *A Commentary, Critical, Experimental, and Practical on the Old and New Testaments.* By Robert Jamieson, A. R. Fausset, and David Brown. 3 vols. Grand Rapids: William B. Eerdmans Publishing Company, n.d.

_____. "Jeremiah-Malachi." In vol. II of *A Commentary, Critical, Experimental, and Practical on the Old and New Testaments.* By Robert Jamieson, A. R. Fausset, and David Brown. 3 vols. Grand Rapids: William B. Eerdmans Publishing Company, n.d.

Feinberg, Charles. *Premillennialism or Amillennialism? The Premillennial and Amillennial Systems of Interpretation Analyzed and Compared.* Grand Rapids: Zondervan Publishing House, 1936.

_____. *The Prophecy of Ezekiel: The Glory of the Lord.* Chicago: Moody Press, 1969.

Findlay, G. G. "St. Paul's First Epistle to the Corinthians." In vol. II of *Expositor's Greek Testament.* Edited by W. Robertson Nicoll. 5 vols., reprinted. Grand Rapids: Wm. B. Eerdmans Publishing Company, 1970.

Fischer, Loren. "Parables of Instruction for Servants and Stewards." Mimeographed class notes for CE 310 Seminar, Western Conservative Baptist Seminary, 1972.

Fishburne, Charles W. "I Corinthians 111.10-15 and the Testament of Abraham." *New Testament Studies* 17 (October 1970): 109-15.

Ford, Jess A. "The Church in Glory." Unpublished Th.M. thesis, Dallas Theological Seminary, 1954.

Friesen, Melvin R. "What Is the Cause for Shame in I John 2:28?" Unpublished M.Div. monograph, Grace Theological Seminary, 1969.

Gaebelein, A. C. *The New Testament: Romans-Ephesians.* Vol. II. *The Annotated Bible: The Holy Scriptures Analyzed and Annotated.* New York: Publication Office "Our Hope," 1916.

"Games." *The People's Bible Encyclopedia.* 1921.

Gardiner, E. Norman. *Athletics of the Ancient World.* Oxford: Clarendon Press, 1930.

Gates, John R. "Arminianism." *Wycliffe Bible Encyclopedia.* Edited by Charles F. Pfeiffer, Howard F. Vos, John Rea. 2 vols. Chicago: Moody Press, 1975.

_____. "Crown." *Pictorial Bible Dictionary.* Edited by Merrill C. Tenney. Grand Rapids: Zondervan Publishing House, 1964.

Geiger, Wallace W. "A Critical Investigation of II Corinthians 5:11a." Unpublished B.D. monograph, Grace Theological Seminary, 1955.

Geikie, Cunningham. *New Testament Hours.* Vol. III: *The Apostles: Their Lives and Letters.* New York: James Potts & Company, Publishers, 1895.

Gingrich, Raymond E. *An Outline and Analysis of the First Epistle of John.* Grand Rapids: Zondervan Publishing House, 1943.

Godet, F. *Commentary on St. Paul's First Epistle to the Corinthians.* Vol. I. Translated by A. Cusin. In Vol. XXVII of Clark's Foreign Theological Library. Edinburgh: T. & T. Clark, 1893.

_____. *Commentary on St. Paul's First Epistle to the Corinthians.* Vol. II. Translated by A. Cusin. In Vol. XXX of Clark's Foreign Theological Library. Edinburgh: T. & T. Clark, 1890.

Gray, James M. "Christ the Executor of All Future Judgments." *Christ and Glory: Addresses Delivered at the New York Prophetic Conference, Carnegie Hall, November 25-28, 1918.* Edited by Arno C. Gaebelein. New York: Publication Office "Our Hope," n.d.

_____. *Prophecy and the Lord's Return: A Collection of Popular Articles and Addresses.* New York: Fleming H. Revell Company, 1917.

Gromacki, Robert Glenn. *Are These the Last Days?* Old Tappan, NJ: Fleming H. Revell Company, 1970.

_____. *Salvation Is Forever.* Chicago: Moody Press, 1973.

Grosheide, F. W. *Commentary on the First Epistle to the Corinthians: The English Text with Introduction, Exposition and Notes.* In *The New International Commentary on the New Testament.* Edited by F. F. Bruce. Grand Rapids: Wm. B. Eerdmans Publishing Company, 1953.

Grundmann. *"stephanos, stephanoō" Theological Dictionary of the New Testament.* Vol. VII. Edited by Gerhard Friedrich. Translated and edited by Geoffrey W. Bromiley. Grand Rapids: Wm. B. Eerdmans Publishing Company, 1971.

Guille, George E. *The Judgment Seat of Christ: Who Stands There? When? What For?* Chicago: Bible Institute Colportage Association, 1916.

Gundry, Robert H. *The Church and the Tribulation.* Grand Rapids: Zondervan Publishing House, 1973.

Haldeman, I. M. *Ten Sermons on the Second Coming of Our Lord Jesus Christ.* New York: Charles C. Cook, 1917. Reprint ed. Grand Rapids: Baker Book House, 1963.

Hale, William Harlan. *The Horizon Book of Ancient Greece.* Edited by William Harlan Hale. New York: American Heritage Publishing Company, Inc., 1965.

Hamilton, Floyd E. *The Basis of Millennial Faith.* Grand Rapids: Wm. B. Eerdmans Publishing Company, 1942.

Hamilton, Gavin. *Maranatha! Highlight of the Twentieth Century.* New York: Loizeaux Brothers Publishers, n.d.

Hamilton, Richard Winter. *The Revealed Doctrine of Rewards and Punishments.* London: Jackson and Walford, 1847.

Harris, H. A. *Greek Athletes and Athletics.* With an Introduction by the Marquess of Exeter. N.p.: Indiana University Press, 1964.

Haupt, Erich. *The First Epistle of St. John: A Contribution to Biblical Theology.* Clark's Foreign Theological Library, Vol. LXIV. Translated, with an Introduction, by W. B. Pope. Edinburgh: T & T Clark, 1879.

Henry, Carl F. H. *Christian Personal Ethics.* Grand Rapids: Wm. B. Eerdmans Publishing Company, 1957.

Henry, Patrick David. "What Are the Works That Shall Be Burned as Mentioned in I Corinthians 3:15." Unpublished B. D. monograph, Grace Theological Seminary, 1946.

Herrstrom, W. D. *Judgment Day for Everybody.* Grand Rapids: Zondervan Publishing House, 1939.

Hewitt, P. E. *Coming Events: A Handbook of Bible Prophecy.* Grand Rapids: Zondervan Publishing House, 1942.

Hobbs, Herschel H. *The Epistles to the Corinthians: A Study Manual.* Shield Bible Study Series. Grand Rapids: Baker Book House, 1960.

Hodge, A. A. *Outlines of Theology.* Chatham, Great Britain: W. & J. Mackay Limited, 1879. Reprint ed. Grand Rapids: Zondervan Publishing House, 1972.

Hodge, Charles. *An Exposition of the First Epistle to the Corinthians.* Grand Rapids: Wm. B. Eerdmans Publishing Company, n.d.

_____. *An Exposition of the Second Epistle to the Corinthians.* Grand Rapids: Wm. B. Eerdmans Publishing Company, n.d.

_____. *Systematic Theology.* 3 vols. Grand Rapids: Wm. B. Eerdmans Publishing Company, 1940.

Hodges, Jesse Wilson. *Christ's Kingdom and Coming.* Grand Rapids: Wm. B. Eerdmans Publishing Company, 1957.

Hodges, Zane C. *The Gospel Under Siege: Faith and Works in Tension.* Dallas: Redención Viva, 1981.

_____. *Grace in Eclipse: A Study on Eternal Rewards.* Dallas: Redención Viva, 1985.

_____. "Hebrews." In *The Bible Knowledge Commentary: New Testament.* Edited by John F. Walvoord and Roy B. Zuck. Wheaton, IL: Victor, 1983. Reprinted, Colorado Springs: Cook, 1996.

_____. *The Hungry Inherit: Refreshing Insights on Salvation, Discipleship and Rewards.* Chicago: Moody Press, 1972.

Hogg, C. F., and Watson, J. B. *The Promise of His Coming: Chapters on the Second Advent.* London: Pickering & Inglis Ltd., n.d.

Horne, Thomas Hartwell. *An Introduction to the Critical Study and Knowledge of the Holy Scriptures.* Vol. II. New ed. Philadelphia: Desilver, Thomas & Company, 1836.

Horsefield, F. J. *The Church and the Coming King.* London: Marshall Brothers, Ltd., 1926.

Hough, Robert Ervin. *The Christian after Death.* Chicago: Moody Press, 1947.

Howitt, F. E. "The Coming Judgeship of the Saints." *The Coming and Kingdom of Christ.* Chicago: Bible Institute Colportage Association, 1914.

Hoyt, Herman A. *The End Times.* Chicago: Moody Press, 1969.

_____. "The Examination and Rewarding of the Church." Unpublished sermon text, Winona Lake, IN, n.d.

_____. *I and II Corinthians.* Winona Lake, IN: Grace Theological Seminary, n.d.

_____. "The Marriage and Exaltation of the Church." *Focus on Prophecy.* Edited by Charles L. Feinberg. Westwood, NJ: Fleming H. Revell, 1964.

_____. "The Occupation of the Redeemed: Revelation 21:22-27." Unpublished sermon text, Winona Lake, IN: n.d.

Hughes, Philip Edgcumbe. *Paul's Second Epistle to the Corinthians: The English Text with Introduction, Exposition and Notes.* In *The New International Commentary on the New Testament.* Edited by F. F. Bruce. Grand Rapids: Wm. B. Eerdmans Publishing Company, 1962.

Hunter, A. M. *Exploring the New Testament.* Edinburgh: Saint Andrew Press, 1971.

Huther, Joh. Ed. *Critical and Exegetical Handbook to the General Epistles of James, Peter, John, and Jude.* Translated from the third German edition by Paton J. Flong, D. B. Croom, and Clarke H. Irwin. With a Preface and supplementary notes to the American edition by Timothy Dwight. New York: Funk & Wagnalls, Publishers, 1887.

Ironside, H. A. *Addresses on the Epistles of John.* New York: Loizeaux Brothers, Bible Truth Depot, 1931. Oakland, CA: Western Book and Tract Company, 1931.

_____. *Addresses on the First Epistle to the Corinthians.* New York: Loizeaux Brothers, Publishers, 1938. Oakland, CA: Western Book and Tract Company, 1938.

_____. *Addresses on the Second Epistle to the Corinthians.* New York: Loizeaux Brothers, Publishers, n.d. Oakland, CA: Western Book and Tract Company, n.d.

_____. *Care for God's Fruit Trees and Other Messages.* Grand Rapids: Zondervan Publishing House, 1941.

_____. "The Judgment Seat of Christ." *Our Hope* 46 (April 1940): 668-72.

_____. *Miscellaneous Papers.* 2 vols. New York: Loizeaux Brothers, Inc., Publishers, 1945; Oakland, CA: Western Book and Tract Company, Inc., 1945.

_____. *Sailing with Paul: Simple Papers for Young Christians.* New York: Loizeaux Brothers, Bible Truth Depot, n.d.

Johnson, Carl G. *Prophecy Made Plain for Times like These.* Chicago: Moody Press, 1972.

Johnson, S. Lewis, Jr. "The Gospel That Paul Preached." *Bibliotheca Sacra* 128 (October-December 1971): 327-40.

_____. "The Out-Resurrection from the Dead." *Bibliotheca Sacra* 110 (April-June 1953): 139-46.

Jonas, Rudolf. "A Diadem of the Cult of Kybele from the Neapolis Region (Samaria)." *Palestine Exploration Quarterly* 94 (July-December 1962): 118-28.

Judge, E. A. "Judgment-Seat." *The New Bible Dictionary.* Edited by J. D. Douglas. Grand Rapids: Wm. B. Eerdmans Publishing Company, 1962.

"Judgment Seat." *The International Standard Bible Encyclopedia.* 1955.

"Judgment Seat." *Pictorial Bible Dictionary.* Edited by Merrill C. Tenney. Grand Rapids: Zondervan Publishing House, 1962.

Kelly, William. *Notes on the Second Epistle of Paul the Apostle to the Corinthians, with a New Translation.* London: G. Morrish, 1882.

Kent, Homer A., Jr. *The Epistle to the Hebrews: A Commentary.* Grand Rapids: Baker Book House, 1972.

_____. "The Gospel According to Matthew." *The Wycliffe Bible Commentary.* Edited by Charles F. Pfeiffer and Everett F. Harrison. Chicago: Moody Bible Institute, 1962.

John. Winona Lake, IN: BMH Books, 1974.

_____. *Light in the Darkness: Studies in the Gospel of John.* Winona Lake, IN: BMH Books, 1974.

_____. *The Pastoral Epistles: Studies in I and II Timothy and Titus.* Chicago: Moody Press, 1958.

Ketcham, Robert T. *Why Was Christ a Carpenter? and Other Sermons.* Des Plaines, IL: Regular Baptist Press, 1966.

Kieran, John, and Daley, Arthur. *The Story of the Olympic Games: 776 B.C. to 1972.* Rev. ed. Philadelphia: J. B. Lippincott Company, 1973.

Kling, Christian Friedrich. "The First Epistle of Paul to the Corinthians." Translated by Daniel W. Poor. In vol. VI of *Commentary on the Holy Scriptures.* Edited by John Peter Lange. New York: Charles Scribner's Sons, 1915.

Kunkel, Wolfgang. *An Introduction to Roman Legal and Constitutional History.* Translated by J. M. Kelly. Oxford: Clarendon Press, 1966.

"Labor and Reward." *Our Hope* 22 (June 1916): 717-19.

Ladd, George Eldon. *The Blessed Hope.* Grand Rapids: Wm. B. Eerdmans Publishing Company, 1956.

Lang, G. H. *Pictures and Parables: Studies in the Parabolic Teaching of Holy Scripture.* London: The Paternoster Press, 1955.

Larkin, Clarence. *Dispensational Truth or God's Plan and Purpose in the Ages.* Philadelphia: Rev. Clarence Larkin Est., 1918.

Laurin, Roy L. *I Corinthians: When Life Matures.* 3rd ed. Findlay, OH: Dunham Publishing Company, 1957.

Lenski, R. C. H. *The Interpretation of St. Paul's First and Second Epistles to the Corinthians.* Minneapolis: Augsburg Publishing House, 1963.

Lewis, C. S. *The Weight of Glory and Other Addresses.* 1st American paperback ed. Grand Rapids: Wm. B. Eerdmans Publishing Company, 1965.

Lias, J. J. *The First Epistle of St. John with Exposition and Homiletical Treatment.* London: James Nisbet & Company, 1887.

Liddell, H. G. *An Intermediate Greek-English Lexicon Founded upon the Seveneth Edition of Liddell and Scott's Greek-English Lexicon.* Reprinted. Oxford: Clarendon Press, 1968.

Lightfoot, J. B. *Notes on the Epistles of St. Paul: I and II Thessalonians, I Corihthians 1-7, Romans 1-7 Ephesians 1:1-14.* Classic Commentary Library. Grand Rapids: Zondervan Publishing House, 1957.

Lloyd-Jones, D. M. *Romans: An Exposition of Chapters 7.1–8.4: The Law: Its Functions and Limits.* Grand Rapids: Zondervan Publishing House, 1973.

Logsdon, S. Franklin. *Profiles of Prophecy.* Grand Rapids: Zondervan Publishing House, 1970.

Lutzer, Erwin. "Are We Making Sin Too Easy?" *Moody Monthly* (July-August 1976): 45-47.

McClain, Alva J. *Christian Theology: Biblical Eschatology.* Revised by John C. Whitcomb, Jr. Winona Lake, IN: Grace Theological Seminary, n.d.

Mackintosh, C. H. *Papers on the Lord's Coming.* Chicago: Moody Press, n.d.

Manley, G. T. *The Return of Jesus Christ.* Chicago: InterVarsity Press, 1960.

Marchbanks, John B. "Question Box." *Our Hope* 62 (January 1956): 415-17.

Marsh, F. E. "Christ's Coming for and with His Saints." *Our Hope* 14 (September 1907): 205-19.

Marsh, Frederick E. *Fully Furnished or The Christian Worker's Equipment.* Fincastle, VA: Bible Study Classics, 1924.

_____. *What Will Take Place When Christ Returns?* 2nd ed. London: Chas. J. Thynne, n.d.

Martin, James P. *The Last Judgment in Protestant Theology from Orthodoxy to Ritschl.* Grand Rapids: Wm. B. Eerdmans Publishing Company, 1963.

Martin, Walter R. "The Christian and the Judgment." *Eternity,* July, 1958, pp. 30-32.

Mason, Clarence E., Jr. "A Study of Pauline Motives as Revealed in 2 Corinthians 4:16-6:4a." *Bibliotheca Sacra* 111 (July 1954): 213-28.

Masterman, E. W. G. "Gabbatha." *The International Standard Bible Encyclopedia.* 1955.

Maxwell, L. E. "The Judgment Seat of Christ." *The Prairie Overcomer* 30 (April 1956): 132-38.

Mayor, Joseph B. *The Epistle of St. James: The Greek Text with Introduction Notes and Comments.* 2nd ed. London: Macmillan and Company, Limited, 1897; New York: Macmillan Company, 1897.

Metzger, Bruce M. *A Textual Commentary on the Greek New Testament.* London: United Bible Societies, 1971.

Missler, Chuck and Nancy. *Kingdom, Power, & Glory: The Overcomer's Handbook.* Coeur d'Alene, ID: King's High Way, 2008.

Morgan, G. Campbell. *The Corinthian Letters of Paul: An Exposition of I and II Corinthians.* New York: Fleming H. Revell Company, 1946.

_____. *Studies in the Four Gospels.* Old Tappan, NJ: Fleming H. Revell. Company, 1931.

Morris, L. L. "Crown." *The New Bible Dictionary.* Edited by J. D. Douglas. Grand Rapids: Wm. B. Eerdmans Publishing Company, 1962.

Morris, Leon. *The Biblical Doctrine of Judgment.* London: Tyndale Press, 1960.

_____. *The First Epistle of Paul to the Corinthians: An Introduction and Commentary.* Tyndale New Testament Commentaries. Edited by R. V. G. Tasker. Grand Rapids: Wm. B. Eerdmans Publishing Company, 1958.

Moule, Handley C. G. *The Second Epistle to the Corinthians: A Translation, Paraphrase, and Exposition.* Edited with Appendices by A. W. Handley Moule. Grand Rapids: Zondervan Publishing House, 1962.

Moulton, James Hope, and Milligan, George. *The Vocabulary of the Greek Testament Illustrated from the Papyri and Other Non-literary Sources.* Grand Rapids: Wm. B. Eerdmans Publishing Company, 1930.

Mueller, J. Theodore. "The Saint's Reward and God's Grace." *Christianity Today* 3 (January 5, 1959): 14-15.

Murray, George L. *Millennial Studies: A Search for Truth.* Grand Rapids: Baker Book House, 1948.

Murray, John. *The Epistle to the Romans: The English Text with Introduction, Exposition and Notes.* In *The New International Commentary on the New Testament.* Edited by F. F. Bruce. Grand Rapids: Wm. B. Eerdmans Publishing Company, 1965.

Narum, William H. K. "A Study of the Eschatological Motifs of the Christian Life." Unpublished Th.D. dissertation, Princeton Theological Seminary, 1951.

Neighbour, R. E. *What About Eternal Security; The Virgin Birth; Pentecostalism; Coming, Cataclysms; The Abode of the Dead; Rewards for Saints? A series of Seven Sermons on Vital Questions of the Hour.* Elyria, OH: Gems of God Publishing Company, n.d.

Nicholas, Barry. *An Introduction to Roman Law.* Oxford: Clarendon Press, 1962.

Nicol, Thomas. "Games." *A Dictionary of the Bible Dealing with Its Language, Literature, and Contents Including the Biblical Theology.* Edited by James Hastings. 4 vols. New York: Charles Scribner's Sons, 1909. Edinburgh: T. & T. Clark, 1909.

Olford, Stephen F. "The Judgment Seat of Christ." *Prophecy and the Seventies.* Edited by Charles Lee Feinberg. Chicago: Moody Press, 1971.

Orr, James. *The Progress of Dogma: Being the Elliot Lectures, Delivered at the Western Theological Seminary, Allegheny, Penna., U.S.A., 1897.* 4th ed. London: Hodder and Stoughton, 1901.

Pache, Rene. *The Future Life.* Translated by Helen I. Needham. Chicago: Moody Press, 1962.

Patterson, Alexander. *The Greater Life and Work of Christ as Revealed in Scripture Man and Nature.* New York: Christian Alliance Publishing Company, 1896.

Pentecost, J. Dwight. "The Judgment Seat of Christ." Taped sermon from Bible Believers' Cassettes, Inc., Springdale, AR, n.d. (Transcribed.)

_____. *Prophecy for Today: An Exposition of Major Themes on Prophecy.* Grand Rapids: Zondervan Publishing House, 1961.

_____. *Things to Come: A Study in Biblical Eschatology.* With an Introduction by John F. Walvoord. Grand Rapids: Dunham Publishing Company, 1958.

Peters, George N. H. *The Theocratic Kingdom of Our Lord Jesus, the Christ, as Covenanted in the Old Testament and Presented in the New Testament.* With a Preface by Wilbur M. Smith. 3 vols. Grand Rapids: Kregel Publications, 1952.

Pettingill, William L. *God's Prophecies for Plain People.* Wilmington, DE: Just a Word Incorporated, 1923.

Pfitzner, Victor C. *Paul and the Agnon Motif: Traditional Athletic Imagery in the Pauline Literature.* Leiden: E. J. Brill, 1967.

Philpott, P. W. "Will There Be Any Tears in Heaven, and Why?" *Light on Prophecy: A Coordinated, Constructive Teaching: Being the Proceedings and Addresses at the Philadelphia Prophetic Conference, May 28-30, 1918.* New York: Christian Herald Bible House, 1918.

Pink, Arthur W. *The Redeemer's Return.* Ashland, KY: Calvary Baptist Church Book Store, n.d.

Pinnock, Clark H. "The Structure of Pauline Eschatology." *The Evangelical Quarterly* 37 (January 1965): 9-20.

Plummer, A. *The Epistles of St. John with Notes, Introduction and Appendices.* In the *Cambridge Bible for Schools and Colleges.* Edited by J. J. S. Perowne. Cambridge: University Press, 1884. London: C. J. Clay, M. A. & Son, 1884.

Plummer, Alfred. *A Critical and Exegetical Commentary on the Second Epistle of St. Paul to the Corinthians.* In *The International Critical Commentary.* Edinburgh: T & T Clark, 1915.

Radmacher, Earl D. *The Nature of the Church.* Portland, OR: Western Baptist Press, n.d.

_____. "Why Should I Work for Rewards?" Taped sermon from Bible Believers' Cassettes, Inc., Springdale, AR, n.d. (Transcribed.)

Raffety, William Edward. "Crown." *The International Standard Bible Encyclopedia.* 1955.

Ramm, Bernard. *Protestant Biblical Interpretation: A Textbook of Hermeneutics for Conservative Protestants.* Complete rev. ed. Boston: W. A. Wilde Company, 1956.

Raud, Elsa. *Introduction to Prophecy.* Findlay, OH: Dunham Publishing Company, 1960.

Redpath, Alan. *Blessings Out of Buffetings: Studies in II Corinthians.* Westwood, NJ: Fleming H. Revell Company, 1965.

_____. *The Royal Route to Heaven: Studies in First Corinthians.* Westwood, NJ: Fleming H. Revell Company, 1960.

Renfer, Rudolf Albert. "The Judgment-Seat of Christ." Unpublished Th.M. thesis, Dallas Theological Seminary, 1939.

Rice, John R. *Tears in Heaven.* Murfreesboro, TN: Sword of the Lord Publishers, 1941.

Ritchie, John. *The Second Advent of the Lord Jesus with Subsequent Events in Heaven and on Earth: Ten Lectures Illustrated by A Coloured Chart.* 3rd ed. Kilmarnock, Scotland: John Ritchie, Publisher of Christian Literature, n.d.

Robertson, A. T. *The Glory of the Ministry: Paul's Exultation in Preaching.* With an Introduction by Ralph G. Turnbull. Grand Rapids: Baker Book House, 1967. Westwood, NJ: Fleming H. Revell Company, 1911.

_____. *A Grammar of the Greek New Testament in the Light of Historical Research.* Nashville: Broadman Press, 1934.

_____. *Word Pictures in the New Testament.* Vol. IV: *The Epistles of Paul.* Nashville: Broadman Press, 1931.

Robertson, Archibald, and Plummer, Alfred. *A Critical and Exegetical Commentary on the First Epistle of St. Paul to the Corinthians.* In *The International Critical Commentary.* Edited by C. A. Briggs, et. al. 2nd ed. Edinburgh: T. & T. Clark, 1914.

Robinson, Wm. Childs. *Christ-The Hope of Glory: Christological Eschatology.* Grand Rapids: Wm. B. Eerdmans Publishing Company, 1945.

Roetzel, Calvin J. *Judgment in the Community: A Study of the Relationship between Eschatology and Ecclesiology in Paul.* Leiden: E. J. Brill, 1972.

Rogers, E. W. *Concerning the Future.* Chicago: Moody Press, 1962.

Ross, Arthur M. "Games." *Pictorial Bible Dictionary.* Edited by Merrill C. Tenney. Grand Rapids: Zondervan Publishing House, 1964.

Rosscup, James E. "The Overcomer of the Apocalypse." *Grace Theological Journal* 3 (Fall 1982): 261-86.

Rupprecht, A. "Corinth." *The Zondervan Pictorial Encyclopedia of the Bible.* 1975. Vol. I.

Ryrie, Charles Caldwell. *The Basis of the Premillennial Faith.* Neptune, NJ: Loizeaux Brothers, 1953.

_____. *Dispensationalism Today.* With a Foreword by Frank E. Gaebelein. Chicago: Moody Press, 1965.

Sale-Harrison, L. *The Judgment Seat of Christ: An Incentive and a Warning.* London: Pickering & Inglis, 1938. Harrisburg, PA: Evangelical Press, 1938.

Sauer, Erich. *From Eternity to Eternity: An Outline of the Divine Purposes.* Translated by G. H. Lang. Grand Rapids: Wm. B. Eerdmans Publishing Company, 1963.

_____. *In the Arena of Faith: A Call to a Consecrated Life.* Grand Rapids: Wm. B. Eerdmans Publishing Company, 1955.

_____. *The Triumph of the Crucified: A Survey of Historical Revelation in the New Testament.* Translated by G. H. Lang. With a Foreword by A. Rendle Short. Grand Rapids: Wm. B. Eerdmans Publishing Company, 1951.

Savage, H. H. "What Will the Faithful Do in Heaven?" *Moody Founder's Week Conference Messages: February 5-11, 1962.* Chicago: Moody Bible Institute, n.d.

Savage, Henry H. *The Heavenlies: Purified Places, Perfected Peoples, Perpetual Plans.* Grand Rapids: Diadem Music and Publishing Company, 1964.

Schaff, Philip. *The Evangelical Protestant Creeds, with Translations.* Vol. III. *The Creeds of Christendom with a History and Critical Notes.* 4th ed. Grand Rapids: Baker Book House, 1966.

_____, ed. *A Select Library of the Nicene and Post-Nicene Fathers of the Christian Church.* Vol. XXII: *Saint Chrysostom: Homilies on the Epistles of Paul to the Corinthians.* Revised by Talbot W. Chambers. New York: Christian Literature Company, 1889.

Schep, J. A. *The Nature of the Resurrection Body: A Study of the Biblical Data.* Grand Rapids: Wm. B. Eerdmans Publishing Company, 1964.

Schultz, Arnold C. "Judge, Judgment." *Baker's Dictionary of Theology.* Edited by Everett P. Harrison. Grand Rapids: Baker Book House, 1960.

Scofield, C. I. *Rightly Dividing the Word of Truth (2 Timothy 2:15); Ten Outline Studies of the More Important Divisions of Scripture.* Old Tappan, NJ: Spire Books by the Fleming H. Revell Company, n.d.

_____, ed. *The Scofield Reference Bible.* New York: Oxford University Press, 1945.

Scroggie, W. Graham. *What About Heaven? Comfort for Christians.* London: Pickering & Inglis, Ltd., n.d.

Shedd, William G. T. *Dogmatic Theology.* 3 vols. New York: n.p., 1888-94. Classic reprint ed. Grand Rapids: Zondervan Publishing House, 1971.

Silver, Jesse Forrest. *The Lord's Return*. 5th ed. New York: Fleming H. Revell Company, 1914.

Smith, Wilbur M. *The Biblical Doctrine of Heaven*. Chicago: Moody Press, 1968.

Smith, William Taylor. "Games." *The International Standard Bible Encyclopedia*. 1955.

Spencer, Duane Edward. *Crowns*. Word Keys which Unlock Scripture. San Antonio: Word of Grace, n.d.

_____. *Judgment*. Word Keys which Unlock Scripture. San Antonio: Word of Grace, n.d.

_____. *Rewards*. Word Keys which Unlock Scripture. San Antonio: Word of Grace, n.d.

Sproule, John A. "The Christian and Future Judgment." Unpublished term paper for the course CTA 302, Grace Theological Seminary, 1974.

Stanley, Arthur Penrhyn. *The Epistles of St. Paul to the Corinthians with Critical Notes and Dissertations*. 4th ed. London: John Murray, 1876.

Stanley, Charles. *Eternal Security: Can You Be Sure?* Nashville: Oliver-Nelson, 1990.

Stanton, Gerald B. *Kept from the Hour: A Systematic Study of the Rapture in Bible Prophecy*. Grand Rapids: Zondervan Publishing House, 1956.

Stanton, Horace C. *The Starry Universe, the Christian's Future Empire: The Scriptural Indications that God's Children Are to Inherit All His Illimitable Kingdom; from Heaven as a Metropolis, Exploring and Enjoying Them at Will*. New York: Fleming H. Revell Company, 1909.

Strauss, Lehman. *The Book of the Revelation: Outlined Studies*. Neptune, NJ: Loizeaux Brothers, 1964.

_____. *God's Plan for the Future*. Grand Rapids: Zondervan Publishing House, 1965.

_____. *We Live Forever: A Study of Life After Death*. New York, Loizeaux Brothers, 1947.

Strombeck, J. F. *First the Rapture*. 3rd ed. Moline, IL: Strombeck Agency, Inc., 1951.

Strong, Augustus Hopkins. *Systematic Theology*. Valley Forge, PA: Judson Press, 1907.

Stuart, M. "The White Stone of the Apocalypse." *Bibliotheca Sacra or Tracts and Essays on Topics Connected with Biblical literature and Theology*. Edited by Edward Robinson. New York: Wiley and Putnam, 1843.

Suelzer, A. "Judgment, Divine (in the Bible)." *New Catholic Encyclopedia*. 1967. Vol. VIII.

Tan, Paul Lee. *The Interpretation of Prophecy*. With a Foreword by John C. Whitcomb, Jr. Winona Lake, IN: BMH Books, Inc., 1974.

Tasker, R. V. G. *The Second Epistle of Paul to the Corinthians: An Introduction and Commentary*. The Tyndale New Testament Commentaries. Edited by R. V. G. Tasker. Grand Rapids: Wm. B. Eerdmans Publishing Company, 1958.

Tatham, C. Ernest. "Three Bible Judgments." *Our Hope* 63 (October 1956): 237-39.

Tcherikover, Victor. *Hellenistic Civilization and the Jews*. Translated by S. Applebaum. New York: Atheneum, 1970.

Tenney, Merrill C. "The Gospel According to Luke." *The Wycliffe Bible Commentary*. Edited by Charles F. Pfeiffer and Everett F. Harrison. Chicago: Moody Bible Institute, 1962.

_____. *Interpreting Revelation*. Grand Rapids: Wm. B. Eerdmans Publishing Company, 1957.

_____. New Testament Survey. Rev. ed. Grand Rapids: Wm. B. Eerdmans Publishing Company, 1961.

Thalleen, Waldor Edward. "The Christian Doctrine of Rewards." Unpublished Th.M. thesis, Dallas Theological Seminary, 1950.

Thatcher, G. W. "Judgment Seat." *Dealing with Its Language, Literature, and Contents including the Biblical Theology*. Edited by James Hastings." 4 vols. New York: Charles Scribner's Sons, 1909. Edinburgh: T & T Clark, 1909.

Thayer, Joseph Henry, trans. *Greek-English Lexicon of the New Testament*. By C. L. Wilibad Grimm. Grand Rapids: Zondervan Publishing House, 1962.

Thiessen, Henry C. "Will the Church Pass through the Tribulation?" *Bibliotheca Sacra* 92 (April-June 1935): 187-205.

_____. "Will the Church Pass through the Tribulation?" *Bibliotheca Sacra* 92 (July-September 1935): 292-314.

Thomas, W. H. Griffith. "The Influence of the Study of Prophecy upon the Life and Service of a Christian." *Christ and Glory: Addresses Delivered at the New York Prophetic Conference, Carnegie Hall, November 25-28, 1918*. Edited by Arno C. Gaebelein. New York: Publication Office "Our Hope," n.d.

_____. *The Principles of Theology: An Introduction to the Thirty-nine Articles*. London: Longmans, Green and Company, 1930.

Travlos, John. *Pictorial Dictionary of Ancient Athens*. New York: Praeger Publishers, 1971.

Trench, Richard Chenevix. *Synonyms of the New Testament*. Marshallton, DE: National Foundation for Christian Education, n.d.

Tweeddale, William Frank. "An Examination of the Judgment Seat in 2 Corinthians 5:10." Unpublished B. D. monograph, Grace Theological Seminary, 1957.

Unger, Merrill F. *Archaeology and the New Testament*. Grand Rapids: Zondervan Publishing House, 1962.

_____. *Beyond the Crystal Ball*. Chicago: Moody Press, 1973.

_____. "The Doctrine of the Believer's Judgment." *Our Hope* 58 (November 1951): 269-76.

_____. "The Doctrine of the Believer's Judgment." *Our Hope* 58 (December 1951): 375-80.

_____. "The Doctrine of the Believer's Judgment." *Our Hope* 58 (January 1952): 433-39.

_____. "The Doctrine of the Believer's Judgment." *Our Hope* 58 (February 1952): 500-6.

_____. *Great Neglected Bible Prophecies.* Chicago: Scripture Press Book Division, 1955.

Vacendak, Robert. "Revelation." In *The Grace New Testament Commentary.* Edited by Robert N. Wilkin. Denton, TX: Grace Evangelical Society, 2010.

Van Gorder, Paul R. *The Judgments of God.* Grand Rapids: Radio Bible Class, 1972.

Vincent, M. R. *Word Studies in the New Testament.* 2 vols. MacDill AFB, FL: MacDonald Publishing Company, n.d.

Vine, W. E. *The Epistle to Romans: Doctrine, Precept, Practice.* lst rev. ed. London: Oliphants Limited, 1948.

_____. An Expository Dictionary of New Testament Words with Their Precise Meanings for English Readers. Westwood, NJ: Fleming H. Revel Company, 1940.

Vos, J. G. "Crown." *The Zondervan Pictorial Encyclopedia of the Bible.* 1975. Vol. I.

Walton, Arthur B. "The Judgment Seat of Christ: A Study of the Doctrinal Importance of the Judgment." Unpublished theology paper, Dallas Theological Seminary, January, 1968.

Walvoord, John F. "Amillennial Ecclesiology." *Bibliotheca Sacra* 107 (October-December 1950): 420-29.

_____. "Amillennial Eschatology." *Bibliotheca Sacra* 108 (January-March 1951): 7-14.

_____. "Amillennial Soteriology." *Bibliotheca Sacra* 107 (July-September 1950): 281-90.

_____. "Amillennialism as a System of Theology." *Bibliotheca Sacra* 107 (April-June 1950): 154-67.

_____. "The Church in Heaven." *Bibliotheca Sacra* 123 (April-June 1966): 99-103.

_____. *The Church in Prophecy.* Grand Rapids: Zondervan Publishing House, 1964.

_____. *Daniel: The Key to Prophetic Revelation.* Chicago: Moody Press, 1971.

_____. "Judgments and Rewards to Christians, to Gentiles and to Jews." *Light for the World's Darkness.* Compiled and edited by John W. Bradbury. New York: Loizeaux Brothers, 1944.

_____. *The Millennial Kingdom.* Grand Rapids: Dunham Publishing Company, 1959.

_____. *The Rapture Question.* Grand Rapids: Dunham Publication of Zondervan Publishing House, 1957.

_____. "The Relation of the Church to the Great Tribulation." *Focus on Prophecy.* Edited by Charles L. Feinberg. Westwood, NJ: Fleming H. Revell, 1964.

_____. *The Return of the Lord.* Grand Rapids: Zondervan Publishing House, 1955.

Warfield, Benjamin Breckinridge. *Biblical and Theological Studies.* Cited by Samuel G. Craig. Philadelphia: Presbyterian and Reformed Publishing Company, 1952.

Wesley, John. *Sermons*, Vol. I. With numerous translations, notes, and preface by John Emory. *The Works of the Rev. John Wesley, A. M.* 3rd American ed. New York: Eaton & Mains, n.d. Cincinnati: Jennings & Graham, n.d.

Wessel, Walter W. "The Resurrection of the Dead and Final Judgment." *Contemporary Evangelical Thought: Basic Christian Doctrine.* Edited by Carl F. H. Henry. New York: Holt, Rinehart and Winston, 1962.

West, Nathaniel. *The Thousand Years: Studies in Eschatology in Both Testaments.* Fincastle, VA: Scripture Truth Book Company, n.d.

Wheaton, D. H. "Money." *The New Bible Dictionary.* Edited by J. D. Douglas. Grand Rapids: Wm. B. Eerdmans Publishing Company, 1962.

Wilkin, Robert N. *The Road to Reward: Living Today in Light of Tomorrow.* Irving, TX: Grace Evangelical Society, 2003.

_____. *The Ten Most Misunderstood Words of the Bible.* Denton, TX: Grace Evangelical Society, 2012.

Willmington, H. L. *The King Is Coming: An Outline Study of the Last Days.* With a Foreword by Jerry Falwell. Wheaton: Tyndale House Publishers, 1973. London: Coverdale House Publishers Ltd., 1973.

Wilson, C. "Second Epistle to the Corinthians." *The Zondervan Pictorial Encyclopedia of the Bible.* 1975. Vol. I.

Wood, Leon J. *The Bible & Future Events: An Introductory Survey of Last-Day Events.* Grand Rapids: Zondervan Publishing House, 1973.

Woychuk, N. A. *For All Eternity: Being a Devotional Exposition of I Cor. 3:8-15.* With a Foreword by L. S. Chafer and a Foreword to the second edition by T. R. Dunham. 2nd ed. New York: Books, Inc., 1955.

_____. "Life in Heaven." *Bibliotheca Sacra* 107 (April-June 1950): 227-36.

_____. "What Will We Do in Heaven?" *Bibliotheca Sacra* 108 (October-December 1951): 458-502.

_____. "Will We Have Bodies in Heaven?" *Bibliotheca Sacra* 108 (January-March 1951): 98-104.

_____. "Will We Know Each Other in Heaven?" *Bibliotheca Sacra* 108 (July-September 1951): 347-54.

Wright, Fred H. *Manners and Customs of Bible Lands.* Chicago: Moody Press, 1953.

Wuest, Kenneth S. *Wuest's Word Studies from the Greek New Testament for the English Reader. Vol. IV: Golden Nuggets, Untranslatable Riches, Bypaths, In These Last Days.* Grand Rapids: Wm. B. Eerdmans Publishing Company, 1966.

Young, Edward J. *The Prophecy of Daniel: A Commentary.* Grand Rapids: Wm. B. Eerdmans Publishing Company, 1949.

Zeller, George. "Weeping and Gnashing of Teeth: Will This Be the Fate of True Christians?" http://www.middletownbiblechurch.org/doctrine/hodgesgn.htm.

_____. "Who Is the Overcomer in Revelation 2-3?" http://www.middletownbiblechurch.org/doctrine/hodgesov.htm.

# AUTHOR & PERSON INDEX

# SCRIPTURE INDEX

## ALSO BY SAMUEL L. HOYT

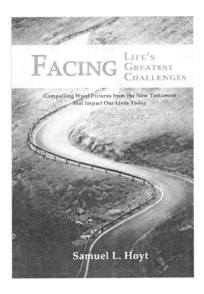

### FACING LIFE'S GREATEST CHALLENGES:
#### COMPELLING WORD PICTURES FROM THE NEW TESTAMENT THAT IMPACT OUR LIVES TODAY

Study Biblical Metaphors to Grow through Your Daily Challenges.

Life is full of challenges as we seek to navigate our lives and grow to be more like Christ. Jesus and the apostle Paul describe the Christian as an athlete, a soldier, a letter, an ambassador, a priest, a temple, a steward, and a handful of other pictures. This book examines 13 New Testament word pictures of the Christian life that give us insights in dealing with challenges we face daily. This book is perfect for personal and group study, Sunday School curriculum, or as part of a sermon series. Questions are provided at the end of each of the thirteen chapters for personal reflection or group discussion.

"When we get a biblical picture of our internal self, we are likely to try and live out that perception in daily life." – Elmer Towns

available through
amazon.com & barnesandnoble.com

*10 Principles to Ponder When the Unexpected Happens* by Shawn Laughlin

*Bad News for Good People and Good News for Bad People: "You Must Be Born Again!" (John 3:1-21)* by Dennis M. Rokser

*David: A Man after the Heart of God* by Theodore H. Epp

*Disciplined by Grace* by J. F. Strombeck

*Don't Ask Jesus into Your Heart: A Biblical Answer to the Question: "What Must I Do to Be Saved?"* by Dennis M. Rokser

*Faith & Works: A Clarification of James 2:14-26* by Dennis M. Rokser

*Freely by His Grace: Classical Grace Theology* edited by J. B. Hixson, Rick Whitmire, and Roy B. Zuck

*The Epistle to the Galatians* by C. I. Scofield

*Getting the Gospel Wrong: The Evangelical Crisis No One Is Talking About* by J. B. Hixson

*The Gospel of the Christ: A Biblical Response to the Crossless Gospel Regarding the Contents of Saving Faith* by Thomas L. Stegall

*The Gospel of Grace and Truth: A Theology of Grace from the Gospel of John* by Michael D. Halsey

*Grace: The Glorious Theme* by Lewis Sperry Chafer

*Holding Fast to Grace* by Roy L. Aldrich

*I'm Saved! Now What?* by Dennis M. Rokser

*I'm Saved But Struggling With Sin! Is Victory Available? Romans 6-8 Examined* by Dennis M. Rokser

*Interpreting 1 John* by Dennis M. Rokser

*Job: A Man Tried as Gold* by Theodore H. Epp

*Let's Preach the Gospel: Do You Recognize the Importance of Preaching the Gospel to Both the Unsaved and the Saved?* by Dennis M. Rokser

*LifeQuakes: God's Rescue Plan in Hard Times* by Leah Weber Heling

*Must Faith Endure for Salvation to Be Sure?* by Thomas L. Stegall

*The Need of the Hour: A Call to the Preaching of the Supremacy and Sufficiency of Jesus Christ, Verse-by-Verse, from a Grace Perspective* by Dennis M. Rokser

*Never Alone: From Abandoned to Adopted in Christ* by Becky Jakubek

*Planting & Establishing Local Churches by the Book* by Dennis M. Rokser

*The Powerful Influence of the Christian Woman* by Donna Radtke

*Promises of God for the Child of God* by Dennis M. Rokser

*Repentance: The Most Misunderstood Word in the Bible* by G. Michael Cocoris

*Salvation in Three Time Zones: Do You Understand the Three Tenses of Salvation?* by Dennis M. Rokser

*Seven Key Questions about Water Baptism* by Dennis M. Rokser

*Shall Never Perish Forever: Is Salvation Forever or Can It Be Lost?* by Dennis M. Rokser

*Should Christians Fear Outer Darkness?* by Dennis M. Rokser

*The Strombeck Collection: The Collected Works of J. F. Strombeck* by J. F. Strombeck

*A Tale of Two Thieves* by Shawn Laughlin

*Trophies of God's Grace: Personal Testimonies of God's Gift of Salvation*

*Truthspeak: The True Meaning of Five Key Christian Words Distorted through Religious Newspeak* by Michael D. Halsey

*Where Faith Sees Christ* by C. I. Scofield

For other helpful resources from a biblically-based, Christ-honoring, and grace-oriented perspective, please visit us at:

www.gracegospelpress.com

CPSIA information can be obtained
at www.ICGtesting.com
Printed in the USA
FSOW01n1931060815
9696FS